Cornel West
& PHILOSOPHY

Cornel West
& PHILOSOPHY

THE QUEST FOR SOCIAL JUSTICE

Clarence Sholé Johnson

Routledge
Taylor & Francis Group
New York   London

Published in 2003 by
Routledge
711 Third Avenue
New York, NY 10017

Published in Great Britain by
Routledge
2 Park Square, Milton Park
Abingdon, Oxon OX14 4RN

Routledge is an imprint of the Taylor & Francis Group, an informa business

Portions of chapter 2 were previously published as "Reading Cornel West as
Humanistic Scholar: Rhetoric and Practicing" in *Cornel West: A Critical Reader*,
ed. George Yancy. Copyright © 2001 by Blackwell. Portions of chapter 3 were pre-
viously published as "Cornel West, African American Critical Thought and the
Quest for Social Justice," in *Journal of Social Philosophy*, vol. 32, no. 4 (winter
2001), 547-572. Copyright © 2001 by Blackwell. Other portions of chapter 3 also
will be published as "A Critique of Cornel West's Christo-Marxian Prescription for
Social Justice," in *Social Philosophy Today*, vol. 16, *Race, Social Identity, Human
Dignity*, ed. Cheryl L. Hughes. Copyright © 2002 by the Philosophy
Documentation Center.

Cataloging-in-Publication Data is available from the Library of Congress.

ISBN 0-415-94073-7 — ISBN 0-415-94074-5 (pbk.)

CONTENTS

FOR TINA,
KOJO,
AND EFFIE

ACKNOWLEDGMENTS

Many individuals, in no small measure, helped make this book a reality, and I would like to thank each and every one of them. First is my wife and companion, my very best friend and intellectual sparring partner, Tina, for her encouragement and support throughout this project, and particularly for being the sounding board for my ideas when I was striving to formulate them. I also wish to thank her for her penetrating and incisive criticisms and thorough and careful reading of the entire manuscript, as well as suggestions for improvement that have been absolutely invaluable. I could not have done this without you, dear.

Second, I thank our children, Kojo and Effie, sometimes my volunteers, at other times my conscripts and captives, for giving me audience as I pursued the objective of trying to make clear my thoughts on specific issues on social justice in a manner that is simple and straightforward without being simplistic. If anything, I hope that the various challenges that I put to them will serve to inspire them to think critically about the issue of social justice.

And third, I discussed some aspect or the other of the topics examined in this book with a number of friends and colleagues, either in conversation or in writing (or both), from whom I benefited greatly and thus to whom I must express my sincere thanks. In no particular order, they are Harry M. Bracken, Robert Bernasconi, Gloria Wade-Gayles, Robert (Bob) Gurland, George Carew, Don

Klinefelter, George Yancy, Andrew Schoedinger, Michael Gomez, Thaddeus Smith, Thea Smith, Sheldon Wein, Percy Johnson, Violet Johnson, and Donald Hamelberg.

My departmental colleagues here at Middle Tennessee State University (MTSU) gave their support and fellowship during the period in which I was engaged in this project, for which I thank each of them: Mary Magada-Ward, Michael Hinz, Jack Purcell, Robert Hood, Ronald Bombardi, and Michael Principe. I also thank Mrs. Terry Ferrell, the department's secretary, for various forms of assistance in preparing the manuscript, and Deljuania Martin and Wayne Green, our work-study students, for running a number of short-notice library errands ever so willingly, which gave me time to focus on other things. In this regard also, I thank the staff of the Inter-library Loan Department of MTSU Library for their assistance, especially the promptness with which they obtained from other libraries much-needed materials that were essential to my research.

I presented parts of this book in various forums and would like to acknowledge participants in those forums, collectively and severally, beginning with the MTSU community: the African American Lecture Series of MTSU under the guidance of Professor Bonnie Shipp, former director of the African American Studies Program. I thank both the students and my faculty colleagues for vibrant discussions that followed my various presentations. In this regard, I especially wish to acknowledge the many students over the years with whom I shared my enthusiasm for some of the issues I discuss here in my courses in Ethics, Modern Philosophy, and Philosophy and the African American Experience.

I had the honor and privilege of being invited by the philosophy clubs of various institutions, through their faculty advisors, to present aspects of my research at their campuses. I would like to acknowledge those clubs, through their respective institutions, and the faculty advisors: University of Tennessee at Chattanooga, under Professor Donald Klinefelter; University of the South, under Professors James Peterman and Christopher Conn; Tennessee State University, under Professors Bill Hardy and Jim Montmarquet; and Boise State University, under Professor Andrew Schoedinger.

I thank participants at the following professional conferences in which I discussed significant aspects of my research: the Second

University-wide Faculty Research Symposium at MTSU (spring 2001); the 33rd Annual Meeting of the Tennessee Philosophical Association, held at Vanderbilt University, November 2–3, 2001; the National Association of African American Studies (NAAAS) annual conference in Houston, Texas; the Sixteenth International Conference of the North American Society for Social Philosophy (NASSP) held at Villanova University, Pennsylvania; and the 1997 Eastern Division Meetings of the American Philosophical Association (APA) book symposium on Lewis Gordon (ed.), *Existence in Black* (Routledge, 1997).

I would like to express my profound gratitude to Lewis Gordon for inviting me to undertake a book-length study of Cornel West as a philosopher for the Routledge series on Africana Thought, of which Gordon is co-editor with Paget Henry. This book is obviously the result of that invitation. Gordon also gave me necessary support, editorial advice, and critiques of parts of the manuscript that I found absolutely invaluable. In this context, I also wish to thank my Routledge philosophy editor, Damon Zucca, for his support and patience, as well as his willingness to accommodate my suggestions for improving the manuscript.

I effectively commenced the research for this book in spring 1998 as a scholar-in-residence at New York University under the auspices of the NYU Faculty Resource Network. I wish to thank the administrators and staff of the network for making my stay at NYU worthwhile and quite productive. I especially wish to thank Robert (Bob) Gurland, my faculty host, of NYU's Philosophy Department, for those stimulating discussions about my research project.

My ability to continue with the research here at MTSU was owing to several research grants that I received from the university, through the College of Graduate Studies and the Faculty Research and Creative Activity Committee (FRCAC). I thank Dr. Donald Curry, Dean of the College of Graduate Studies, and the FRCAC for their support, on behalf of the institution, without which I might not have been able to complete the work in a timely manner.

Finally, I thank Dr. John McDaniel, dean of the College of Liberal Arts at MTSU, for his keen interest in my research and for his support, which have enabled me to pursue my research goals with much success.

Variant forms of my discussions in chapters 2 and 3 appeared respectively in George Yancy (ed.), *Cornel West: A Critical Reader* (Blackwell, 2001) and in the *Journal of Social Philosophy*, vol. 32, no.4 (winter 2001), 547–572, also a Blackwell publication. I would like to thank Blackwell Publishers for permission to reproduce those essays here.

Cornel West's Philosophical Writings and Social Justice

This study is the first extended, systematic, and thoroughgoing philosophical interrogation of Cornel West's diverse corpus as a cohesive whole and with a specific focus on social justice.[1] By this I mean that the present study elaborates, articulates, and analyzes the theoretical framework that is central to and thus gives unity to West's diverse intellectual preoccupations. That theoretical framework is an admixture of pragmatism, existentialism, Marxism, and Black prophetic Christianity. West's intellectual preoccupations crystallize around the theme of social justice. Or, alternatively put, social justice is the guiding preoccupation of West's philosophy. Accordingly, any serious discussion of West's philosophical views cannot but examine his various claims about social justice. In light of this fact, my proposed aim is both to elaborate West's position on social justice and to advance a penetrating critique of some of the concrete issues on social justice that West examines in light of his subscription to pragmatism, existentialism, Marxism, and Black prophetic Christianity.

In general, discussions of social justice are formulated responses to the question: "What kind(s) of institutional arrangements and configurations are necessary in society for the existence and promotion of human dignity?" Fundamentally, this question is about the type(s) of social arrangements that should regulate the distribution of societal benefits and burdens in a manner compatible with justice, thereby promoting social stability and upholding human dignity.

1

Justice in this sense simply means fairness and equity. Philosophers since Plato and Aristotle have been grappling with this question in one form or another.[2] More recently, noted social and political philosopher John Rawls has responded to the demands of the question by positing an ideal condition, called a veil of ignorance, from which rational agents in an original position of equality would establish a system of justice that would uphold and promote human dignity. The original position is one in which the parties to the discussion and subsequent agreement about the principle of justice they should adopt, *prior* to establishing a system of justice, are ignorant of whatever advantages or disadvantages they each may have before deliberating and hence choosing a principle of justice. For Rawls, this condition of ignorance is necessary to prevent each individual member's contingent situation entering into and thus influencing the deliberation and subsequent outcome in terms of their choice of principle. The principle of justice that follows upon this procedure of ignorance is what Rawls calls "justice as fairness."[3] Others such as Marx, on the other hand, have approached the issue from the backdrop of an already unjust (read unfair) *status quo* in the sense of bourgeois appropriation of capital and exploitation of labor. And for Marx, such a status quo ought to be dismantled by means of a violent proletarian revolution for justice even to begin to be achieved.[4] In significant ways, Cornel West's philosophical preoccupations, both theoretical and practical, are an attempt to address this question. And West approaches the task from the presupposition of the existence of injustice in society that he thinks must be eradicated to uphold human dignity.

From a moral point of view, a society is unjust if, among other things, both the mechanism that it establishes to administer the distribution of benefits and burdens and the very distribution itself disadvantage some of its members. Put otherwise, the society has a legal (or constitutional) framework in terms of which its institutions are established and governed, yet, concerning the establishment and distribution of benefits and burdens, the legally sanctioned institutional arrangements disadvantage some members of the society. It is important to stress the legality of the institutional framework through which some members of society are disadvantaged. What this shows is that it does not follow from the fact that a social arrangement is legally sanctioned that it is morally acceptable. Well-known examples are slavery and gender discrimination. Significantly, the lived reality of the disadvantaged members is tantamount to social degradation and devaluation. And this constitutes a grave moral infraction against them because it violates the principle of dignity that befits them as persons. West's concern with social justice is to propose measures to address what he considers grave moral transgressions against the disadvantaged members of society in light of societal/institutional organization, and thus to uphold and promote their dignity as persons. For this reason, West's concern derives from ethical considerations. I shall amplify this point shortly, but for now I simply wish to call attention to certain empirical factors that I believe played a role in orienting West toward the issue of social justice.

West's preoccupation with social justice may be traced back to his formative years in Sacramento, California. Growing up in a segregated part of Sacramento, West began to be conscious of the disparities in society at a very early age. There was no library where he lived, so that access to reading material was by way of a bookmobile.[5] West reports that his first exposure to philosophy was at about age thirteen or fourteen through material on Kierkegaard that he had obtained from the bookmobile. What struck him the most about Kierkegaard's writing, he says, was Kierkegaard's struggle with "a certain level of melancholia," a struggle with a profound sadness, sorrow, and terror about the human condition. Kierkegaard's preoccupation "resonated deeply"[6] with him particularly because of Kierkegaard's endeavor both to grapple with the issue of "what it means to be human" and "to come to terms with despair and dread . . . that was inescapable" (Osborne 1996, 128). Considering that at this teenage period West's experiences were limited largely to the segregated part of Sacramento, one can only surmise that Kierkegaard's writing resonated with him because it offered him a philosophical representation of the social and existential situation of Blacks in the United States at the time. Through the writing of Kierkegaard, in other words, West was able to give meaning to the pervasive sorrow, sadness, and terror that enveloped his community and by extension the rest of Black America. In this way, Kierkegaard's writing enabled West to relate philosophical reflection and speculation to the existentially concrete situation of the human being. It is in light of this influence of Kierkegaard's writing that West later will characterize the lived reality of African Americans in the United States as the absurd, in the existentialist sense, with the society itself being the grand theater in which the absurd is enacted. By the absurd West means the Black experience of disappointment, despair, dread (or anxiety), disease, and (social) death owing to Black subordinate status, the latter of which derives from anti-Black racism. In short, Kierkegaard's writing was "decisive" to West's philosophical development (Yancy 1998, 33).

Although Kierkegaard's writing highlighted the existential dimension of suffering that appealed to West and provided West with the concept of the absurd to capture the suffering that typifies the Black experience, it was the Black church that established the foundation for West's awareness of Black suffering. This is because the Black church has always been concerned with Black oppression and liberation. Or, as West puts it, the Black church has as its central concern "the problem of evil and the confrontation with social misery" (Osborne 1996, 128). What this means is that the Black church was central to attuning West's mind, as it did that of most Blacks, to Black social misery owing to White–supremacist policies. The Black church articulated Black experience of vilification, degradation, and suffering and put forward critiques of the society as it also provided African Americans with the mechanism to remake themselves in the context of their social condition. It is in light of this fact about the role and significance of the Black church in his intellectual life that West says that the Black church is "fundamental" to his intellectual development. And it is in this context that we should see West's own philosophic quest as, among other things, an attempt "to make sense of the world" (Yancy 1998, 47). He undertakes this quest through a concern with social justice.

In pursuit of this quest for social justice West further draws upon the theoretical outlooks of Marxism and American pragmatism, especially John Dewey's variant of the latter, because he considers both philosophical positions as being concerned with the plight of the socially disadvantaged. During his teenage years in Sacramento and prior to attending Harvard for his undergraduate studies, West was exposed to Marxist literature disseminated by the Black Panther

Party through the writings of Black revolutionary writers such as Amilcar Cabral, Kwame Nkrumah, and Franz Fanon. And later in college he studied the views of Karl Marx and other Marxists such as Antonio Gramsci (Osborne 1996, 128). This exposure to Marxism later shaped West's politicoeconomic outlook and engendered in him the belief that capitalism is the cause of social misery in society. And this belief in turn is at the core of the proto-Marxian solution he proposes as remedy to the condition of the socially disadvantaged.

West's exposure to American pragmatism was as an undergraduate student at Harvard. However, it was as a graduate student at Princeton University, under the influence of Richard Rorty, that he developed an acute interest in Dewey's version of the doctrine. What appealed to West was Dewey's preoccupation with the plight of the socially underprivileged and disadvantaged in nineteenth-century United States during the industrial revolution. West drew upon Dewey's brand of pragmatism and synthesized it with features of his Christian background and his Marxist orientation to define his own philosophical outlook, which he calls prophetic pragmatism. Prophetic pragmatism is the theoretical foundation on which West anchors his analyses of social issues in contemporary society. I therefore proceed in chapter 1, "Pragmatism and Existentialism," with a discussion of West's prophetic pragmatism infused with his existentialist concerns. I then give an illustrative treatment and examination of a social concern that West articulates in the claim that the existential predicament of African Americans in contemporary urban society consists of a form of nihilism.

In chapter 2, "Humanistic Scholarship and Praxis," I show that West's diverse intellectual engagements transcend disciplinary boundaries, as they also are concerned with praxis. This is because West believes that humanistic theory should always have a cash value in praxis, a position he articulates through the concept of the humanistic intellectual as a critical organic catalyst in society. In West's view, humanistic studies that fail to uphold this principle are ends in themselves and make no difference to society. Similarly, he thinks, practitioners of humanistic studies that fail to establish a relation between theory and praxis are of little intellectual relevance to society. To illustrate this claim, West singles out for special scrutiny the early

Black cultural critics in American society, contemporary Black intellectuals, and Black political leadership. In light of his view about the role of the humanistic scholar to society, I argue that what drives West's diverse intellectual engagements is a desire to define himself as a humanistic scholar and thus to establish his practical relevance to society in the sense of addressing social concerns. However, I challenge West's criticism of the early Black cultural critics as misguided and his criticism of Black intellectuals (as opposed to the Black intellectual leadership) as misplaced even as I endorse his attack on the Black political leadership. But notwithstanding my trenchant critique of West on these issues, I conclude that his praxis bears out his rhetoric insofar as the issue of social justice is concerned. In other words, there is a consistency between West's rhetoric and practice.

I take up the subject of social justice in detail in chapter 3, "Black Prophetic Christianity and Marxist Social Thought." Here I examine, among other things, West's claim that social justice for Blacks in particular, but generally for people of color, can only be realized through a synthesis of the insights of Black prophetic Christianity and Marxist social thought. I show that this position offers a reductivist, simplistic, and false account of Black oppression. The position is reductivist because it erroneously represents all forms of oppression as a function of class. And it is simplistic and false because it explains Black oppression in terms of class subordination when in fact it is by virtue of race that Blacks occupy the lower class they do. In short, oppression is much more complex than West seems willing to acknowledge. Finally, I posit some conceptual and practical difficulties against West's view that capitalism is inherently (read logically) incompatible with social justice and argue, contra West, that the pursuit of social justice can be effected within a reformed liberal capitalism.

The subject of the Black quest for social justice is incomplete, however, without also an examination of the conflict between Blacks and Jews in the society at large. This is because Blacks and Jews are the most despised and vilified groups in Western society, both the targets of White supremacist assault and treatment, yet both groups have been unable to forge a common bond that should enable them to resist oppression. Instead, there are charges of Black anti-Semitism and of Jewish anti-Black racism. What is the reason for this tense relation between the two groups? And how, in particular, is the Black quest for social justice, as that of Jewish people, affected by this friction between the two groups? It is these issues that I examine in chapter 4, "Black-Jewish Conflict and Dialogue." West's diagnosis of the problem is in terms of a mutual misperception between the two groups and thus a mutual misrepresentation by each group of the other. Accordingly, he proposes dialogue as a solution.

I begin by delineating the mutual misperception that West thinks is the cause of the problem between Blacks and Jews. I then go on to supplement West's diagnosis of the problem by drawing upon some recent scholarship in which it is argued that one of the influential items that led to the disintegration of the relation between Blacks and Jews was a socioeconomic clash of interests between them. The conflict was over the administration of a local school board in the Ocean Hill-Brownsville section of New York City. In this regard, I note that the parties to this and similar conflicts were recent Jewish and Black immigrants, from Eastern Europe and the Caribbean, respectively. These new immigrants were not linked to and by the "historical" Black-Jewish alliance prior to and during the 1960s, the period of the civil rights movement. Furthermore, the new members of the respective groups were integrated very quickly into the pervasive and conflict-oriented *racial* dynamics of the larger society. And to add to the complexity of the situation is the fact that in American society Blacks and Jews are differently situated in the socioeconomic hierarchy, with Jews at the top and Blacks at the bottom. Thus, this socioeconomic clash of interests between the two groups, inscribed within the racial dynamics of the larger society, got recast into a Black-Jewish conflict, with charges of Jewish anti-Black racism and countercharges of Black anti-Semitism.

Against this expanded backdrop of the putative cause of the problem between Blacks and Jews, I proceed to critique West's proposed solution of dialogue as remedy. In particular, I argue that his proposed solution does not go far enough to the heart of the matter in the society. Contra West, I suggest that any proposed solution to the conflict must go beyond dialogue between the two groups to confront the larger issue of the possibility of a deracialized society. Finally, I call attention to certain inherent limitations to and presuppositions of dialogue that West simply glosses over but that make his proposed solution appear simplistic if not downright naive.

Central to the pursuit of social justice by Blacks is affirmative action. This is a federal government-mandated policy implemented in the 1960s to remedy the systemic race and gender social injustice meted out against Blacks and women in the sphere of employment, education, and other aspects of life in both the public and private sectors. Yet this policy has met with virulent opposition since its inception, especially from White males. Some have even charged that affirmative action is reverse discrimination because, they say, it is preferential treatment and has nothing to do with qualifications, competence, and merit. Although West is aware of this kind of viewpoint, he does not attempt to challenge it in any protracted manner. Instead, he advances a Marxian class-based alternative affirmative action proposal as a remedy to social inequities. I take up this matter in chapter 5, "Affirmative Action and Proto-Marxism."

First, I challenge the identification of affirmative action with preferential treatment. Second, I elaborate West's motivation for a class-based alternative policy and show that his proposal is consistent with his humanistic endeavors and so has the advantage of being more inclusive than the current race and gender policy. However, I go on to argue that West's alternative is out of step with the specific challenges that historically have circumscribed Black and women's demands for social justice, namely, race and gender oppression, and to which the current policy is thus a response. I articulate the specific form of oppression experienced by Blacks by invoking a Du Boisean theoretical framework in terms of which blackness is synonymous with being *the* problem in and to society. Using this framework, I argue that the systemic institutional exclusion of Blacks from the public domain *in light of their blackness* (which is deemed an aberration to the society) is at the core or Black oppression, not class, as West would have us believe. Accordingly, his class-based affirmative action proposal just does not apply as a solution to a problem that is race and gender based.

In chapter 6, "Modernity, Philosophy, and Race(ism)," I examine the views of "enlightenment" philosophers on the subject of race and what I consider the propagation and dissemination of White supremacy. This subject is fitting at this juncture because West's discussion of the ethics of social justice is in essence a targeted response to the ubiquitous ethos, culture, and praxis of White supremacy that pervade contemporary society. More particularly, the various ways in which White supremacy is manifested in contemporary society are all traceable to "enlightenment" discourses of race and personhood. These discourses themselves, presented under the guise of science, created a hierarchy of the different races as an ontological "given," with Whites at the apex and Blacks at the base. Within this framework, Whites are constructed and presented as cognitively, emotionally, and aesthetically superior to all others but especially Blacks, their supposed natural antithesis. Put otherwise, we have in enlightenment discourse a polarity between the "best" and "worst" of nature, constructed and represented respectively as Whites and Blacks. It was in light of this framework or representation that African slavery was promulgated and perpetuated. Since contemporary anti-Black racism derives from the intellectual superstructure created in enlightenment discourse, it is therefore worth exploring the contributions of philosophers in upholding and sanctifying that structure.

My focus on the philosophers is for two reasons. First, I show that even as philosophers often profess to speak on behalf of humanity, they sometimes articulate the most virulent forms of racism and bigotry usually associated with the ignorant and uneducated. Ironically, they supposedly are the pioneers and champions of knowledge and of all that is good, right, and just in society. What makes this phenomenon most frightening and disturbing is that philosophers are trained to take a critical approach to issues. Yet the critical eye that enlightenment philosophers should have brought to bear on the subject of race was severely jaundiced and plagued with cataract. Such a global critical deficiency (or illness) on the issue of race is exemplified in the views of key enlightenment figures such as John Locke (1632–1704), David Hume (1711–1776), Immanuel Kant (1724–1804), Georg Wilhelm Friedrich Hegel (1770–1831), and others. Second, and more importantly, philosophical views (e.g., about the nature of society, the human good, etc.) undoubtedly influence public policy. How, if at all, did the racist positions of enlightenment philosophers help shape the public policies and sustain the White supremacist ethos, culture, and superstructure that are responsible for the social injustice experienced by people of color, especially Blacks? It is with a speculation on this matter that I close this chapter.

Finally, I conclude this study with a postscript entitled "West, Public Intellectualism, and the Harvard Controversy." This conclusion is fitting in light of a purported tension between Lawrence H. Summers, president of Harvard, and West over the nature of West's scholarship. It is reported that Summers criticized West's sociopolitical involvement as well as his engaging in the production of a rap music CD entitled *Sketches of My Culture* as anything but scholarship. And this criticism has fostered tension between both West and the department of Afro-American Studies, on the one hand, and President Summers, on the other. In light of this issue, I address the following questions: (1) What is the nature of the scholarship of a public intellectual? (2) How, if at all, is West's sociopolitical engagement and musical adventure consistent with his self-definition as a public intellectual? (3) Finally, is a college or university president in a position singularly to evaluate the scholarship of a faculty member without transgressing or undermining academic freedom?

The Ethical Basis of West's Concern with Social Justice

I claimed earlier that West's concern with social justice has an ethical basis. Given West's explicit affirmation about the role and influence of his Christian background in his intellectual development, it might perhaps be thought that the ethical basis of his concern with social justice is a variant of the Divine Command theory of morality that is central to religions. But this is not the case, as I shall show presently. The Divine Command theory of morality claims that our ideas of right and wrong, good and bad, and related notions of morals derive from a Supreme Being in the form of a set of commandments prescribed by such a being for humans to follow. An action is moral, then, to the extent that it conforms to the prescriptions of the deity and is immoral to the extent that it contravenes those prescriptions. We find an illustration of a morally right action, according to the Divine Command theory, in the willingness of the biblical Abraham to sacrifice his only child, Isaac, simply upon being informed by an angel that God had required such an act of Abraham. It really does not matter that Abraham may have been hallucinating. The point is that if Abraham had questioned this requirement, which supposedly was from God, or had shown an unwillingness to follow the commands, he would have disobeyed

God, and such disobedience would have constituted a moral trans-gression against God.

Despite his insistence on his Christian background and even his invocation of the notion of "prophet" in his claim to being a prophetic pragmatist, the ethical consideration that informs West's concern with social justice is not a variant of the Divine Command theory. On the contrary, we find a secular ethics at the heart of West's concern, an ethics that I go on to describe as humanistic. By secular ethics I mean one that is not defended on religious grounds, and hence is only tan-gentially related to a religious outlook. At the same time it is a posi-tion that is compatible with a nonreligious outlook. Alternatively put, if the psychological motivation behind West's engagement with social justice is his religious background, the arguments he advances for social justice are not themselves rooted in religion.

A work of this nature undoubtedly is limited in scope. There are a variety of issues into which I cannot go here given the focus on social justice. For example, is there a shift in West's philosophical position between the publication of his proto-Marxian *Prophecy Deliverance* and his pragmatist-oriented *American Evasion of Philosophy?*[7] (For this reading of West see Wood 2000, esp. chap. 4; cp. chap. 1, esp. 45–62.) The implication of this question is that there is an inconsistency between West's self-declared Marxist view, prominently articulated in the former work and his *Ethical Dimensions of Marxist Thought,* and his pragmatist-motivated out-look in the latter work.[8] Specifically, in *Prophecy Deliverance,* West maintains that the chief source of social injustice is the monopolistic stranglehold that capitalists have on the resources of society, hence causing an overall maldistribution of capital. Accordingly, he calls for a dismantling of capitalism to achieve social justice. However, in *American Evasion of Philosophy* and subsequent works, it is argued, West seems to be advocating a *reform* and not a destruction of the current liberal capitalist structure to achieve social justice. Thus, either he has shifted from his earlier Marxian position in favor of a pragmatist position or he is logically inconsistent. The demand there-fore is for West to reconcile his supposed proto-Marxian orientation and his supposed pragmatist outlook.

Another issue that may call for examination is the following: How consistent is West's claim to being antifoundationalist with his avowed Christian outlook? This question is significant because religious claims are inherently unempirical and so are not open to revision in light of new data. But then, to the extent that all such claims are grounded on faith, and faith is a subjective psychological condition of its practitioner, they are both dogmatic and foundationalist. The argument here, seen differently, is that religious claims or, better still, the propositions in which they are formulated, are not in any way different from propositions about sense data. Sense data themselves are not open to public inspection but yet have sometimes been taken to be about the external world. Indeed, some philosophers, such as G. E. Moore, even claim that propositions about sense data are unproblematic by construing their proper analyses as claims about parts of the surface of material objects and then appeal to common sense as guide to determine the veracity of such claims.[9] Even so, such reliability as Moore claims for the judgments of common sense is nothing short of dogmatism because it assumes the veracity of common sense itself. In like manner, it might be said, West's purported antifoundationalism would seem to be logically inconsistent with his avowed Christian outlook precisely because the latter is invariably dogmatic. Finally, in light of these conceptual issues that warrant explication and reconciliation, how secure then is the basis on which West depends for his discussion of social justice?

These undoubtedly are philosophically interesting issues. However, in view of my focus here they must await another discussion. This work is premised on the assumption that West's prophetic pragmatism is consistent with both his proto-Marxian and Christian outlooks, and I have even tried to motivate such a consistency. Still, I ask, what are the consequences of the triage for West's engagement with the issue of social justice? It is an answer to this question that I have tried to sketch in this work. And in pursuing this task, my methodology consists in conceptual analyses of West's views with the goal of establishing whether or not they are consistent, plausible, problematic, or otherwise.

CHAPTER ONE

Pragmatism and Existentialism

Introduction

Although Cornel West is generally acknowledged to be a pragmatist, in light of his own very identification with that position, very little attempt has been made thus far to relate his pragmatism to his existentialist preoccupations.[1] It is with this task that I shall be concerned in this chapter. In particular, I propose to elaborate how West draws upon his concept of prophetic pragmatism to address social concerns such as what he deems a nihilistic threat to Black America. To realize this goal, I will begin by giving a general but detailed overview of West's philosophical orientation in order to situate him within the pragmatist tradition. I then will go on to elaborate his discussion of nihilism in Black America and to critique his philosophy of prophetic pragmatism as a viable strategy to resolve the nihilistic threat to Black America.

Situating West as Pragmatist

A useful starting point for my discussion is West's own exemplary historical, if brief, account of the genealogy of pragmatism in *The American Evasion of Philosophy* (1989). In this work West delineates some of the most distinctive, perhaps even the defining, attributes of pragmatism. Essentially, he says, pragmatism, as a philosophical movement begun by Ralph Waldo Emerson, marked a radical departure in the United States from the dominant philosophy in Europe as reflected in the writings of the continental rationalists and the so-called British empiricists. The concern of rationalists and empiricists alike was epistemological; specifically, to subvert skepticism by providing a sound foundation for knowledge. The foundation was sought in the criterion of certainty. The point of deviance between these two competing schools, however, was over the method by which the purported certainty could be attained. For the rationalists it was through the employment of reason unaided by experience, whereas for the empiricists it was by means of sensation. What is significant is that this issue dogged philosophy with no sign of a resolution. Besides, there was also a metaphysical import to the whole enterprise in that the quest for certainty was a quest for apprehending (i.e., attaining knowledge of) the nature of reality. Thus, the issue between the rationalists and the empiricists was about the method by which knowledge of reality could be attained—whether through the employment of reason unaided by experience or through atomistic sensation.[2] According to West, this unresolvable issue that engaged the European philosophers provided, indeed constituted, the point of departure for pragmatism, the only authentic Western philosophy native to America. What then does pragmatism advocate?

Pragmatism, says West, in its historical evasion of epistemologically centered philosophy, is "a future-oriented instrumentalism that tries to deploy thought as a weapon to enable more effective action." Or, better still, pragmatism advances "a conception of philosophy as a form of cultural criticism in which the meaning of America is put forward by intellectuals in response to distinct social and cultural crises" (1989, 5). It is this characteristic of pragmatism, namely, of its having as an end *knowledge as it relates to action*, that clearly distinguishes the doctrine from European philosophy, the latter of which was concerned either with knowledge as such or with being as an extrasensory phenomenon.

It is not my aim here to identify let alone discuss any of the crises in reaction to which pragmatism originated as response and/or tried to side-step. I mention this fact about the point of departure of pragmatism only to call attention to the following features of the position. First, pragmatism is action oriented. Second, it is concerned with consequences. And third, as a social and cultural critique, pragmatism is a dynamic (as opposed to a static) philosophical position. This last point is of the utmost significance because it brings out very clearly the relevance of pragmatism to the contemporary United States. As society undergoes change—social, economic, and cultural—pragmatisms come to bear on the ongoing discussion about the nature of the change. It is in this connection that one sees clearly the rationale for West's identification of himself as a Deweyan, rather than a Piercean or Jamesian, pragmatist. As he tells us, "the thoroughgoing historical consciousness and emphasis on social and political matters found in John Dewey speaks more to my purpose than the preoccupations with logic in Pierce and the obsessions with individuality in James" (ibid., 6). This remark immediately begs a central question of the present study: "What is Cornel West's purpose in his philosophy?" To answer this question I will have to answer yet another, even more fundamental, question: What, in West's view, is the nature of Dewey's pragmatism?

West characterizes Dewey as "the greatest of the American pragmatists" (ibid., 69) because, among other things, Dewey's pragmatism expresses "a mode of historical consciousness that highlights the conditioned and circumstantial character of human existence in terms of changing societies, cultures, and communities" (69–70). West goes on to elaborate his meaning in a note explaining the difference between the pragmatism of William James and that of Dewey, saying that Dewey's is concerned with "the social and historical forces that shape the creative individual" (ch. 3, note 1). The central causal agents of change that help shape the individual are the economic structures that had emerged in a nineteenth-century society undergoing rapid industrialization. Inversely proportionate to the rapid industrialization of society and the tremendous economic success of the industrial capitalist investors was a sharp decline in the living conditions of the new industrial working class that consisted largely of immigrants and African Americans. Put baldly, the industrial working class experienced economic poverty and social misery at a time when the capitalist investors and organizations were experiencing huge economic successes. West sums up the socioeconomic reality of the industrial underclass as "principally that of economic deprivation, cultural dislocation, and personal disorientation" (80). It is directly to this crisis of the human condition that Dewey's pragmatism speaks. Thus, in a sense, Dewey's pragmatism, in its bid to formulate strategies to ameliorate the predicament thus described, is a form of social activism.

West lists three ways in which Dewey attempted to address the socioeconomic crisis of nineteenth-century America. (1) Through journalism Dewey endeavored to popularize critical intelligence (or critical thinking) so as to be able to educate the masses. (2) Dewey affiliated himself with influential middle-class humanitarian organizations that worked with the underclass in a bid "to assimilate and acculturate immigrants into the American mainstream." And (3) Dewey exercised leadership over a rapidly growing teaching profession both by practical examples and through his writing (ibid., 79–80).

It is arguable of course that Dewey succeeded in these ventures. For example, West points out that while Dewey's commitment to cultivate critical intelligence, especially in children, led him to set up a laboratory school in Chicago, popularly known as the "Dewey School," his endeavor to take philosophy to the people through the newspaper was scarcely helpful to his cause. Dewey outraged the mainstream media, which lampooned his idea, and he was unwilling to engage them in any manner whatsoever. True, Dewey was involved directly with humanitarian groups and organizations that were concerned about the social and economic condition of the industrial working class, as attested to by his participation in Hull House (founded by Jane Addams). According to Richard J. Bernstein, "Dewey mixed with workers, union organizers, and political radicals of all sorts."[3] Yet Dewey's reluctance to engage the very core middle-class establishment from which his income and status as a professional originated seems to have cast a shadow on his social activism. Thus, although he believed that social and economic redemption for the underclass could be obtained through a democratization process facilitated by education, he was most unwilling to invest the hard capital, using his professional career as collateral, for this end.

West contrasts Dewey's unwillingness to risk his professional career in support of his political beliefs with the willingness of his friend and former classmate Henry Carter Adams to do just that. Adams was dismissed from his teaching position at Cornell University because of his public support of the Knights of Labor. What is significant is that Adams had considerable difficulty securing a job because of his socialist beliefs (ibid., 80). Yet this difficulty in obtaining a job did not quell his desire to give expression to his political beliefs *after* he had landed a job. To be sure, Dewey did try to exercise leadership over his professional colleagues by even castigating them for their complacency, indolence, and ivory-tower mentality. As West puts it, "Dewey castigated the ivory-tower scholar frightened by the dirty world of politics and afraid of the consequences of active engagement" (82).[4] But when one considers that Dewey just was not prepared to face the consequences of subscribing to a political belief, his criticism of his professional colleagues seems to ring hollow. Surprisingly, West describes as "quite understandable" (82) Dewey's unwillingness to risk his career in promoting and defending his political beliefs against press criticism, especially his belief of taking philosophy to the masses. And continuing his apology for Dewey, West says that "Dewey practiced professional caution and political reticence. He remained deeply engaged in civic affairs, but shunned controversy" (83).[5] No doubt all of this is true. Yet it remains an open question whether or not Dewey was prepared to confront and engage the real culprits, the causes of the problems he was presumably working to resolve, namely, the very middle-class institutions and establishments that supported his economic and social lifestyle.

To sum up the key points of the discussion thus far, West regards the following as central to Dewey's pragmatism. First, it is action oriented in endeavoring to provide strategies through education for the amelioration of the dismal socioeconomic condition of the emergent underclass in nineteenth-century industrial America. Second, it utilized existing middle-class institutions, such as universities and humanitarian organizations, to sound a note of urgency in its critique of social and economic injustice that was meted out to the underclass. And third, for Dewey philosophy had an instrumental rather than an intrinsic worth; he felt that its value consists in its ability to be employed in the resolution of human problems rather than in its celebration of ideas as much, as the the European epistemologists believed. It is in this context that, for West, Dewey was as much a social reformer as he was a philosopher.

West's Purpose in His Philosophy

Drawing upon the foregoing discussion, I now can attempt to answer the question raised earlier about West's purpose in his philosophy. Essentially, and in a similar Deweyan spirit, West's philosophy (or his pragmatism) is unquestionably a form of cultural criticism and social activism. His principal motivation in outlining his philosophical views in *Evasion* (1989) is, in his words, "my disenchantment with intellectual life in America and my own demoralization regarding the political and cultural state of the country." In the intellectual sphere, West is disenchanted by what he describes as "the transformation of highly intelligent liberal intellectuals into tendentious neoconservatives owing to crude ethnic identity-based allegiances and vulgar neonationalist sentiments." On the political sphere, West is concerned about and disappointed with "the professional incorporation of former New Left activists who now often thrive on a self-serving careerism while espousing rhetoric of oppositional politics of little serious integrity." And on the cultural domain, he is "depressed about the concrete nihilism in working-class and underclass American communities—the pervasive drug addiction, suicides, alcoholism, male violence against women, white violence against black, yellow, and brown people, and the black criminality against others, especially other black people" (7–8).

There can be no doubt but that these concerns about the human predicament in contemporary America situate West squarely within the pragmatist tradition of Emerson and Dewey. Some parallelisms are certainly in order. For example, West's avowed interest in the plight of the underclass parallels Dewey's concern with the new industrial underclass in nineteenth-century United States. West's declared disappointment with intellectual colleagues is but a reflection or a replay of Dewey's indictment of Dewey's own professional colleagues. And West's membership in the Democratic Socialists of America is reminiscent of Dewey's affiliation with unions and organized labor.

As with Dewey, West gives a practical use to philosophy by deploying it to resolving concrete issues that affect human beings in their day-to-day struggles. His aim in so doing is to effect change in society through a reconfiguration of the structures that delimit or exclude individuals from participating in its political and economic systems. He characterizes his philosophy as "prophetic pragmatism," a position he elaborates in a variety of ways, of which the following is a succinct statement:

> Prophetic pragmatism understands the Emersonian swerve from episte-
> mology—and the American evasion of philosophy—not as a wholesale

rejection of philosophy but rather as a reconception of philosophy as a form of cultural criticism that attempts to transform linguistic, social, cultural, and political traditions for the purposes of increasing the scope of individual development and democratic operations. Prophetic pragmatism conceives of philosophy as a historically circumscribed quest for wisdom that puts forward new interpretations of the world based on past traditions in order to promote existential sustenance and political relevance. Like Emerson and earlier pragmatists, it views truth as a species of the good, as that which enhances the flourishing of human progress. This does not mean that philosophy ignores the ugly facts and unpleasant realities of life and history. Rather, it highlights these facts and realities precisely because they provoke doubt, curiosity, outrage, or desperation that motivates efforts to overcome them. These efforts take the forms of critique and praxis, forms that attempt to change what is into a better what can be. (ibid., 230)[6]

West's pragmatism is "prophetic" precisely because he draws upon his Christian background to articulate and engage the problems that confront the powerless in contemporary America with a view to their amelioration and as a spiritual vocation. Central to this vocation is an ethic of love of the kind expressed in the Bible requiring us to love our neighbors as (we do) ourselves. As I will demonstrate in the sections that follow, this concept of love will play an important role in West's discussion of the problem of Black nihilism. But what I want to stress here is that West, as both proponent and practitioner of prophetic pragmatism, envisions himself a modern-day prophet, comparable to the biblical prophets, advocating on behalf of "the wretched of the earth."

In sum, then, West, like Dewey in the nineteenth-century United States, is concerned with the social, economic, cultural (in the broadest sense), and spiritual afflictions of the powerless in contemporary society. And like the biblical prophets, West sees himself as bringing urgency to the conditions of the powerless, advocating their amelioration with honesty and integrity. With this in mind, I shall characterize West's prophetic pragmatism as a philosophical position concerned with cultural criticism, imbued with a moral content and anchored in West's Christian background. This characterization draws support from West's own very remark:

> I hold a religious conception of pragmatism. I have dubbed it
> "prophetic" in that it harks back to the Jewish and Christian tradi-
> tion of prophets who brought urgent and compassionate critique to
> bear on the evils of their day. The mark of the prophet is to speak the
> truth in love with courage—come what may. Prophetic pragmatism
> proceeds from this impulse. It neither requires a religious foundation
> nor entails a religious perspective, yet prophetic pragmatism is com-
> patible with religious outlooks. (*Evasion*, 233)

It scarcely needs any argument to show that West's primary object in
Evasion is to contextualize prophetic pragmatism as an authentic
variety of American pragmatism. He suggests as much in his con-
cluding remarks in the introductory chapter of *Evasion*. "I began this
work as an exercise in critical self-inventory, as a historical, social,
and existential situating of my own work as an intellectual, activist,
and human being. I wanted to make clear to myself my own contra-
dictions and tensions, faults and foibles as one shaped by, in part, the
tradition of American pragmatism." Or again: "I have written this
text convinced that a thorough examination of American pragmatism, stripping it of its myths, caricatures, and stereotypes and viewing it as a component of a new and novel form of indigenous
American oppositional thought and action, may be a first step
toward fundamental change and transformation in America and the
world" (8). These remarks, taken in light of the preceding discussion,
validate further the point that West's philosophical concerns situate
him squarely within the pragmatist tradition. I now will give an illustrative treatment of one specific issue about human existence that
West interrogates from the perspective of an existentialist informed
by the motivations of prophetic pragmatism. Specifically, I will consider his treatment of nihilism among African Americans in his book
Race Matters.[7]

West and Black Nihilism

One existentialist concern that West raises in *Race Matters* (1994) is
what he describes as the pervasive sense of utter meaninglessness,
despondency, self-loathing and impotence that permeates Black
America, especially its youth (1994, 22–23). It is this horrifying phenomenon that West characterizes as nihilism in Black America. Black
nihilism, in short, is a life without hope that constitutes a severe

threat to the very survival of Black America. And it is precisely because of the severe threat that nihilism poses for Black America that West says nihilism needs to be confronted.[8]

West identifies two main causes of this nihilism: (1) the preponderance of market morality in America and (2) the serious and deleterious crisis of leadership in the Black community. Concerning the first, the preponderance of market morality, West contends that the market forces promote, even advocate, an ethic of consumerism that subordinates, instrumentalizes, or objectifies others as a means of pleasure for one's own profit. Another way of putting this point is to say that market morality commodifies human beings, thereby treating them as a means to an end, the end being profit, rather than (in Kant's well-known terminology) ends in themselves.[9] This morality construes bestial hedonism as a virtue, for it takes the end in life to be indulgence in the seductive transient pleasures of the body. Furthermore, and more importantly, this market morality is transmitted through the airwaves and dominates popular culture—radio, television, movies, and so on—thereby creating a form of environmental and psychological pollution for all who exposed to the American environment. It is in this regard that the market morality is a partial cause of Black nihilism. For, to the extent that Blacks in the United States coexist with others in the environment whose atmosphere is overwhelmed by this pollution, their behavior is thus environmentally and psychologically determined by the influences of the market morality. In other words, there is a form of environmental and psychological determinism according to which the behavior of Blacks, and all others in the American atmosphere, is a direct consequence of the preponderance of market forces. Among Blacks, in particular, this determinism gives rise to either of two forms of behavior, depending on the economic (and hence social) stratum of society to which the individual belongs: (1) excessive, tasteless, and nauseating consumerism, if the individual belongs to the Black middle class; or (2) drugs, crime, alcoholism, and violence, if the individual belongs to the underclass. Since the majority of Blacks in American society occupy the lower stratum in the socioeconomic ladder, it is therefore among them that the nihilistic behavior is most virulent. The reason is that they cannot be active participants in the market forces that shape their lives and to which they nonetheless are exposed constantly. Thus they cannot enjoy the seeming benefits, albeit banal, that market morality glorifies and presents as the virtues of self-worth and personal success. The individual's perception of his or her failure to experience via the market medium the bodily titillations glorified and worshiped by market morality occasions a sense of utter despair and meaninglessness, an existential anguish. And the net result of such anguish is crime, drugs, alcoholism, and violence. In sum, we have in the Black community, particularly among the underclass, self-destructiveness brought on by a sense of utter powerlessness.

In saying this West is not excusing the immoral conduct of some Blacks or attempting to absolve them from personal responsibility for their actions. He clearly states that "black murderers and rapists should go to jail" (ibid., 25; cf. 85), a position that would be difficult to maintain if he subscribed to, because it is incompatible with, rigid determinism. On the other hand, he notes that failing to offer a causal explanation of the conduct of Blacks in terms of the socioeconomic forces that impinge upon their very being, forces that affect individual decisions, and yet condemn them, is to ascribe blame or responsibility to them unfairly. And it is this charge of unfairness that West brings against the new Black conservatives for what he considers their unevenhanded indictment of Black behavior and their argument for the wholesale dismantling of those social programs upon which individuals in the Black underclass depend for sheer survival. (Black conservatives argue against social programs because, in their view, those programs have bred nothing but a mentality of dependency in the Black community.) As West says,

> My aim is not to provide excuses for black behavior or to absolve blacks from personal responsibility. But when the new black conservatives accent black behavior and responsibility in such a way that the cultural realities of black people are ignored, they are playing a deceptive and dangerous intellectual game with the lives and fortunes of disadvantaged people. We indeed must criticize and condemn immoral acts of black people, but we must do so cognizant of the circumstances into which people are born and under which they live. By overlooking these circumstances, the new black conservatives fall into the trap of blaming black poor people for their predicament. It is

imperative to steer a course between the Scylla of environmental determinism and the Charybdis of a blaming-the-victims perspective. (85)

The second partial cause of Black nihilism, says West, is the absence of effective (in the sense of quality) leadership, both politically and intellectually, among Blacks. Briefly stated, West's point is that post-civil rights Black leadership has failed to undertake a critical discussion of issues, actual and potential, affecting the Black community with a view toward putting forth concrete solutions, even in a preemptive way, to some of the ills that wreak havoc in the community. Among these ills are the disintegration of the Black family, sexism and violence toward Black women, homophobia, and xenophobia.

According to West, nowhere was this absence of Black leadership voice more pronounced than in the 1992 Senate Confirmation Hearings of Clarence Thomas, then President George Herbert Walker Bush's nominee for the Supreme Court. Among other things, West argues, the Black leadership was silent on the issue of Thomas' (in)competence and hence (un)suitability to serve in the Supreme Court; they did not examine Thomas' proven track record in any of the offices in which he had served prior to being nominated, nor did they even discuss Thomas' character, especially in light of the charge of sexual harassment that Anita Hill had brought against him during the Confirmation Hearings, either to absolve him from or convict him of wrongdoing.

West attributes this immoral silence of the Black leadership to what he describes as racial reasoning, a Black "closing-ranks mentality" (ibid., 37–38) that demands that Blacks should rally behind their fellow Blacks in a racist society where the opportunity to serve in such a highly respected capacity is rare. Thus, even if the leadership had reservations about the suitability of Thomas to serve as the representative of the Black intellectual leadership in matters of jurisprudence in the highest court of the land, they nevertheless allowed racial reasoning to override their better, honest, and truthful judgment about Thomas' very (un)qualification for the office. And this, says West, is "most disturbing," for it reflects a "failure of nerve of [the] black leadership" (35).

More generally, concerning Black leadership in dealing with the threat of nihilism in the Black community, West remarks that contemporary political leaders seem too anxious to call attention to themselves, in particular to their being successful in America, rather than to the afflictions of the less fortunate. And he deems this aspect of current Black leadership a mark of moral degeneracy (ibid., 54), since for such leadership politics functions instrumentally to the realization of *each leader's* own individual selfish ends. Thus, contrasting contemporary Black leadership with the leadership of the not-too-distant past, West states:

> [M]ost present-day black political leaders appear too hungry for status to be angry, too eager for acceptance to be bold, too self-invested in advancement to be defiant. And when they do drop their masks and try to get mad (usually in the presence of black audiences), their bold rhetoric is more performance than personal, more play-acting than heartfelt. Malcolm, Martin, Ella, and Fannie made sense of the black plight in a poignant and powerful manner, whereas most contemporary political leaders' oratory appeals to black people's sense of the sentimental and sensational. (58)

It is in this context that West laments the nonexistence of *quality* individuals of the likes of Frederick Douglass, Sojourner Truth, Martin Luther King Jr., Malcolm X, and Fannie Lou Hamer among today's crop of Black political leaders (53).

West proceeds to characterize contemporary Black political leadership into the following three groups. First are the race-effacing managerial leaders such as Wilson Goode (ex-Mayor of Philadelphia) and the late Thomas Bradley (ex-Mayor of Los Angeles). Second are the race-identifying protest leaders such as Louis Farrakhan of the Nation of Islam and Marion Barry (ex-Mayor of Washington, D.C.). And third are the race-transcending prophetic leaders such as the late Harold Washington (ex-Mayor of Chicago) and, to some extent, at least in terms of effort, "The Jesse Jackson of 1988." Noting that "the first type is growing rapidly," West points out that, on the positive side, this group "survives on sheer political savvy and thrives on personal diplomacy." On the negative side, however, because this group's chief interest is "the practical mainstream as the only game in town," it therefore "tends to stunt progressive development and silence the prophetic voices in the black community" (ibid., 58–59).

In contrast, race-identifying protest leaders typically carve out a

Black turf over which they set themselves as war-lords, "vowing to protect their leadership status over it, and serving as power brokers with powerful nonblack elites (usually white economic or political elites . . . to 'enhance' this black turf)." Continuing, West says that these leaders "function as figures who white Americans must appease *so that the plight of the black poor is overlooked and forgotten*" (ibid., 60, emphasis added).

It is significant, however, that neither of these two groups can meet the challenge of the Black nihilistic threat. The race-effacing leadership is too busy attempting to endear itself to the dominant (read White) establishment to have enough commitment to address the most urgent and burning ills afflicting the Black community. Besides, it would not be *politically practical* to devote the time and commit the resources necessary to address such problems. For the race-identifying group, it would seem that the threat to Black survival ceases to exist once the dominant establishment has appeased the leadership. And one would imagine such "appeasements" to occur regularly. Little wonder then that West says quite rightly that of the two types of leadership the former is the lesser evil when the alternative is a conservative, invariably a White, politician.

Finally, West discusses race-transcending prophetic leadership. It is this group that West credits with the credentials, both political and moral, to avert Black nihilism. He lists the following as the prerequisites for membership into this group: "personal integrity and political savvy, moral vision and prudential judgment, courageous defiance and organizational patience." But no sooner has West specified these attributes than he hastens to add, "The present generation has yet to produce such a figure" (ibid., 61)—that is, one who would meet these requirements. Paradoxically, it is this type of leadership that has the authority to meet and hopefully resolve the existential crisis in the Black community.

West's criticism of the lack of quality individuals among Black political leadership extends also to Black intellectuals. In a tone reminiscent of Dewey, West indicts contemporary Black intellectuals with, among other things, mediocrity, narrow specialization and a lack of engagement with "the battles of the streets" (ibid., 62), meaning with concrete issues affecting Black America. Among the reasons he gives for this phenomenon is that many Black scholars isolate themselves from mainstream academy; they "distance themselves so far from the mainstream academy that they have little to sustain them as scholars" (63). And it is precisely in this way that Black scholars marginalize themselves, producing only work of mediocre quality.

Corresponding to each of the three categories of Black politicians already noted, West draws a similar category among Black intellectuals. These are the race-distancing elites, the race-embracing rebels, and the race-transcending prophets. The first, usually found in the most exclusive universities and colleges, view themselves as having a near monopoly on the knowledge of "what is wrong with black America." Furthermore, says West, "They revel in severe denigration of much black behavior yet posit little potential or possibility in Afro-America." West's criticism of this group is particularly severe not because of their attack on Black conduct as such, but because, as he says, their criticism, although trenchant, "often degenerates into a revealing self-hatred" (ibid., 64). In other words, the virulence of their criticism reflects their self-hatred (at being Black?) as much as it is a condemnation of Black conduct. On the other hand, race-embracing Black intellectuals, says West, reject the White academy and its hierarchies only to reproduce similar hierarchies headed by themselves in the (Black) institutions in which such individuals function. In such contexts, West continues, "rhetoric becomes a substitute for analysis, stimulatory rapping a replacement for serious reading, and uncreative publications an expression of existential carthasis" (65).

Finally are "the few race-transcending prophets" among whom West lists the late James Baldwin, noting, however, that "With the exception of Toni Morrison, the present generation has yet to produce such a figure" (ibid., 66).

Prophetic Pragmatism and the Resolution of Black Nihilism

Given this crisis of leadership in the Black community, the question that arises is "What then needs to be done?" This question is raised in various places in West's discussion of the aforementioned issue of Black nihilism (see ibid., 11, 28, and 66.) In this section I will show that the suggestion West puts forward to this existential *angst* in the Black community is grounded in both his philosophical orientation as a pragmatist of the Deweyan persuasion and in his Christian background. I begin with West's discussion of the crisis of leadership.

West begins by lamenting the absence of credible (read quality) political leadership in the Black community. Historically, such leadership functioned as custodians of traditional cultural (or institutional) pillars of strength and support in the community—the church, schools, and mosques and other civic organizations. These institutions served as a source of empowerment, transmitting and reinforcing values in the community. Thus, it was in and through these institutions that individuals drew support to affirm their self-worth. Both the centrality and the vitality of these institutions in Black communal life during trying times of economic deprivation, political exclusion, and social anguish were owing to effective leadership. The erosion of the influence of these institutions in present-day Black communal life, but particularly among youths, added to the self-serving kind of political leadership in the Black community, cannot but count as major factors for the moral crisis among Black youths. Thus, against this background, West calls for bold leadership in the spirit of Sojourner Truth, Martin Luther King Jr., Malcolm X, Fannie Lou Hamer, and others. Not only must such leadership be genuinely angry about the plight of the wretched of the earth, but it must also be provoked (in the Emersonian sense) to act on its anger so as to effect social change. In this context, it is worth noting West's insistence that effective leadership of the kind described must build race-transcending coalitions. The point here is not simply that West is invoking a historical accident of the kind witnessed in the social movement of Martin Luther King Jr. Rather, and more importantly, he sees such a coalition as a pragmatic measure to anchor the moral crisis in the Black community to the economic reality of American life that is its partial cause. This point can be expressed alternatively as follows. To the extent that the economic circumstances of the Black community, felt disproportionately by its youth, are determined directly or indirectly by White-owned corporate institutions over which those communities have no control, the only way to alter those economic circumstances and hence partly to resolve the existential crisis in the Black community is to involve White and other (usually liberal) like-minded individuals concerned with justice and fairness in exerting pressure on those corporate institutions to respond to the affliction that they bring on the powerless.

Critics may perhaps charge that West is naively optimistic in relying on such transracial coalitions to resolve the crisis in the Black community. They may cite recent attempts by the dominant (White) race, White males in particular, and even some Black conservatives, to dismantle the token gestures of the 1960s, in the form of affirmative action programs, to redress some historical wrongdoings. In light of such endeavors, once referred to as "the angry White male syndrome," is it realistic to hope that the crisis in the Black community will be resolved by a transracial alliance? It might then be suggested that Black people should cease depending on others to help solve their problems.[10]

Yet a credible defense can be made in West's favor, at least for now. (Later I will discuss certain limitations of West's solution to the nihilistic threat.) In the context of his philosophical position, West's proposal acknowledges a brute fact about America, namely, both its diversity and the logical connectedness of its various constitutive elements. Put otherwise, West's prophetic pragmatism recognizes that although America is diverse no one group can exist atomistically—i.e., logically independent of the others. Accordingly, no one group can address its own problems without the support and involvement of the others. It is in this spirit that West's prophetic pragmatism importunes progressive Black political and intellectual leadership to be *race*-transcending in building coalitions to deal with the nihilism among Black youths. If West celebrates Martin Luther King Jr.'s race-transcending strategy for social change (as he does), it is precisely because he thinks that the strategy exemplifies the idea he is articulating as central to prophetic pragmatism even as he notes that King was not a prophetic pragmatist:

> The social movement led by Martin Luther King, Jr., represents the best of what the political dimension of prophetic pragmatism is all about. Like Sojourner Truth, Walter Rauschenbusch, Elizabeth Cady Stanton, and Dorothy Day, King was not a prophetic pragmatist. Yet like them he was a prophet, in which role he contributed mightily to the political project of prophetic pragmatism. *His all-embracing moral vision facilitated alliances and coalitions across racial, gender, class, and religious lines.* (1989, 235, emphasis added)

In addition to building race-transcending coalitions, West urges Black political leadership to promote and practice "a politics of conversion." A politics of conversion is a mechanism that inspires people "to believe that there is hope for the future and a meaning to struggle" (1994, 29). More importantly, and central to this politics, says West, is "an affirmation of one's self-worth *fueled by the concern of others*" (29, emphasis added). In other words, one's self-worth is affirmed through and measured by one's concern about the predicament of others.

West's view of a politics of conversion echoes the biblical exhortation for a person to love her or his neighbor as herself or himself. I submit that it is to this exhortation that West is alluding in saying that an ethic of love is at the heart of a politics of conversion. Indeed, this ethic is unquestionably at the heart of West's own prophetic pragmatism. Apropos is West's already-noted unequivocal remark about the rootedness of his version of prophetic pragmatism in the Judeo-Christian tradition.

Accordingly, West sees prophetic pragmatism, at least in terms of its advocacy of an ethic of love, as having a natural appeal to African Americans because of their spirituality and their attachment to the cultural institutions in the community around which life centers, viz. the church, school, and similar organizations. Furthermore, West believes that, given bold leadership of the prophetic kind he has described, these cultural institutions can be used effectively to stave off the self-hatred and self-devaluation that nihilism engenders in the psyche (or the souls) of Black youths.

A similar insight about the need for prophetic voices among Black intellectual leaders underlies West's criticism of the current Black intellectual leadership. Indeed, West's criticism of the Black intellectual leadership is no less a comment on what he deems the vocation and moral obligation of the intellectual to his or her community and how effectively the intellectual will discharge these responsibilities.

I believe that, again, as with his engagement of the political leadership, West is right in arguing that the vocation of Black intellectuals is constantly to put forward and critique ideas about, among other things, issues affecting their communities. Among the issues in the Black community are crime, drugs, violence, sexism, intolerance toward certain forms of sexual orientation, and racial diversity. The Black intellectual has a moral duty to his or her community to engage these issues. To treat these matters as "taboo subjects" is, for West, to acquiesce in the preposterous belief that they cannot be interrogated. Yet failure to interrogate *any* matter whatsoever is a grave moral crime an intellectual could commit both against his or her vocation and against his or her community. The reason is that, since an intellectual is obligated to investigate ideas, the view that some matters ought not be investigated implies a contradiction, for it is logically at odds with the vocation of the intellectual. But furthermore, an intellectual who fails to engage in a critical discussion of the issues affecting his or her community is committing a moral crime against the community because there can be no solution to the ills that afflict the community in the absence of such discussion. It is for this reason that I think West is right in condemning those intellectuals whom he alleges disengage themselves from "the battles of the streets." (ibid., 62).

Yet there is the often raised objection about the credentials of intellectuals to speak on behalf of the afflicted, especially since those intellectuals do not live in the communities and hence do not have the experiences of individuals whose interests they are supposed to be representing. Some may argue that the intellectuals do not have an appreciation of the complexity of the situation they are supposed to be critiquing in light of the fact that they are not members of the underclass. The thrust of such criticism is that intellectual leadership, the absence of which West bemoans, is empty without the actual underclass experiences on which to ground it. Thus the discussion in which West engages and his call for intellectual leadership in the Black community are purely academic.

This objection may even be reinforced by invoking West's own prescription for overcoming intellectual marginalization by Blacks, namely, that Black intellectuals should integrate themselves into mainstream and well-established (read White and wealthy) institutions of learning both in order to have access to resources and to produce respectable material. The argument can then be advanced that, since these institutions are not in Black communities and the experiences in them are foreign to Black underclass experiences, those Black academics who have been integrated into the culture of the mainstream institutions, thriving on the prestige and status conferred upon them, cannot therefore be effective representatives of "the wretched of the earth."

But this objection can very easily be met. Not only is the objection essentially an *ad hominem* against some advocates for the less fortunate in the Black community, but it also commits the fallacy that one cannot appreciate the plight of any victim unless one also is a victim in similar circumstances. But does one need to be raped to appreciate the physical violence toward, the psychoemotional trauma of, and the moral transgression against a rape victim? Or, to take a different example, did the *White* abolitionists have to be transformed into Black slaves and then experience the savagery, barbarity, and dehumanization of slavery to be legitimate antislavery advocates? Yet these are the absurd implications of the objection. It is true that some advocates of the plight of the underclass, including West, are not themselves members of that class, nor do they live in underclass communities. But it does not follow that they cannot interrogate and then contribute substantively to discussions about ameliorating the problems confronting the underclass, problems that culminate in despair, emptiness, and self-loathing. If anything, the contrary argument can very easily be made, namely, that it is precisely because some advocates have acquired a certain status in the society, especially those who are known to have personal moral integrity, that their calls for social justice are heeded by the power structures that otherwise have a natural propensity to ignore the cries of the underclass.

In light of this view, then, I endorse West's contention that intellectuals, especially those who have access to mainstream institutions, like the prisoner in Plato's allegory of the cave who had escaped and symbolically apprehended reality, have a moral obligation to provide leadership in the Black community by engaging the issues that plague the communities and putting forward ideas and strategies for social change. An implied moral judgment in West's view is that failure to do so is an egregious breach of a moral obligation to the community. And I take such judgment to be implicit further in West's condemnation both of the intellectual isolationism of the radical Black intellectuals and of the philosophical detachment of those intellectuals who pontificate about "the problem *with* black America"—that is, those intellectuals whose penetrating criticisms of so-called Black conduct, according to West, reflect only self-hatred. This said, how effective is West's prophetic pragmatism in meeting the Black nihilistic threat?

The Effectiveness (or Otherwise) of West's Proposed Solution

Recall that nihilism, at least as it applies to Black youths, is a state of mind that views life as meaningless. It is a state of mind that bespeaks self-loathing, despair, emptiness, and an utter loss of hope. The result of such an existential predicament is senseless Black-on-Black violence, violence against Black women, drugs, alcoholism, crime, and ultimately premature death. This is the mode of existence of the underclass Black youth. On my reading of West, there are two levels on which his prophetic pragmatism has attempted to meet this crisis: (1) the sociopsychological and (2) the politico-economical.

On the sociopsychological level, prophetic pragmatism urges a rejuvenation of the traditional cultural pillars in Black life—namely, the family, church, school, and similar civic organizations—under moral leadership. I understand West as saying that these institutions should respond to the crisis in the community with a sense of urgency. Furthermore, as in previous times, these institutions should help instill in Black youth positive self-valuation, a sense of self-worth, and in so doing inspire hope in life. In his essay "Philosophy and the Urban Underclass" (1992) West makes this point indirectly in accounting for the existence and severity of the crisis in the Black community:

> This level of self-destruction exists because for the first time there are now no longer viable institutions and structures in black America that can effectively transmit values such as hope, virtue, sacrifice, risk, and putting the needs of others higher or alongside one's own needs. In the past we've seen black colleges in which every Sunday they were forced to sit in those pews and Benjamin Mays would get up and say, "You must give service to the race," reminding these black, petit-bourgeois students that even as they went out into the world they had a cause, an obligation and a duty to do something beyond simply their own self-interest. What they did may have been narrow, myopic, and shortsighted, but the point is they had an institution that was transmitting that value. And it is not just the black school. We can talk about the black church, fraternities, and whole hosts of other institutions in black civil society. We no longer have these to the degree we did in the past, and they are being eroded slowly but surely. This is what is most frightening. This is why we get

the exponential increase in black suicides between eighteen and thirty-five, unprecedented in black history. This is why we get escalating black homicides in which you get some of the most cold-hearted, mean-spirited dispositions and attitudes displayed by black people against other black people as well as nonblacks. It is a breakdown in the moral fabric."

I noted earlier that central to West's prophetic pragmatism is an ethic of love. I interpret West's conception of love to mean both a self-regarding and an other-regarding disposition in the individual. It is such a disposition that he expects the cultural apparatus to help cultivate in Black youths. The need for cultivating such a disposition in the individual can be seen easily once it is realized that a condition of one esteeming or showing respect toward others is that one respects or esteems oneself. If I have a sense of self-worth, then I am more likely to value the personhood of others than if I do not. Conversely, if I lack a sense of self-worth then, I would devalue others. From this psychological point of view, an important remedy to the nihilistic threat to Black America is to promote self-love, in the sense of self-esteem, in youths. In this regard, I believe that, on the sociopsychological level, the recommendation West puts forward to meet the threat of nihilism among Black youths is reasonable.

To some extent, West's recommendation compares with Jesse Jackson's well-known exhortation to Black youths to value themselves, usually expressed in the chant "I am somebody." This exhortation is Jackson's own attempt at instilling a sense of self-worth in youths. Of course, there are significant differences between West's prophetic pragmatism and Jackson's endeavor in the search for a solution to the existential crisis in the Black community. For example, West's prophetic pragmatism sees the importance of the traditional Black cultural institutions in helping to delimit if not eliminate the threat to Black survival. Furthermore, West presents a challenge to all forms of Black leadership, but especially the political and intellectual, to engage the crisis. It is not clear to me that Jackson, besides founding the civic organization Operation PUSH and making televised appearances in which he makes exhortations, confronts the crisis with a sophisticated strategy for effecting profound long-term psychological change in the youths.

On the politicoeconomical level, however, prophetic pragmatism is found wanting in the solution it proposes to the nihilistic threat to Black America. To see this, consider that West prioritizes coalition politics to resolve the crisis in the (correct) belief that eliminating the cause of the crisis, which he takes to be economic, is indeed eliminating the crisis itself. However, he entertains the false notion that the cause can only be removed through a coalition effort of various racial groups. This belief is false simply because, among other things, it does not follow that if one belongs to a coalition one therefore necessarily wields power to address one's concerns. One may lack stature and hence influence within the coalition. Alternatively put, one may indeed be a partner in a coalition, but an *unequal* partner. And given such a situation one always has to depend on the goodwill and generosity of other members in the coalition for support. As this is undoubtedly the case concerning Blacks in such coalitions, West's undue emphasis on coalition politics to eliminate the economic cause of the nihilistic threat is therefore problematic.

To be sure, West's motivation for promoting coalition politics is the recognition that the underclass problem cuts across race and gender; therefore to meet it effectively requires that liberals from all races band together to exert pressure on the political and economic structures of the society. But, then, the nihilistic threat to Black America is distinct and different from, even though related to, the problems confronting the underclass. To the extent that the underclass problem is transracial, coalition politics may be necessary for its resolution. However, a similar necessity cannot be claimed for the involvement of such politics in resolving the Black nihilistic problem on pain of begging the question. Quite the contrary, the very fact that the nihilistic problem is peculiar to Blacks would seem to suggest, if anything, that coalition politics may only be contingently relevant to its resolution. If I am right, then West should not emphasize coalition politics as he does in the elimination of the economic cause of the Black nihilistic crisis. Instead, his call for transracial coalitions should be subordinate to all other considerations.

Furthermore, it can be argued against West's undue emphasis on coalition politics to remove the economic cause of Black nihilism that for too long Blacks have been too dependent on governments and others for economic uplift in terms of providing investments in their communities. The consequence of such dependency is that, except only fairly recently, politicians have either taken the Black vote for granted or simply have dismissed it as inconsequential to the whole political process. It may be suggested, therefore, that perhaps if Blacks, especially middle-class Blacks, began to view themselves in entrepreneurial rather than in consumerist terms—and act accordingly—they would gain the economic clout that invariably translates into political power. The argument here, in sum, is not that coalition politics is to be dismissed as such. Rather, it is that Blacks need not be overly dependent on the goodwill of other races to solve a problem that, at least for now, is acknowledged to be peculiar to the Black race in America.

The criticism in this argument is all the more pertinent considering that, even as West argues for the formation of race-transcending coalitions to exert pressure on the politicoeconomic structures so as to meet the economic issue that underlies the nihilism in Black America, he fails to offer a protracted discussion on the need for economic leadership in the Black community by Blacks, while correctly denouncing the consumerism of the Black middle-class. Surely such leadership is just as critical to ameliorating the problems he has identified.

On balance, then, prophetic pragmatism advances some very good suggestions on how to meet the nihilistic crisis in Black America, especially on the sociopsychological (including the moral) level. However, on the politicoeconomic level the position is found wanting because of the emphasis that West places on coalition politics over race-based solutions to the problem. It is debatable of course whether or not the difficulty I am highlighting for West's prophetic pragmatism is unavoidable for any version of prophetic pragmatism. I find it curious, however, that West makes the following observation in a discussion in which he elaborates some of the difficulties confronting Black prophetic practices that attempt to bring to the center of American liberal discourse the concerns of Black people. (These practices are activities of trade unions and feminist, populist, socialist, and other forms of political organizations.)

> The design and operation of the American social system requires that
> this quest for democracy and self-realization be channeled into unfair

competitive circumstances such that opportunistic results are unavoidable. In fact, in an ironic way, opportunistic practices become requisite to sustain the very sense of prophetic sensibilities and values in the USA. This is so primarily because deliverance is the common denominator in American society and culture—and a set of practices of whatever sort cannot be sustained or legitimated over time and space without some kind of delivery-system or some way of showing that crucial consequences and effects (such as goods and services) flow from one's project. *This "delivery prerequisite" usually forces even prophetic critics and actions to adopt opportunistic strategies and tactics in order to justify themselves to a disadvantaged and downtrodden constituency.*[12]

I submit that West's observation in this passage accurately reflects his awareness of the difficulties inherent in race-transcendent strategies. In my view, these difficulties impose a severe constraint on his prophetic pragmatism, especially in its attempt to address the nihilistic crisis under consideration.

Conclusion

In this chapter I have shown that West's philosophical preoccupation situates him squarely within the American pragmatist tradition. Specifically, I have elaborated West's own variant form of American pragmatism, namely, prophetic pragmatism. Prophetic pragmatism is a contemporary variant of Deweyan pragmatism in that it views philosophy instrumentally both in its concern with social criticism and with ameliorating social ills. I showed how West deploys his prophetic pragmatism to address a contemporary existential crisis in the Black community, namely, nihilism among the Black youths, and then went on to discuss his proposed solution. The upshot of my discussion is that West's proposed solution to this existentialist crisis in the Black community, although largely commendable, betrays a serious limitation because of the undue emphasis he puts on coalition politics over race-based solutions to the problem. This said, it is to be remarked that, overall, West's diverse intellectual preoccupation, articulated through his doctrine of prophetic pragmatism, is an attempt to establish himself as a humanistic scholar. I turn now to a consideration of his humanistic scholarship.

CHAPTER TWO

Humanistic Scholarship and Praxis

Introduction

A survey of Cornel West's writings cannot but reveal the diversity of his preoccupations. The issues West engages range from philosophy and theology to literary and cultural criticism. Specifically, they include an elaboration of the genesis and development of American pragmatism, a critique of neopragmatism, an analysis of postanalytic philosophy, an examination of the rise and decline of the philosophy of religion in the academy, the place and role of humanistic studies in the academy and society at large, race and social theory, critical legal theory, cultural studies, issues affecting people of color generally and other unrepresented groups, and Black-Jewish relations.

The relative ease with which West traverses traditional disciplinary boundaries in some ways is evidence that these boundaries are largely artificial and only promote intellectual parochialism. For West, a significant consequence of such parochialism is that it disconnects the intellectual life from praxis. And in his view this disconnect is inconsistent with the role of the intellectual, especially the humanistic scholar, to society. West's own examination of the role and significance of the humanistic scholar to society may be read, therefore, as a reaction, if not indeed a corrective, to intellectual parochialism and isolationism. At the very least, he implicitly considers the separation of the theoretical and the practical life as partly responsible for the failure of academics, especially those in the humanistic disciplines, to define their relevance to society. This disconnect underlies his comment in "The Dilemma of the Black Intellectual" about "common perceptions [in the black community] of the impotence, even uselessness, of black intellectuals."[1] And it is also against this background that West's speculation about the resurgence of neopragmatism in contemporary America is to be understood. In "The Limits of Neopragmatism," he attributes this resurgence of neopragmatism to what he claims is "the crisis of purpose and vocation in humanistic studies and professional schools." And he adds:

> [T]he recent hunger for interdisciplinary studies—or the erosion of disciplinary boundaries—promoted by neopragmatisms, poststructuralisms, Marxisms and feminisms is not only motivated by the quest for truth, but also activated by power struggles over what kinds of knowledge should be given status, be rewarded and be passed on to young, informed citizens in the next century. *These power struggles are not simply over positions and curriculums, but also over ideals of what it means to be humanistic intellectuals in a declining empire*—in a first-rate military power, a near-rescinding economic power and a culture in decay. (1993b, 137–138, emphasis added)

Thus he endorses Richard Rorty's attack on academic professionalization and specialization, saying that Rorty's *Philosophy and the Mirror of Nature* is, among other things, "a challenging narrative of how contemporary intellectuals have come to be contained within professional and specialized social spaces, with little outreach to a larger public and hence little visibility in, and minimal effect on, the larger society" (138). In light of the foregoing observations I submit that what drives Cornel West's diverse intellectual engagements is the quest to define his own relevance to society as a humanistic scholar. Furthermore, it is toward the realization of this quest that his most significant discourses are geared. My aim in this chapter, therefore, is to elaborate how West, by employing his theory of prophetic pragmatism, endeavors to establish himself as a humanistic scholar. I shall engage this task by addressing two key questions: (1) What does it mean to be a humanistic scholar? And (2) how, if at all, is West a humanistic scholar?

The Central Features of Humanism

Humanism is first and foremost an anti-establishmentarian philo-sophical position that stresses the value of the individual over those institutions in society that often have primacy and ascendency over individual life.[2] Humanism is motivated by challenge and crisis, and it is animated by a critical temper. The establishments to which humanism is reacting may be religious; economic, in the sense of the etherealization and transcendence of market forces that affect the life of the ordinary individual and over which he or she has no control; or political, in the sense of the primordial and immanent institutions of power that determine the lives of ordinary citizenry but over which the ordinary citizen has no control. The net effect of this con-trolling influence of the institutions on individual life is that it ren-ders the individual powerless and thus dispossesses her or him of the agency to determine the direction of her or his life. Humanism thus seeks to liberate the individual from such dominating and oppressive forces that deprive her or him of individuality so that she or he can realize her or his potential. Paul Kurtz (1969) aptly expresses this point as follows:

> The problem for the humanist is to create the conditions which would emancipate man [woman] from oppressive and corruptive social organization, and from the denigration and perversion of his [her] human talents, which would liberate him [her] from one-sided and distorted development, and which would enable him [her] to achieve an authentic life. (11)

Kurtz identifies four distinctive features of humanism, some or all of which any variant form of the doctrine may espouse. First, humanism rejects a supernaturalistic conception of the universe and denies the claim that humans have a privileged and special place in the cosmos. Alternatively put, humanism conceives of both the human being and the rest of the entire cosmos as a part of nature; consequently, everything that happens both to human beings and to the rest of the cosmos can be given a naturalistic explanation, one grounded in experience (3). Second, humanism affirms that moral values have no meaning in the absence of human experiences. Indeed, a necessary and sufficient condition for the existence of morality is that there are human beings and hence human experiences. It follows from this view that humanistic ethics reject the notion that morality originates from and even requires religion. On the contrary, as Kurtz points out, humanistic ethics "asks that we, as human beings, face up to the human [experiential] condition" (4).

But is not the rejection of the supernatural just what it takes to say that life is meaningless and hopeless, especially when the individual is pitted against the inscrutable, overwhelming, and ever-revolving forces of nature? In other words, does not a subscription to a humanistic philosophy entail a pessimistic outlook on life? The answer, according to Kurtz, is no. Although some humanists have adopted a pessimistic outlook on life in view of a rejection of a theistic universe, "most humanists have found a source of optimism in the affirmation that value is related to man" (4). This optimism derives from a proper appreciation (or cognition) of the human condition, its challenges, problems, and hence its possibilities. Through a proper deployment of her or his powers of thought and intelligence, the human being is able to build a good (or better) life for herself or himself.

The third principle to which at least some humanists subscribe is that ethical judgments are open to rational scrutiny and that such judgments can be given empirical warrant. This principle is consistent with the rejection of a religious-based conception of ethics. Whereas a religious-based conception of morality, such as the Divine Command theory, advances an absolutist and hence universalistic principle of morality, one that is grounded on a priori considerations, a humanistic ethic views moral norms as general guides to be applied and modified in light of the contingent (or empirical) circumstances and conditions of individuals. The role of reason in the moral domain is limited both to scrutinizing the circumstances in which humans find themselves and in determining whether or not existing norms need to be applied or modified in the quest to provide at least a provisional basis for action.

The fourth and final attribute of humanism is that it involves some form of social humanitarianism. What this means is that humanists often are committed to a form of social justice principle in which they seek at least to promote the happiness of the greater number of people and at most the happiness of humanity as a whole. This humanist concern with social justice derives from the belief that all human beings are members of the same human family; thus it is the humanist's obligation to advance the welfare of humankind (ibid., 9). Humanistic positions with a humanitarian strain include liberal, democratic, utilitarian, and socialist. Each of these positions is driven by a double humanist ideal of the development of individual potentialities and of the promotion of social harmony and justice. To quote Kurtz,

> If liberal, Renaissance and Enlightenment humanisms emphasized the perfectability of the individual and had faith in the instrumentality of reason and education, utilitarian, democratic, and especially socialist humanism have emphasized that many or most of the problems of man can only be resolved by social action, by changing the social system, the underlying economic structure, the forces and relationship of production. Humanists today attack all those social forces which seek to destroy man; they deplore the dehumanization and alienation of man within the industrial and technological society, the conflict and tension, poverty and war, racial discrimination and hatred, inequality and injustice, overpopulation and waste, the emphasis on the mere quantity rather than on the quality of life. In effect, they condemn all the contradictions of modern life, and the failure of modern man to achieve the full measure of his potential excellence. (10–11)

It is clear from this passage that humanism emphasizes the value of human life and human dignity as an end.[3] Thus, a humanistic scholar is an intellectual who is concerned with defending the dignity of humanity against the abusive and oppressive societal power structures that alienate, dehumanize, and denigrate the individual. To that end, a humanistic scholar is not only anti-establishmentarian, but he or she also is motivated by ethical and sociopolitical concerns. Given these considerations, how then, if at all, is Cornel West a humanistic scholar?

The Elements of West's Humanism

There is no question that West's views are anti-establishmentarian, as is clear from the theme of social justice that permeates his writings. In both his philosophical and theological writings, West consistently bemoans what he deems the social injustice that is meted out to the ordinary individual in society, especially in a capitalistic environment, by the dominant institutions of power. For instance, in the essay "Prophetic Theology" (1988b), he elaborates the doctrine of *imago Dei*, the doctrine that humans are made in the image of God, as espousing among other things an egalitarian principle in which God identifies with all stripes of humanity. In this connection, he says, the doctrine targets "those who are denied dignity and a certain minimum of humane treatment." He explains humane treatment in terms of "a Christian mandate for identification with the downtrodden, the dispossessed, the disinherited, with the exploited and the oppressed."[4] And in his essay "The New Cultural Politics of Difference," West declares that the aim of the new cultural politics of difference is that of "locating the structural causes of unnecessary forms of social misery, [of] depicting the plight and predicaments of demoralized and depoliticized citizens caught in market-driven cycles of therapeutic release—drugs, alcoholism, consumerism—and [of] projecting visions, analyses and actions that proceed from particularities and [to] arrive at moral and political connectedness" (1993b, 30). In particular, he declares that the purpose of the new cultural politics of difference is to "expand the scope of freedom and democracy" in a civilization that revolves around market forces (31).

I will shortly examine some of the issues West addresses in the essay "The New Cultural Politics of Difference" if only to demonstrate why, in my view, this concern establishes him as a humanistic scholar. For the present it is only worth emphasizing that the principal target of his critique is the sociopolitical and economic forces that are reified in Western societies. These are the forces that shape the life and the existential circumstances of the ordinary individual and over which the latter has little or no control. This means then that the philosophical position within which West treats the issues he raises, namely, prophetic pragmatism, evidently satisfies at least the fourth characteristic of humanism—viz., the concern with social justice. Indeed, for West, the whole point of prophetic pragmatism is that it "analyzes the social causes of unnecessary forms of social misery, promotes moral outrage against them, organizes different constituencies to alleviate them, yet does so with an openness to its own blindnesses and shortcomings" (ibid., 139).

But to the extent that West's engagements are generally articulated through his doctrine of prophetic pragmatism they also satisfy the other requirements of humanism. For instance, implicit in most forms of humanism is an optimistic outlook on life. There certainly is no shortage of optimism in West's sociopolitical engagements. As I have shown in the previous chapter, West often articulates this optimism in the notion of hope and in his advocacy for improving the life and lot of the ordinary individual. To illustrate, the solution West proposes to what he thinks is a nihilistic threat to the Black community, even with its limitations, is meant to occasion hope and optimism as against despair and meaninglessness. And the hope and optimism he wishes to inspire is not just for Black America, but instead is for all of "the working-class and underclass American communities" (1989, 7). The reason is that it is this entire group that constitutes "the wretched of the earth" within America.

Although West grounds this optimism in his Christian background, so that in a sense he anchors his humanism in religion, he does not consider religion a necessary prerequisite for optimism. Nor for that matter does he consider religion a requirement for morality. He states that prophetic pragmatism is perfectly compatible with a nonreligious outlook (ibid., 233). What this means is that prophetic pragmatism is only contingently related to a religious outlook. It follows therefore that although prophetic pragmatism embodies a moral outlook, that outlook too is perfectly compatible with a nonreligious perspective. But even if West did not assert that prophetic pragmatism is compatible with a nonreligious outlook, it is doubtful that he would claim that moral values have meaning in the absence of human experiences. The empirical grounding of prophetic pragmatism would certainly argue against such a position. It is a contingent fact that humans exist and hence that *human societal experiences* call for moral valuation. From this it would follow that morality would be absolutely unintelligible for human beings in the absence of human experiences.

The third characteristic of humanism noted earlier is that ethical judgments are open to rational scrutiny and can be given empirical warrant. It is clear that the humanism I am attributing to West, based as it is on his prophetic pragmatism, would uphold this characteristic. Consider that West is constantly calling for a critique of the status quo. This call is motivated by what he deems a moral outrage against the perceived suffering of and injustice meted out to others.

Implicated in this call then is a demand that we deploy our rational faculty to analyze the cause of human suffering and to search for solutions to human misery. One can assume that, for West, the ethical judgments we form at any given moment are subject to the Emersonian empirical principles of revisability, contingency, and experimentalism. After all, he tells us that it is these principles that undergird American pragmatism, of which prophetic pragmatism is a contemporary variant (ibid., ch.1). I turn now to West's discussion in "The New Cultural Politics of Difference" for further amplification of this thesis.

Illustrations of West's Humanistic Concerns: Challenges to Social Change

The central idea in "The New Cultural Politics of Difference "is that, at any given historical period, cultural critics are responding to what they consider the numbing crisis of their time. For example, in the mid-nineteenth century, a period West describes as the decline of the Age of Europe, Matthew Arnold, one of the cultural giants of the time, proposed a way of addressing the crisis of a potential conflict between, on the one hand, the rapidly eroding aristocracy and an emerging arrogant middle class and, on the other hand, a massive, restless working class with anarchic tendencies. According to West, Arnold's proposal consisted in a dissolution of classes and the establishment of a secular humanist culture. Arnold believed that the secular reconceptualization of culture—that is, wresting culture away from the dominant religious-based institutions in favor of secular institutions—"could play an integrative role in cementing and stabilizing an emerging bourgeois civil society and imperial state" (1993b, 6). In this regard, Arnold conceived of the cultural critic as "the true apostles of equality" (7).

Arnold's response is significant because it expresses his belief that a revision of culture, consisting in a reconstitution of the power structure, would ensure stability (as against anarchy) and hence preserve European civilization. West quotes Arnold as saying, "Through culture seems to lie our way, not only to perfection, but even to safety" (ibid., 7). The operative words here are "our" (versus them), "perfection" (versus imperfection and ugliness), and "safety" (versus barbarism and mob conduct). As West correctly observes, the questions that immediately arise are: Who are the "we" whose "perfection" and "safety" must be preserved? And who are the "them" (they) whose imperfection and barbarism must be guarded against? These questions are significant because, says West, they exhibit the typical Eurocentric White male character of the cultural critic's response to the crisis of the period. The "us" to whom Arnold refers were the White males, and the "them" referred to others. Indeed, the "us" / "them" distinction in Arnold's response is clearly exclusionary, says West, especially in light of Arnold's "negative attitudes toward British working-class people, women and especially Indians and Jamaicans in the Empire" (8). West thus concludes correctly that, for Arnold, culture was meant to be a weapon for bourgeois White (read European) male safety (8). In West's view, it was this Arnoldian conception of culture that has come to inform Western society. And it is this conception of culture that motivates and infuses the new cultural politics of difference. In other words, it is this conception of culture that provides the crisis to which the new cultural politics of difference is responding in contemporary society.

According to West, the major crisis of contemporary society is the misrepresentation and marginalization of the Other—i.e., people of color, women, homosexuals, the elderly, and Jews—by the established institutions of power. The various forms of representation of these groups (or their members) as "different" has led to a depoliticization and exclusion of their members from so-called mainstream society. For West, it is these forms of representations and their consequences that comprise the crisis to which the new cultural politics of difference is responding. And the object of the response from marginalized peoples is to overhaul or dismantle the very institutions of power responsible for the crisis in question. As West puts it, the objective is "to empower and enable social action and, if possible, to enlist collective insurgency for the expansion of freedom, democracy and individuality" (ibid., 4).[5]

West identifies what he characterizes as three distinct challenges confronting the practitioner of the new cultural politics of difference: intellectual, existential, and political. The intellectual challenge is: How does the cultural critic respond, at least in terms of proposals put forward, to the crisis of the period? The existential challenge is: How does the practitioner of the new cultural politics of difference acquire the "self-confidence, discipline and perseverance necessary for success without an undue reliance on the mainstream for approval and acceptance?" (ibid., 25). And the political challenge is that of making relevant to the larger society one's intellectual engagements by forming alliances with, and utilizing, those extraparliamentary organizations whose sole purpose is to agitate and advocate on behalf of the less fortunate. I shall treat his discussion of these challenges in turn.

To the extent that the new cultural politics of difference is responding to the crisis of marginalization and downright exclusion in contemporary society, contends West, its inception can be traced to the post-World War II period. This period marked the end of the Age of Europe, with much of Europe ravaged by war and the former European colonies agitating for and gaining political independence. But the period also marked the birth of the United States as a major Western power, for while Europe was struggling economically to recover from the war, the United States was enjoying tremendous economic success. This success in turn occasioned a new American middle class. Of significance, however, is that temporally contiguous with the emergence of this new mass middle class, says West, was "the first major emergence of subcultures of American non-WASP [White Anglo-Saxon Protestant] intellectuals: the so-called New York intellectuals in criticism, the Abstract Expressionists in painting and the bebop artist in jazz music" (ibid., 11). According to West, the emergence of these new subcultures signaled a challenge to the dominant American White male elite that was still loyal to an older and eroding European culture. Outside of the United States, Blacks in the former European colonies were challenging White hegemonic cultural practices.[6]

It is not difficult to see why both New World and Old World Blacks would be mounting intense challenges to White hegemonic practices. Since colonialism (and its predecessor slavery) were legitimated on a deliberate White supremacist denial of the humanity of Black people and an attendant blatant and systematic (mis)representation of Blacks, post-World War II Black cultural critics, both within and outside the United States, were driven, therefore, by the quest to validate Black humanity against the preponderant racist cultural practices. In other words, the early Black cultural critics embarked upon the task of reconstituting Black identities and articulating Black humanity.[7] However, West considers highly deficient the intellectual response of the early Black cultural critics within the United States. He alleges that those critics were driven by a moralistic motivation to combat White supremacist and racist misrepresentations of Black peoples, and in light of this motivation they posited what they considered positive images of Blacks.[8] But he thinks that this strategy is problematic for two reasons. First, he says, the positing of the so-called positive images presupposes a moral judgment about what exactly constitutes a positive Black image. In other words, the notion of a positive Black image is value laden. But, then, whose value judgment was being used as the norm for determining positive Black image(s)? No doubt, it was the value judgment(s) of those critics. What this all means, concludes West, is that the early Black cultural critics betrayed the same tendency of the dominant White male power elite, namely, to universalize their own experiences as the experiences of all people. In the present situation, the early Black cultural critics universalized their own conception(s) of positive Black images as that (those) of all Black people.

Second, these critics, according to West, betrayed a homogenizing impulse in representing Black peoples as of a kind. This means that they essentialized blackness or, what is the same thing, dissolved Black specificities and so elided differences among Black peoples. West attributes this essentialization of blackness to a fundamental assumption of these early critics, namely, that every Black person was an equal candidate for the same kind of racist characterization and treatment. Given this assumption, together with the additional assumptions (1) that Blacks were of a kind, (2) that Blacks were psychologically similar to Whites, and (3) that Whites considered themselves human, the critics then concluded that Blacks too were human. But West thinks the generalization that Blacks are of a kind is false because, even though in principle every Black person was (and is) an equal candidate for the same kind of racist treatment, in practice considerations of class, gender, sexual orientation, and the like often influenced (and still influence) the way one Black person was (and is) treated in contrast to another. For example, a lower-class Black person was (and is) often treated less favorably than her or his middle-class Black counterpart. Of course, West is not contesting the claim that Blacks are similar to Whites *qua* humans in light of psychological makeup. It is only the claim about the similarity of Black experiences that he is challenging. To that end, he explains what he considers the supposed facile generalization of the early Black cultural critics by saying that such a generalization was motivated by the critics' preoccupation with gaining White acceptance. Consequently, they advanced an assimilationist account of Black humanity by creating a mythological reified Black homogeneity. In short, West's contention is that the early Black cultural critics uncritically accepted the prevailing norms in their defense of Black humanity (ibid., 16–19).

There is no doubt that West is sympathetic to the antiracist motivations of the early Black cultural critics. Nevertheless, I believe that his criticism is unfair at best and misses the point at worst. Let us begin by considering closely the charge of essentializing blackness or, as he puts it, of dissolving Black particularities. West's criticism seems rooted in the belief that the critics in question *should have been* concerned with drawing attention to Black specificities as they defended Black humanity. But the question is why should they be concerned with Black specificities at all? An elaboration of Black specificities presupposes Black humanity in the first place. And since the point at issue was not whether there were specific kinds of Blacks—gays or lesbians, rich or poor, men or women—but instead the larger question of whether or not Blacks were humans, to elaborate Black particularities would have been to lose sight of the crucial objective, namely, the representation of Blacks as *human*. Thus, West's criticism seems to miss the point.

To reinforce my argument, consider how we normally proceed with the task of *classifying* objects (in the broadest sense of the term). Here we may invoke the Aristotelian concepts of *genus* and *species* whereby the former is broader in extension than the latter.[9] To begin, I can classify myself as an animal and go on to say that I belong to the same genus as horses, cows, cats, dogs, owls, and so on, for these too are animals. But then I may go on to point to the characteristics, whatever they are, that differentiate me from these other animals and in virtue of which I classify myself further as human and classify them as beasts. Then, further, within the human *species* I may go on to identify those specific features that distinguish me (and others like me) as male from those that distinguish a female. And so on. What this all means is that to classify oneself as X, Y, or Z is to identify oneself as a member of the class of entities that belong to X, Y, or Z. It is to say that one instantiates (or exemplifies) those attributes that are essential to, and thus are shared by, all the members of the class of X, Y, or Z.

Now, since the racist misrepresentation to which the early Black cultural critics were responding was not whether any Black was male or female, rich or poor, gay or lesbian, *but instead whether Blacks belonged to the same species as Whites—namely, the human species*—it was imperative, therefore, that the response be directed at this specific issue and not whether within the species some members had other traits. Of course, it follows that if a thing is human *ceteris paribus* it also is either male or female, gay or lesbian (or may be neither), rich or poor, and so on. But the converse is not true. It does not follow, for example, that because a thing is male or female it is therefore human. Thus, West's criticism simply does not apply.

Suppose, however, one assumes that West was correct in his criticism. Still, I believe that one can make the case for treating the response of the early Black cultural critics more sympathetically than he seems to allow. To do this let us turn to the existential challenge that West suggests the new cultural politics of difference should meet. The challenge, recall, is how the cultural critic of a marginalized, misrepresented, and disenfranchised group can develop the psychological fortitude, in the form of self-confidence, discipline, and perseverance, necessary for success without an undue reliance on the mainstream for acceptance and approval (ibid., 25).

The most significant effect on African diasporic peoples of the assault on Black humanity is the undermining of their self-confidence and the questioning of their abilities and potentialities. Roy D. Morrison II makes this point very poignantly in respect of postemancipation Black Americans, saying: "Postemancipation blacks had social and economic inferiority imposed upon them by Jim Crow laws and racism. In many cases, they internalized such negative notions and came to regard themselves as innately inferior to whites."[10] West is fully aware of this problematic nature of Black existence, for he reminds us that "To be a black artist in America is to be caught in what I have called elsewhere 'the modern black diasporan problematic of invisibility and namelessness.' This problematic requires that black people search for validation and recognition in a culture in which white-supremacist assaults on black intelligence, ability, beauty and character circumscribe such a search" (ibid., 59; cp. 74). This psychological damage of racist practices is much more visible and protracted in the West because of mass media—movies, television, radio, and so on—through which popular culture is disseminated. And contemporary Western societies still propagate "old" stereotypes of Blacks as intellectually inferior to Whites even in somewhat sanitized ways but often with a pretended intellectual sophistication.[11] To be sure, such stereotypes are regularly and quickly challenged. But that is beside the point. The point, for my present purpose, is that a casual reflection upon contemporary racist practices cannot but lead one to imagine the kind of nearly insurmountable odds with which the early Black cultural critics had to contend in their endeavor to defend Black humanity, *especially in the absence of a cultural infrastructure or apparatus of their own.* One can assume, for example, that if their views were deemed "too radical," those views would not be given an avenue for expression. On the contrary, if those views gave a semblance of credence to the standard stereotypes and beliefs about Blacks, then they would readily find expression. It is pertinent to note, for instance, the circulation in the White academy of Leopold Senghor's absurd declaration that emotion is to Blacks as reason is to Whites and of John Mbiti's erroneous assertion that African conception of time is limited to the past and the present and that Africans have no conception of the future.[12] These remarks perfectly harmonize with the prejudices that inform White denial of Black intelligence, rationality, and, ultimately, humanity. It is not surprising therefore that they were so readily circulated by mainstream intellectual outlets.

Against this background, then, it would seem that the early Black cultural critics who endeavored to defend Black humanity had little choice but to do so within the very cultural apparatus through which Black humanity was assaulted. In other words, it was impossible for the early Black cultural critics to pursue the task in question outside of the mainstream cultural apparatus, given that they did not have a cultural infrastructure of their own. They had to challenge the mainstream "from within," a method that West himself endorses in his frequent calls for transracial alliances with White liberals and others to address issues. (Recall my discussion in the preceding chapter.)

Moreover, the early cultural critics had to engage the task without at the same time antagonizing the custodians of the apparatus. In sum, the early Black cultural critics had to practice political reticence—to adapt West's characterization of Dewey's maneuvering tactics in affiliating with humanitarian organizations that were sympathetic to the plight of the industrial underclass while Dewey himself was still under the patronage of the very middle-class establishment that was largely responsible for the status quo (1989, 80–81; cf. 108).

I have highlighted this difficulty that the early Black cultural critics had to negotiate because I believe that it provides a basis for understanding and appreciating the alleged assimilationist and homogenizing impulses (to use West's terminologies) of those critics. It is in this light that I consider unfair West's condemnation of the motivations of the critics as originating simply from "a quest for white approval and acceptance and an endeavor to overcome the internalized association of blackness with inferiority" (1993b, 16). Indeed, a contemporary variant of the predicament of the early Black diasporic cultural critic can be seen in the endeavor of Black studies and women's studies to gain recognition and acceptance in the academy. These studies arose largely as a result of sociopolitical agitations in the 1960s. Before these studies were recognized as legitimate areas of intellectual inquiry, however, they had to go through many hurdles, the most fundamental of which was to be sanctioned by the various curriculum committees of academic institutions. To be sanctioned means to be accepted and approved by those committees. And the politics of gaining such acceptance and approval involved, among other things, modifying and moderating the rhetoric in which the arguments were made for the legitimacy of those studies as genuine areas of intellectual inquiry. Sometimes the politics of gaining acceptance and approval may even require diluting the content of the proposed syllabi of the studies so as not to "offend" the custodians of the academic "cultural" apparatus.

Notice that the curriculum committees here are analogous to the cultural apparatus in society whose approval and acceptance needed to be won by the early Black cultural critics. The strategic maneuverings of the pioneers of women's studies and Black studies are similar to those of the early Black cultural critics. And the difficulties that confronted the pioneers of women's studies and Black studies—

for example, that of making credible their various programs as legitimate areas of inquiry against the backdrop of hostile criticism and virulent opposition from the custodians of the academic cultural apparatus—correspond to the predicament of the early Black cultural critics. If therefore it would be disingenuous to condemn the pioneers of women's studies and Black studies for their strategic political maneuvers, it would similarly be disingenuous to condemn the early Black cultural critics for their strategic maneuverings in defending Black humanity within the very racist institutional structure that they sought to challenge. The need for sympathy and understanding that I am advocating is accented when one recalls West's own observation about the negotiating that even the prophetic critic, the new cultural worker situated within the umbrella of the new cultural politics of difference, has to undertake.[13]

The Political Challenge and the Black Intellectual

This brings me to the political challenge that West says must be addressed by a practitioner of the new cultural politics of difference. Indeed, it is through his discussion of this challenge that West's humanistic scholarship most poignantly reveals itself. The challenge, to repeat, is for the practitioner to make relevant to society at large her or his intellectual engagements by working with extraparliamentary groups whose purpose is to advocate for the less fortunate in society. Examples of extraparliamentary groups are the church and similar religious organizations, trade unions, the National Association for the Advancement of Colored People (NAACP), academic organizations such as the American Association of University Professors (AAUP), and similar types of civic organizations. A condition for being a practitioner of the new cultural politics of difference, for West, is that the individual be affiliated both with the academy and with extraparliamentary groups of the kind mentioned here. *Qua* intellectual, the practitioner necessarily functions within the academy in order to stay "attuned to the most sophisticated reflections about the past, present and future destinies of the relevant cultures, economies and states of our time" (ibid., 102) and to gain exposure to the "paradigms, viewpoints and methods" that the mainstream has to offer (ibid., 27). On the other hand, in being affiliated with extraparliamentary organizations, the practitioner of the new cultural politics of difference grounds herself or himself in what West describes as subcultures of criticism—that is, those "progressive political organizations and cultural institutions of the most likely agents of social change" (102–103; cp. 27). This simultaneous positioning is essential for the intellectual to connect the life of the mind to praxis. In particular, the ultimate goal of this dual and complementary positioning is to help promote "greater democracy and freedom" (103) in society. And the intellectual accomplishes this feat through providing systematic criticism that demystifies the existing power structure and by implementing in praxis the ideas garnered from the academy. In this connection, a subtext in West's discussion is that the new cultural worker should conceive of herself or himself as a kind of Socratic gadfly to the society and even to the very institutions to which she or he belongs within and outside the academy. As a Socratic gadfly, the new cultural worker must bring to bear all of her or his analytical skills to interrogate existing power structures, institutions, issues, and communal relations in the hope of improving them. The crucial issues on which she or he should focus attention are political, economic, and social—or, more generally, existential. The new cultural worker should be prepared to engage issues such as the following:

> [H]ow to help generate the conditions and circumstances of such
> social motion, momentum and movements that move society in more
> democratic and free directions. How to bring more power and pres-
> sure to bear on the status quos so as to enhance the life chances of
> the jobless and homeless, landless and luckless, empower degraded
> and devalued working people, and increase the quality of life for all?
> (102)

West captures this political role of the intellectual in the concept of the intellectual as a critical organic catalyst of change in society (ibid., 27, 102), a concept he obtained from the critical thought of the Italian Marxist Antonio Gramsci.[14] Following Gramsci, West distinguishes between "organic" and "traditional" intellectuals. The former, he says, are those individuals who are "linked to prophetic movements or priestly institutions, [and] take the life of the mind seriously enough to relate ideas to the everyday life of ordinary folk." For him, organic intellectuals are "activistic and engaged." In contrast, traditional intellectuals "revel in the world of ideas while nesting in comfortable places far removed from the realities of the common life." As such, traditional intellectuals are "academic and detached" (1998a, 271).[15] In light of this distinction one can thus appreciate the severity of West's criticism of Black intellectuals. The thrust of his criticism is that Black intellectuals have little or no respect in the Black community precisely because they are largely "traditional" intellectuals. Thus, Black intellectuals' engagements have little or no instrumental value to the day-to-day predicament of the Black community. What this means, in effect, is that Black intellectual engagements are not humanistically oriented. Yet, before I determine whether or not West's own practice is congruent with his rhetoric, it may be worthwhile to examine the reasons he gives for this lack of humanistic orientation of Black intellectual engagements, and thus whether or not he is justified in condemning Black intellectuals as he does.

West traces the supposed irrelevance of Black intellectual activities, and hence what he perceives as the impotency of Black intellectuals, to the nonexistence of the necessary infrastructure in Black institutions to sustain intellectual life (1993b, 70–71; cp. 1994c, 64). He attributes this state of affairs to two factors: (1) Black integration into mainstream postindustrial elite American universities even as these institutions have shown a tendency to question the abilities and capabilities of Black students as potential scholars (1993b, 74; cp. 70) and (2) a lack of creative imagination among Black scholars, themselves to originate and sustain indigenous institutional mechanisms that promote criticism and self-criticism (70). These two factors, for West, conjunctively inhibit the development of the intellectual apparatus that will yield and sustain the kind of culture that defines intellectual life. Given that Black intellectuals, like other professionals in society, seek fame, recognition, status, and power, the kind of climate in which they function, with little to sustain them intellectually, has made the bulk of them inconsequential to the wider academy (which often marginalizes them) and to the Black community itself.[16] And the situation is exacerbated by an endemic tension and distrust between Black intellectuals on the one hand and the larger Black community on the other, especially since the former refuse to be "organically linked with African American cultural life"

(71) in visible ways. According to West, this refusal is effected through exogamous marriages, abandonment of Black institutions, and a "preoccupation with Euro-American intellectual products [that] are often perceived by the black community as intentional efforts to escape the negative stigma of blackness or [that] are viewed as symptoms of self-hatred" (71).

But what are some of the sociological factors that account for this lack of infrastructure to promote and sustain intellectual activity in the Black community? This question is of the utmost importance since, as West observes, at least two main intellectual traditions are endemic (even intrinsic) to African American life: (1) the Black Christian tradition of preaching—that is, Black orality and oratory; and (2) the Black musical tradition of performance (ibid., 72–73). To characterize as "traditions" the Black practice and methodology of preaching and musical performance is to say the following: (1) that the respective forms of activity in each tradition are executed within an institutional infrastructural framework; (2) that there is a culture that both sustains and in turn is sustained by the infrastructure; (3) that there are very rigorous criteria for excellence, criteria that are applied ruthlessly but very objectively; and (4) that there is an intolerance for mediocrity. It is because of these factors, says West, that the "traditions" in question have been able to produce and immortalize legendary figures both in music and in the Black church.[17] Yet we do not find a similar or equivalent tradition in Black intellectual life. According to West, this is partly because the Black community as a whole conceives of intellectual life as having *only* instrumental value. Thus, they celebrate the intellectual who is a political activist or cultural critic (71).

Assuming that West is correct, his diagnosis suggests that there has been a monumental failure of the Black institutions themselves to define their relevance to the Black community. After all, Black intellectuals are members of academic institutions. Accordingly, the larger Black community's belief that Black intellectuals are useless to their needs, if true, is more a reflection of the failure of the Black institutions than of the Black intellectuals. In other words, the phenomenon West describes is more a statement about the Black institutions themselves than about the Black intellectuals.[18] Of course, the supposed perception of impotence of the Black intellectual, again if true, is a post-Civil Rights phenomenon. The 1960s witnessed all stripes of Black people, intellectuals and nonintellectuals, men and women of different classes and stations in life, banding together at the grassroots level in the advocacy and demand for human freedom and dignity. There was institutional commitment to the struggle for civil rights. But above all, there was a *service ethos* that Black institutions fostered, encouraged and transmitted. Somehow, this spirit that linked the individual with the larger community via the institutions in question seemed to evaporate with post-Civil Rights gains. The importance of institutions has now become subordinate to the (self-)importance of the individual. Consequently, except only nominally, there has been an "erosion of the service ethos," as West calls it, at both the institutional and the individual levels. Echoing a similar sentiment, bell hooks states: "We have experienced . . . a change in that communal ethic of service that was so necessary for survival in traditional black communities. That ethic of service has been altered by shifting class relations. . . . A certain kind of bourgeois individualism of the mind [now] prevails."[19]

This is certainly not to deny that particular individuals, specifically academic intellectuals, sometimes make the effort to be involved with local groups or organizations in their communities. In his challenge of West's attack on Black intellectuals, Lewis Gordon provides instances of academic intellectuals as political activists.[20] Indeed, Gordon faults West's criticism of Black intellectuals on two counts. First, he questions what he deems West's subscription to a postmodernist restrictivist concept of the intellectual as an academician and, consequently, West's claim that Black academic intellectuals detach themselves from their communities. Gordon thinks, on the contrary, that there are nonacademic intellectuals who are also involved in their communities. Second, and more importantly, Gordon charges that West wrongly identifies (all forms of) political activity with the consensus-building type that West himself practices and its modus operandi of "speech and agreement" (or dialogue). Gordon then construes West's charge that academic intellectuals have failed to make themselves relevant to the Black community to mean that, for West, academic intellectuals have failed to perform the *only* kind of political activity, the dialogic, that can lead to change in the community. To counter West's position, Gordon proceeds to identify another form of political activity, the instrumental (or functional), which, he says, emphasizes "building up institutions or simply responding to immediate problems" in the community. In Gordon's view, it is this latter form of political activity that is mostly practiced by Black academics. And it is in this context that Gordon gives examples of Black academic intellectuals who are politically active in their local communities (L. Gordon 1997a, 200–201). Unfortunately, says Gordon, the political activity of this type of academic intellectuals is not as "visible," except of course in the community itself, as is the political activity of what he calls the celebrity-type of intellectuals—meaning people like West.[21]

Yet I do not think that Gordon's examples of political praxis constitute a refutation of West's thesis about the general impotence of Black intellectuals as such.[22] What Gordon demonstrates through the examples is that academic intellectuals *may sometimes* be involved in their communities. By means of these examples, Gordon thus highlights a dimension of political activity that West often downplays or subordinates to the dialogic method of addressing political concerns. Thus, it is not so much that West narrowly conceives of political activity as consensus-building as that he seems to privilege the consensus-building form over other forms of political activity. It is this privileging that leads him to envision political activity of the individual within an institutional framework whose operative methodology is speech and dialogue. Accordingly, he advances the thesis about the general absence of a coherent and systemic involvement of individuals as a call of duty. And he attributes this absence to the nonexistence of the necessary infrastructure in the Black institutions. Of course, it does not follow from the infrastructural problems of the kind West alleges that individual academic intellectuals may not be active in their communities. And this is what Gordon demonstrates. But the two positions are not contradictory; they are complementary.[23]

While I believe that West is quite right in condemning the nature of Black intellectual life as a *function of major infrastructural problems in Black academic institutions,* I think, however, that his criticism is misdirected. He should have directed his criticism at the Black institutions, especially their leadership, however that is defined, not at the intellectuals. The reason is that it is the leadership that has failed to take initiatives to cultivate and promote the kind of culture and climate that drive intellectual activity of the kind exhibited in elite White schools. The caliber of Black faculty (indeed of any scholar) and the nature and scope of their intellectual endeavors (however defined) are a function of the kind of leadership provided. And where such leadership is found wanting in its function the results show in the intellectual life of the community. To illustrate, few Black institutions have taken initiatives to launch a serious African American studies program or an African(a) studies program as part of their core curriculums. Yet it is these academic areas that speak directly to life in the Black community, and it is via these academic areas that a connection can be made with the ground-level activities in the community.[24] It seems that for most Black schools African American studies or African(a) studies exist only nominally. Thus, until the situation is corrected, Black intellectual activity will have no organic link of the kind West envisions, and so, assuming West is correct in his criticism, Black intellectuals will continue to be perceived collectively as useless to the larger Black community. Since it is the leadership that is vested with the authority and responsibility to create and/or alter the climate in which intellectual activity takes place, it is that body therefore that West should have targeted for criticism, not the Black scholars, who are themselves victims of leadership ineptitude. It is that body that must generate and support the ethos of service in the collective consciousness of Black academics, an ethos that informs praxis in the form of duty.

West's Humanism: Congruence or Divergence between Rhetoric and Practice?

The preceding discussion of West's attack on Black intellectuals within the context of his analysis of the new cultural politics of difference clearly helps bring into focus the humanistic orientation of his scholarship. The existential, intellectual, and political concerns that he thinks drive the new cultural politics of difference also inform his castigation of the Black intelligentsia. It is of course arguable that West is justified in his criticism of the Black intellectuals or even that his claim of the perception of their supposed impotency is accurate. Gordon's criticism is meant to show that West got it all wrong. Regardless of how one interprets West's views, however, there can be no doubt that his concerns are humanistic, especially since they are inscribed within the parameters that govern humanistic enterprises. After all, his targets in both "The New Cultural Politics of Difference" and "The Dilemma of the Black Intellectual" are specific kinds of structures that delimit the scope of individual agency. In "The New Cultural Politics of Difference," these are structures that incapacitate the individual from participating effectively in political, economic, and other forms of social activity. In "The Dilemma of the Black Intellectual," his critique is of the absence of those structures that he considers vital to empowering individuals so that they may realize their duty in the Black community.

Obviously, West wishes to contrast the nature of his own intellectual activity with those of other Black intellectuals, especially those in Black institutions. He considers his own scholarship and intellectual life to be directly relevant to the Black community and indeed to the larger American society and believes that he establishes this relevance through an organic link with the community. By "organic link" he means participating in organizations that are concerned with addressing issues that pertain to the Black community. He states: "When I think of my own organic link with the black community, it's not that I am somehow thoroughly immersed in the black community, in some pantheistic way. Rather, I'm simply working in a particular organization or institution in which we are contesting among ourselves how we can best generate visions, analysis, and forms of political action. I want to say 'be organized', rather than 'be organic'" (Osborne 1996, 136).

The specific ways in which West says he is organically linked to the Black community is through "black organizations and institutions, from united fronts to churches" (ibid., 136). And he lists among these organizations the Congressional Black Caucus and the Democratic Socialists of America. Germane to the present discussion is West's remark that he and other members of the Democratic Socialists of America had "tried to make health care a major public issue in America for nine years and . . . were unable to do it for the first six or so. Then boom, it just took off [under the Clinton administration, even though without success]" (142). In typical Deweyan fashion, West's membership in the kind of organizations mentioned earns him a voice, he says, in the discussions that shape public policy. And to the extent that whatever public policies are adopted affect different constituencies, West thus says he sees "the need for multi-contextualism." By this he means traversing the different kinds of constituencies "from working people to very poor people, to the academy, as well as other professions" (136), all of whom are affected by public policy of one kind or another.

The foregoing catalog of West's affiliation with groups whose operations and workings have a direct bearing on public policy cannot but lead one to conclude that his practice as a humanistic scholar is congruent with his rhetoric. One can even safely generalize that many of his writings and public engagements are but first-person expressions of the concept of the intellectual as an organic catalyst in society. This generalization is sustained by the kind of issues West addresses in works such as *Race Matters, Prophetic Fragments, Prophecy Deliverance,* and *Keeping Faith,* to name a few.

To sum up, Cornel West's diverse engagements, articulated within his theoretical framework of prophetic pragmatism, establish him as a humanistic scholar. A humanistic scholar is an intellectual who endeavors to give practical application to her or his theoretical engagements in order to uphold the dignity of humanity. Cornel West's immediate concern is with the downtrodden in American society. By examining among other things two of West's essays, "The New Cultural Politics of Difference" and "The Dilemma of the Black Intellectual," I have shown how West pursues his humanistic endeavor. Of importance is that West's challenge that scholars relate the life of the mind to praxis is, indeed, a call for scholars to be humanistic in their orientation. West's own humanistic concern is mostly exemplified in his discussion of social justice largely for African Americans and people of color, but also generally for all those whom he thinks are dispossessed in society. It is this concern I will now address.

CHAPTER THREE

Black Prophetic Christianity and Marxist Social Thought

Introduction

A central theme in African American critical thought is the quest for social justice. As I indicated earlier, it is this quest that drives Cornel West's sociopolitical/philosophical engagements as articulated though his doctrine of prophetic pragmatism. West claims to advocate for dispossessed, exploited, and demoralized individuals in society. The major ills West says he hopes to cure are despair, dread, disappointment, disease, and untimely death (1989, 6–8; see also Osborne 1996, 127). West's contention is that these ills, suffered by people of color and lower-class Whites, result directly from human actions executed in and through the institutions of power and economic control in society. Specifically, the actions that produce these ills express rapacious individualism. And for West, it is these actions that give rise to social injustice. My proposed aim in this chapter, therefore, is to examine West's prescription for overcoming the social injustice wrought by rapacious individualism. In particular, I propose to critique West's suggestion that the liberation of African Americans from socioeconomic oppressive practices can only be effected through an admixture of prophetic Christian outlook and progressive Marxist social criticism.

I will begin by situating West's discussion within what he considers the general aim of African American critical thought and the major tasks that confront theoreticians of African American philosophy. This is because West implies in the Introduction of his

Prophecy Deliverance (1982) that they are these aims and tasks that guide the proposal he advances for Black liberation and social justice. I then will go on to delineate the bases for his advocacy of an admixture of prophetic Christianity and crypto-Marxist theoretical outlook to address the issue of social justice. Finally, I will evaluate his proposal in the context of contemporary discussions on the subject of Blacks and social justice in America.

African American Critical Thought and Liberation from Oppression

The central aim of African American critical thought is to articulate the tragic situation of Blacks in America with a view to engaging it and proposing ways for its amelioration. This is the thrust of West's view in the Introduction of his *Prophecy Deliverance* (1982, 15). By "tragic" West means the existential predicament of Blacks that commenced with the kidnapping of Africans in the middle of the seventeenth century (101) and their enslavement in the West. In the United States, the situation since then has been one of despair, disappointment, dread, disease, and untimely death. The aim of African American critical thought, therefore, is to liberate Blacks from this oppressive existential situation but more so from the factors in contemporary society that nurture and sustain it.[1]

West suggests that to achieve this aim African American critical thought must draw upon the two most fundamental intellectual traditions in American (including Black American) life: the Black church and American pragmatism (ibid., 16–20).[2] The Black church is central to Black life; it is the pillar of African American culture. The Black church is the institution through which Blacks acquired over the years the psychological fortitude to cope with what West often characterizes as "the absurd [of being] in America" (Osborne 1996, 127–28).[3] By the absurd he means a mode of existence that consists in despair, disappointment, dread, disease, and untimely death (127). These, for West, are the five items that form the cornerstone of Black existential predicament in America. The Black church has consistently challenged this absurd by fostering and teaching optimism, courage, strength, and hope. The Black church thus provides spiritual uplifting by celebrating the individual and by restoring the individual's sense of dignity and self-worth.

At the same time, the Black church has been the most vociferous critic of the political and socioeconomic system that denigrates and dehumanizes the individual. Black church leaders construe, articulate, and critique Black oppression as a function of institutional racism. They explain Black dehumanization and the indignity Blacks have suffered over the years as a direct consequence of racist practices in a racist culture. Since racist practices largely account for the prevailing dismal socioeconomic conditions in Black communities (or more generally in communities of peoples of color), the Black church thus provides a site for radical contestation and social criticism of those practices and the culture in which they are embedded. Thus the Black church is the most logical candidate upon which to draw in formulating an African American critical thought.

The second intellectual tradition upon which African American critical thought must draw, according to West, is American pragmatism. This is not just because pragmatism is native to Euro-American philosophy but also, and more importantly, because, as already noted, some forms of the pragmatist tradition are essentially concerned with cultural criticism. And this concern marks a radical departure from the epistemological endeavors that had animated European philosophy since Descartes.[4] Given its aims of critiquing American sociopolitical and economic culture, therefore, African American critical thought cannot but draw upon the critical temper already established and fostered by American pragmatism.

Yet certain additional observations need to be made about these two traditions in American intellectual life if only to appreciate fully West's reason for invoking them as vital to the liberating aim of African American critical thought. According to West, the Black church, particularly the prophetic element within it, is "guided by a profound conception of human nature and human history, a persuasive picture of what one is as a person, what one should hope for, and how one ought to act" (1982, 16).[5] This means that the Black church, in the spirit of prophetic Christianity, articulates a philosophy of existence that is grounded in human nature and that is both anaphoric (in that it views human situation historically) and forward looking (in that it envisions human future possibilities). Central to prophetic Christianity are two norms that, in West's view, are fundamental to African American critical thought. These are (1) the norm of individuality within community and (2) the norm of democracy.

The norm of individuality within community conceives of the individual as a member of a community. The individual's existence within community is an ontological reality. Thus, the norm of individuality within community implies that it is etiologically (or naturally) impossible for the individual to live outside of the community, for this would entail the absurdity that the individual can preexist the community. On the other hand, as a member within community, the individual has a right to her or his self-realization, a right to the fullest development of her or his potential. This is a natural right, a divine gift from God. Because this right is a gift that God bestows on every human, it is thus an egalitarian principle; it expresses the human equality on earth. It is in virtue of this right, therefore, that every human is supposed to pursue her or his happiness on earth. For West, the exercise of this right constitutes existential freedom (ibid., 18). But what needs to be emphasized here is West's view that the norm of individuality, in conceiving of the person relative to the community rather than as a presocial Hobbesian ego or a metaphysical Cartesian ego, "reinforces the importance of community, common good, and the harmonious development of the personality" (17).

The norm of individuality also highlights the dignity of persons and the depravity of persons. The former refers to the human capacity to transform an existing situation and also to be transformed by an existing situation for the better. This transformative capacity, says West, serves to reveal human imperfection and finiteness. The depravity of persons, for West, characterizes a human proclivity "to refuse to transform and to be transformed" (ibid., 17). West describes the dignity of persons and the depravity of persons as elements in a dialectic that informs human personal history. This dialectic is significant to prophetic Christianity because it emphasizes individual agency. An agent has the power or ability to effect change and to resist change. An agent can act or forbear to act; she or he can make or alter a situation. Since the principal aim of African American critical thought is to provide a programmatic strategy for Black liberation and social justice, the concept of agency is therefore of crucial importance to the realization of that aim. The reason is that it is in and through human agency that existential freedom is exercised. And, for West, the exercise of existential freedom in political praxis is "social freedom" (18). It is for this reason that West aptly says, "Existential freedom empowers people to fight for social freedom, to realize its political dimension" (18). Thus we see that social freedom presupposes existential freedom and existential freedom entails human agency. In other words, without existential freedom social freedom is unintelligible in the sense that it is nonexistent.

The second norm that is central to prophetic Christianity is the norm of democracy. By this norm West means a principle of accountability through which individuals can exercise control over those persons and institutions on whom the task and responsibility of leadership are invested. Accountability should be of "institutions to populace, of leaders to followers, [and] of preachers to laity" (ibid., 18). In West's view, the principle of accountability should be the center of any acceptable social vision (18). The reason is that without accountability or a control mechanism individual existential freedom will not be actualized. That freedom, recall, enables individuals to realize and develop their potentials within community to the fullest. If then the institutions whose decisions affect the lives of individuals are not regulated by those individuals, especially in the decision-making processes of those institutions, existential freedom and, by extension, social freedom very easily can be thwarted. West's concern about the lack of control over the institutions of power in contemporary society is rooted in this belief.

What then is the overall significance of prophetic Christianity to a theoretical articulation of Black demand for social justice? For West, prophetic Christianity, by highlighting the norms of individuality and democracy, confronts the tragic character of the history and predicament of African Americans in a very open and honest way and articulates hopes for their liberation. This means that prophetic Christianity takes very seriously "the existential anxiety, political oppression, economic exploitation, and social degradation of the actual human being" (ibid., 19). To that end, prophetic Christianity gives a premium to the notion of struggle, both personal and collective, and accents hope. It is this notion that informs African American critical thought. To quote West, "prophetic Afro-American Christian thought imbues Afro-American thinking with the sobriety of tragedy, the struggle for freedom, and the spirit of hope" (20).

As noted, American pragmatism, especially of the Emerson-Deweyan stripe, is the second intellectual tradition that West says African American critical thought must involve. This is because pragmatism is a form of cultural criticism. It interprets "a people's past for the purpose of solving specific problems presently confronting the cultural way of life from which the people come" (ibid., 20). Its ultimate goal is "amelioration," says West, and its chief consequence is "the transformation of existing realities" (21). Thus, pragmatism speaks to the heart of the African American critical thought. More perspicuously, West believes that African American critical thought must utilize this American philosophical outlook and adapt it (or parts thereof) to the theoretical discussion of Black liberation and social justice.

In addition to the aforementioned intellectual traditions, West also considers Marxist thought central to the liberating aims of African American critical thought. He believes that Marxist thought is significant to the quest for constructing a programmatic strategy for Black liberation and social justice. In the essay "Black Theology and Marxist Thought (1993a)," West contends that Black theologians and Marxist theoreticians have more in common than they seem aware; thus, there is a need for "a serious dialogue" between them.[6] The aim of such dialogue, he says, is "to demystify the deep misunderstanding and often outright ignorance each side has of the other" (1982, 23). And he expresses the hope that such demystification will result in the formation of "an alliance" between prophetic Christianity and progressive Marxist social thought. More importantly, West believes that "the hope of Western civilization" lies in just such an alliance. Concerning the issue of Black liberation and social justice, in particular, he thinks that an alliance between Black theological outlook and progressive Marxist thought will be effective in addressing the crucial task that confronts African American critical thought. This task is "to provide a political prescription for . . . specific praxis in the present historical moment of the struggle for [Black] liberation" (23).[7] Before examining these assertions I will first consider some of the specific claims that drive West's advocacy for a dialogue, and hence an alliance, between prophetic Christianity and progressive Marxist thought.

Black Prophetic Christianity and Progressive Marxist Thought: A Proposed Synthesis

According to West, Black theology and Marxist thought, as intellectual traditions, have a similar goal: They both "focus on the plight of the exploited, oppressed and degraded peoples of the world, their relative powerlessness and possible empowerment" (1993a, 409; 1982, 107). In particular, West establishes three points of commonalities between the two traditions. First, both traditions are concerned with the liberation of the oppressed in society. Second, both traditions employ the same dialectical methodology of negation, preservation, and transformation to achieve their goals. What this means is that both traditions challenge, and hence negate, certain assumptions that undergird the positions they are contesting; they both endeavor to preserve what they perceive as the truth about the situation they are examining; and their analyses provide them with new insights into the nature of the situation they examine. These insights in turn enable them to pursue actions to transform the situation they are contesting. The third point of commonality between both traditions, says West, is that the groups provide trenchant critiques of the socioeconomic system that is responsible for the oppression in society.

To illustrate, Black theologians ground their interpretation of the Bible on the experiences of Blacks. Since these experiences are of suffering and vilification, in contrast to the experiences of Whites, Black theologians therefore question, and hence negate, the viewpoints and interpretations their White counterparts advance of the gospel. A corresponding principle of negation informs Marxist critiques of capitalist theories of the means of production and ownership of materials. According to West, Marxist critiques are aimed at unearthing the misinformation disseminated by bourgeois theoreticians about capitalist society, especially about capital formation, with the goal of correcting such misinformation. Next, Black theologians endeavor to understand and thus preserve what they consider the truth of the biblical text, namely, that God sides with the oppressed, in light of Black experiences of oppression. The corresponding principle of preservation in Marxist thought is that of demonstrating that the bourgeois theories of capitalism support and sanction oppression; thus Marxist thought endeavors to preserve the idea of the conflict-producing nature of social processes (1993a, 411–12). Finally, for Black theologians, the principle of transformation yields newer understandings of the gospel in contrast to past understandings. For Marxist theoreticians, the corresponding principle of transformation provides new insights into the social dynamics of capitalist culture.

But West also brings out certain limitations of each tradition. Concerning Black theologians, for example, he charges that, with only one exception, they have generally failed to advance a social theory that links Black oppression to the capitalist mode of production in American society.[8] What this means is that, in his view, Black theologians have failed to see that Black oppression goes beyond just racist practices to the ownership of wealth and the means of production in American society. For West, it is no accident that Black oppression and powerlessness are inextricably linked in a symbiotic relationship to a lack of wealth. He states that transnational conglomerates own the wealth in American society. These conglomerates, he continues, in a bid to promote their interests—namely, the acquisition of profits—formulate policies that subsequently translate into the domestic and foreign policies of the American government. According to West, not only are the sources of wealth identical with the sources of power, but also, and more importantly, it is through this identity relation of wealth and power that the oppression and exploitation of people of color is effected both within and outside the United States. Thus, in his view, Black theologians, in failing to theorize this relation, fail to identify the real source and nature of the oppression from which they endeavor to liberate Blacks. As he puts it,

> An undisputable claim of Black theology is America's unfair treatment of Black people. What is less apparent is the way in which Black theologians understand the internal dynamics of liberal capitalist America, how it functions, why it operates the way it does, who possesses substantive power, and where it is headed. . . . Black theologians do not utilize a social theory that relates the oppression of Black people to the overall make-up of America's system of production, foreign policy, political arrangement, and cultural practices. (ibid., 414)

West then notes that Marxist theoreticians overcome the limitation of the Black theological outlook in providing a social theory of the relation between ownership of wealth, the source of power, and human exploitation and oppression. Marxist theoreticians address the issue of liberation by advocating a redefinition of the ownership of wealth, the dissolution of the existing power structure, and calling participatory democracy.

But West is even-handed in his criticism in that he is just as critical of the Marxist tradition as he is of the Black theological tradition. For example, he charges that Marxist theoreticians are myopic and mistaken in thinking that the only way to combat oppression is through a redistribution of wealth and demystification of power. Says West, Marxist theoreticians wrongly consider religious values and culture merely as instruments of domination and pacification (ibid., 417). He notes that, although it is true that religious values and culture can be as the Marxists allege, nevertheless, those values can serve also as instruments of resistance to oppression. This use of religious beliefs has been borne out in the role of the Black church in Black liberation struggles. It is this political value of religious belief and culture as instruments of resistance to oppression that Marxist theoreticians fail to see. For West, therefore, Marxist theoreticians could enlarge their understanding of religious culture and value as forms of resistance, taking their cue from liberation theologians. Similarly, Black theologians need to augment their critical outlook by supplying a social theory of Black oppression.

What these limitations to Black theological outlook and Marxist theory suggest is that, in West's view, neither tradition adequately meets the task of providing a theory of liberation of oppressed people. Thus, given their common objective, a dialogue between them is necessary, one that "accents the possibility of mutually arrived at political action" (1982, 107). By "dialogue" West means no less than a synthesis of the virtues (or the positive features) of both traditions to meet their common aim of liberating oppressed people. West's proposed solutions to effect Black liberation and social justice therefore are reflective of such a dialogue. West offers two solutions: (1) collective ownership of the means of production and (2) a counter-hegemonic assault on capitalism. These solutions mutually reinforce each other, and I shall discuss each in turn.

The Seductiveness of Marxian Solutions to Black Oppression

Drawing upon the Marxist social criticism of capitalist culture, West's first solution is that the liberation of oppressed people, but especially people of color, can only come about, in the United States at least, when those people participate "in the decision-making processes of the major institutions that affect their destinies." He explains participation to mean direct involvement in and control of the transnational conglomerates "by the citizenry." In sum, West is calling for a *collective ownership of the means of production* in American society. In his words, "Only collective control over the major institutions of society constitutes genuine power on behalf of the people" (1993a, 415).

West's proposal for collective ownership of the means of production in society expresses the view of one strand of Marxist thinking that affirms the need for justice in society but denies that justice can ever be attained within a capitalistic system. On this view, justice is incompatible with private ownership of the means of production in society. This is because private ownership of the means of production leads to exploitation or alienation of workers. The other strand of Marxist thinking rejects the very idea of justice. This strand views justice as a remedial virtue, a response to some flaw in society. It claims that the very need of justice is to mediate conflicts between individuals. However, in the political society Marxism advocates there will not be a need for justice because there will be no conflicts among members of the society.[9]

While West's call for the participation of hitherto excluded and oppressed people in the decision-making processes of the institutions that affect their lives is unquestionably laudable, his identification of such participation with collectivism cannot but be seriously mistaken. It is seriously mistaken not simply because it equates democratic participation with collectivism but, more importantly, because it assumes without proof that democratic participation cannot occur within capitalism but that it can occur within collectivism. At the very least this is question-begging. Besides, as Will Kymlicka has argued, and quite persuasively, exploitative (read undemocratic and oppressive) conduct can occur just as well under collectivism as under capitalism. Kymlicka illustrates this point by supposing a firm in a socialist system divided between two groups, a majority and a minority, each of whose members has an equal vote (or share or interest). However, in decisions over leisure, work, vacation and the like the majority always wins. According to Kymlicka, in such a situation, if the members in the minority are not allowed to convert into private resources the votes (shares or interests) to which they lay claim, such that they can sell their votes (shares or interests), then they will be unfairly disadvantaged (Kymlicka 1990, 182).[10] The possibility of such a state of affairs in a collectivist system shows that antidemocratic or undemocratic practices are not necessarily peculiar to capitalism. Alternatively, the possibility of the state of affairs described shows that collective ownership of the means of production does not necessarily assure equality in the sense of freedom from exploitation and oppression, as some Marxists, including West, seem to think.[11]

What motivates West's call for a collective ownership of the means of production à la Marxist thinking is the assumption that Black liberation (indeed any form of liberation) and demands for social justice cannot logically be attained within the current capitalist structure in the United States. This is because, on his view, capitalism is intrinsically antithetical to any form of liberating activity, and hence any form of social justice. Bernard Boxill conveys this general belief about the inherent opposition between capitalism and justice as follows: "Marxist theory does not imply that capitalism is, or can be just. On the contrary, it implies that capitalism is not, and cannot be, just, and, moreover, that the workers will come to realize this."[12] For West, the paradox of capitalism is that capitalism promotes "an ethos of rapacious individualism" (1982, 123), and this ethos stifles the norm of individuality within community, the norm that accents individual existential democracy. The individualism that capitalism fosters is that of transnational conglomerates, not the individualism of *persons* as such. Furthermore, the goal of capitalism is to maximize profit, and this profit-oriented nature of capitalism necessarily precludes the democratic participation of workers in investment decisions (122). This antidemocratic nature of capitalism thus translates into exploitation of those in the productive process and hence their oppression. For this reason, West characterizes capitalism as "an *antidemocratic* mode of socioeconomic organization" (122, emphasis in the original). It is to counter the alleged antidemocratic practice of capitalism that West suggests collective owner-ship. The implication is that under collective ownership of the means of production, individuals would be participants in the decision-making processes of the economic institutions that affect their lives. As we have seen, however, even when individuals are participants in the decision-making process for which West clamors they are still not immune from oppression. This shows that oppression is not the sole prerogative of liberal capitalism that West indicts.

The attractiveness of Marxism to liberation theorists is its prom-ise of human economic and social equality. West and countless other theoreticians of oppression and liberation naturally have found this notion appealing. But this notion of equality, premised as it is on a Marxist model, warrants close examination. On the classical view of Marxism, equality has meant the creation of a classless society. The creation of such a society is through collective ownership of the means of production. And collective ownership entails, at least in principle, a democratic participation of all members in the society. But does economic equality, assuming it did occur, necessarily imply social equality and freedom from oppression? Or, alternatively, can economic equality *guarantee* social equality and freedom from oppression? And, more specifically in respect of West's crypto-Marxist suggestion of collective ownership, how will collective own-ership of the transnational conglomerates translate into social equality of the racially and socially diverse body of working people and thus reflect social justice for people of color in particular?

Consider that members of the Black middle class in the United States, even some highly placed on the economic ladder, still experi-ence socially denigrating anti-Black racism. Two recent prominent examples are the notorious Texaco Oil Company incident and the equally notorious racial discrimination incident by the Denny's restaurant chain against some Black Secret Service members of for-mer President Clinton's Secret Service unit. In the Texaco Oil Company incident, some senior White male executives of the com-pany were secretly recorded on audiotape making racial slurs and other denigrating remarks about senior Black employees of manage-rial and higher status with the company. In the Denny's incident, a particular franchise of the restaurant chain refused to provide serv-ice to Black members of the President's Secret Service team but provided service to their White counterparts.[13] What, if anything, these situations highlight is that even as Blacks and other visible minorities have seemingly climbed to higher rungs in the economic ladder, there has not been a corresponding ascent in social acceptability and respectability that could generously be interpreted as a recognition of even near social equality. On the contrary, it would seem that the perception of a significant number of Whites, at least in the social sphere, is not positively affected by the upward economic mobility of Blacks. In other words, notwithstanding Black upward economic mobility, many Whites still view Blacks *as socially unequal* to Whites. It is this perception by some Whites that underlies all too familiar incidents, sometimes reported in the media and even documented, about otherwise respectable- and dignified-looking Blacks in luxury vehicles being routinely stopped by White local and state police officers under some pretext or other.[14] This kind of White police conduct presupposes certain assumptions about Blacks and other visible minorities. West's own experiences (to which I called attention in note 13) is further evidence of this claim.

All of these examples simply show that, even if economic inequality were completely eradicated by some fiat, aided by collective ownership of the transnational conglomerates that currently control the economy, it does not necessarily follow that social equality will result, and hence that Blacks would be liberated from oppression. Collective ownership may highlight existential democracy, as West says, and perhaps even promote social freedom. But it is utopic to believe that collective ownership, and hence economic equality, will eradicate all forms of oppression. Oppression, as West himself is aware, is extremely complex and can be manifested in a variety of ways (ibid., 116). Fairly recent ethnic-cleansing episodes of violence by Serbs against Moslems in Bosnia, and by Hutus against Tutsis in Rwanda and Burundi, clearly show that not all oppression has (or can be linked to) an economic cause. Even if all humans were of the same race and ethnicity and had equal financial resources, we still would find ways to discriminate against, and hence oppress, those to whom we feel superior or over whom we have power. The thrust of my argument, then, is that the Marxian model to which West appeals assumes falsely that eradicating economic inequality (or deprivation) entails ending social inequality and by extension liberating Blacks (and other people of color) from oppression. The evidence (in terms of the experiences) of some (perhaps many) affluent African Americans and Hispanics in contemporary United States exhibits the falsity of that assumption.

West might perhaps retort that the examples I have given, far from constituting a refutation of his position, simply lend support to it. Black theologians, perhaps middle-class Blacks in general, he would insist, tend to (mis)identify their middle-class status with having and exercising control over their lives. They falsely assume that the acquisition of a middle-class status, which is often synonymous with having a well-paying job, translates into possessing and exercising power in the decision-making processes that govern their lives (ibid., 113). It therefore comes as a rude shock to most affluent Blacks when they realize that their seeming material success does not translate into possessing the kind of (regulatory) power that manifests freedom from oppression. (Oppression here includes discriminatory practices.)

Yet, other than the fact that this objection is self-reflective of its proponent, its proper response demands that we ask a specific question that I believe West ought to have raised about the socioeconomic status of Blacks but that he failed to raise. Consider that West was chagrined, and justifiably, that no taxicab would stop for him in New York City. He was chagrined presumably because he realized that, notwithstanding his dignified outward bearing, the taxicab drivers saw him simply as a *Black man and hence a potential criminal*.[15] In other words, it was by virtue of his race that he was discriminated against. But leaving aside this matter, the important point to which I wish to call attention is that the very fact of West confidently hailing a taxicab presupposes a certain conception that he has of himself. This is a conception that, given his socioeconomic status, he ought to be able to hail a taxicab *and* have one pull up. The fact of this conception being rejected for no other reason other than that he is Black is thus the reason West was chagrined. This incident is significant because it shows all the more that West, like most middle-class Blacks, thought that his socioeconomic status gave him a measure of insurance against oppressive practices in the sense of according him power and control over certain decisions in his life. And surely he is not wrong in so thinking. Thus, the question we should ask is why does socioeconomic status not work for Blacks and other people of color by way of conferring acceptability and respectability as it does for Whites? This is the crucial question, I believe, that West ought to have raised about the socioeconomic status of middle-class Blacks rather than claim, as he does, that middle-class Blacks mistakenly conflate their socioeconomic status with possessing power in the society. The answer to this question is obvious: racism. And racism undeniably is the most virulent form of oppression.

The conclusion to draw from the foregoing considerations then is not, as West alleges, that middle-class Blacks misidentify their socioeconomic status with possession of power and control over the decision-making processes that affect their lives. Rather, the conclusion to draw is that oppression manifests itself in many ways. Indeed, the examples of the Denny's restaurant and Texaco incidents exhibit the falsity of the tacit but widely held belief among Marxians that oppression is only of the economically disadvantaged. Concerning people of color generally, the examples show that economic standing is not the major factor in their oppression, and thus must not be given the kind of primacy that West seems to give it in Black liberation struggles. This point needs to be emphasized especially given West's assertion that "class position contributes more than racial status to the basic form of powerlessness in America" (ibid., 115). West makes this assertion in the context of exhibiting what he describes as Black theologians' failure to link Black oppression to the ownership of the means of production in America and thus to the center of power in the society.[16] Noting that oppression is nothing but the result of the dynamics of power in society (112–113), West proceeds to acknowledge that Black powerlessness and oppression in American society are *intensified* by racist practices. And as illustrations he points to the high rate of unemployment among Blacks, the heavy Black concentration in low-paying jobs, and lower-quality housing, education, health care, and police protection (114). But rather than explain Black oppression, as exhibited in his own very illustrations, in terms of racist practices in the society, West switches to a general discussion of oppression and powerlessness in American society at large. And he concludes that the Black situation is not different in kind from the oppression and powerlessness of *all* white-

and blue-collar workers in the society. In other words, West circum-
scribes Black oppression and powerlessness within a general discussion of powerlessness (in the sense of lack of ownership of capital) in
the society at large. Given West's view, white- and blue-collar workers, whether racially White, Brown, or Yellow, are all just as
oppressed as Blacks because none of them have any control over the
economic decisions that affect their lives. True, West insists that the
oppression of Blacks is exacerbated by racism. Even so, he considers
the oppression of Blacks as being only qualitatively different from
the oppression of all others in the society. To quote him:

> [M]ost Americans are, to a significant degree, powerless. They have
> no substantial control over their lives, little participation in the deci-
> sion-making process of the major institutions that regulate their lives.
> Among Afro-Americans, this powerlessness is exacerbated, creating
> an apparent qualitative difference in oppression. (114–115)

It is in this context that West raises a very important question,
namely, whether it is class or race considerations that determine
oppression. To which he responds that it is class *more than* race considerations. I emphasize the comparative expression "more than" to
call attention to the fact that West is not excluding racial considerations from the matter. However, there can be no doubt that, even
despite what he says, West is subordinating race considerations to
class considerations, or, what is the same thing, he is privileging class
over race considerations in determining the factors that influence
oppression in society. Why such privileging as I am alleging? Here is
West's explanation:

> [M]iddle-class black people are essentially well-paid white- or blue-
> collar workers who have little control over their lives because of their
> class position, not their racial status. *This is so because the same lim-*
> *ited control is held by white middle-class people, despite the fact that*
> *a higher percentage of whites are well-paid white- and blue-collar*
> *workers than blacks.* Significant degrees of powerlessness pertain to
> most Americans and this could be so only if class position determines
> such powerlessness. (ibid., 115, emphases added)

If West is correct in his account of the determinant of oppression
in society, then it should make sense for the combined 45 percent of

Whites *and* non-Whites that own only 2 percent of America's wealth to form an alliance to liberate themselves from the shackles of the transnational conglomerates.[17] After all, they should see themselves as an oppressed *class,* and, if so, they should see that the formation of such an alliance would serve their best interest. Yet, as Boxill has rightly noted, even among the working class, racial and ethnic considerations often supercede class interests. Boxill calls attention to Marx's own observation that the attitude of the English working class to the Irish working class during the industrial revolution was of contempt and hatred in much the same way as "that of the 'poor whites' to the 'niggers' in the former slave states of the U.S.A." (Boxill 1984, 55). Speaking of the relation between the English and the Irish working class, Marx continued: "The ordinary English worker has the Irish worker as a competitor who [he believes] lowers his standard of life. *In relation to the Irish worker he feels himself a member of the ruling class*" (55, emphasis added). What these citations from Marx clearly bring out is that ethnicity and racial prejudice often override class considerations as determinants of oppression in society. This observation challenges in many ways the very concept of equality, grounded in economic liberation, at the heart of West's crypto-Marxian thinking. An alliance for liberation from oppression of the kind he describes presupposes mutual recognition of the parties to the alliance as social (and moral) equals. But it is clear from my discussion thus far that such mutual recognition does not occur in the (American) society West is addressing. It is reasonable to say that many Whites do not consider Blacks their social (and moral) equal. So how then can they form an alliance with Blacks even if one grants West's contention that both Whites and Blacks collectively constitute an oppressed *class*?

Next, there is no question that people of color *know* that they are oppressed. But, unless West wishes to have them believe otherwise, it is doubtful that they consider their oppression a consequence of class considerations. Instead, it is reasonable to believe that people of color occupy the lower class that they do precisely because of their race, so that they view their oppression as a function of their race and not their class.

Finally, except for women, do White male workers consider themselves oppressed *in the same way as non-Whites*? The import of these questions is that West's dissolution of Black oppression and powerlessness into a general worker oppression and powerlessness is very misleading if not downright erroneous. Consequently, the solution he proposes to the problem of Black oppression is, in my view, mistaken. Even if one grants that the economic decisions that govern most people's lives are made by the transnational conglomerates, and in that sense most people are oppressed, it is simply not the case that all forms of oppression are reducible to the economic. West exhibits an awareness of this fact from his observation that traditional Marxist analysis of culture narrowly and inaccurately "relates racist practices to misconceived material interests" (1982, 117). He notes that there is more to racism than traditional Marxists are aware and that the Black theologians appreciate. To that end, he affirms that "racism is an integral element within the very fabric of American culture and society. It is embedded in the country's first collective definition, enunciated in its subsequent laws, and imbued in its dominant way of life" (116). The examples drawn from the Texaco and Denny's incidents uphold this observation as they also amply demonstrate that economic elevation does not necessarily eliminate oppression. So it is quite puzzling that West should subordinate or dissolve Black oppression into class oppression when the evidence seems to suggest that, at least for the dominant lower class that is also largely Black, it is their race that explains their class oppression. To conclude, then, the Marxian model to which West appeals in his quest for Black liberation should be rejected on the ground that it provides a false solution to the problem of Black oppression.

Counterhegemonic Activities and Black Liberation

I turn now to the second solution West proposes to effect Black liberation within the context of the liberation of all oppressed peoples, viz., counterhegemonic activities. The point of departure of this solution is West's conception of capitalism not only as an "antidemocratic mode of socioeconomic organization" but also as a hegemonic culture in need of dismantling through a cultural critique. In describing capitalism as a hegemonic culture, West means that capitalism promotes the "dominant world views, sensibilities, and habits that sanction the established order." And worse, contends West, this hegemonic culture seduces its victims to subscribe to its values, mores, beliefs, and attitudes. In the United States, in particular, this seduction takes the form of a belief in the so-called American dream (or a permanent illusion for some?) of an upward economic mobility that translates into higher wages. Thus, by subscribing to the capitalistic culture, oppressed people end up "consenting" to their very oppression and powerlessness. For West, then, the only way to liberate oppressed people from the stranglehold of the capitalistic culture is through a counterhegemonic critique. Invoking the critical thought of Italian Marxist Antonio Gramsci, West explains that critique is not simply "moral criticism" of capitalistic culture. Critique involves among other things a sophisticated understanding of power relations and dynamics within the culture; it is linked with a praxis of faith or political movement; and it is aimed at "ushering forth a new order, of organizing, administering, and governing a more humane social order." In this respect, West suggests that the Black community is already a fertile ground for counterhegemonic praxis. This is because Black people comprise the larger percentage of those oppressed by capitalism and, more importantly, because Black religious leaders enjoy relative autonomy to challenge the establishment in that they are not indebted to the status quo that oppresses Black people (ibid., 121–23).

I agree with West that capitalistic culture ought to be subject to a cultural critique with the goal of empowering its victims. The question, however, is how can such empowerment be effected? West believes that it cannot be effected within the current system. As he says, counterhegemonic activities "cannot be realized within the perimeters of the established order" (ibid., 120). And it is this belief that underlies his call for the complete dismantling of the capitalistic culture. But I disagree with West on this point because there are ways of empowering working-class people within the capitalistic system that he does not acknowledge. One such way is to agitate through trade unions for employees to own stocks and purchase shares in the very national and transnational corporations in which they work. By so doing, they can acquire some measure of controlling interests in the institutions and so will be able to influence, at least to some degree, management decisions in the corporations.[18] The acquisition of stocks and shares in national and transnational corporations already occurs in major corporate organizations such as Home

Depot, Avis Car Rental, and Microsoft. It is instructive that the latter two are among America's transnational corporate giants. If this is a trend, then it suggests that the face of capitalism is gradually changing. And precisely because this putatively new trend is consistent with the norm of democracy and ownership of the resources West is advocating, it thus negates West's contention that counter-hegemonic praxis cannot occur within the status quo.[19] Granted West's contention, it would be impossible for this "new" form of capitalism to occur. In light of this new phenomenon, however, what West should be advocating is a refurbishment of capitalism that humanizes the economic system, not its elimination or destruction. The following are some of the questions he should pose in this regard: (1) How can Blacks and other marginalized and oppressed groups become players rather than spectators in this new form of capitalism? (2) How can so-called Third World countries become participants in the new form of capitalism to help improve the quality of life for their citizens, especially since many such countries have experimented with Marxist thought with disastrous consequences? And (3) how could political pressures be brought to bear on the United States government so that its foreign policies could be made conducive to the economic self-sufficiency of Third World countries and in a democratic context? More generally, my point is that West should investigate the possibility of devising and implementing, within the very capitalistic system, transformative activities that would advance the liberation of people of color instead of proposing a religio-Marxian solution whose very presuppositions raise more problems than they solve.

The position I am advancing in some ways is compatible with that of contemporary Marxists such as John Roemer.[20] For example, Roemer, as with West, belongs to the second strand of Marxists who advocate justice within a Marxian framework. But Roemer does not subscribe to the traditional account of exploitation offered by Marxists. According to that account, exploitation consists in an asymmetrical relation between capitalists and labor. It is a relation in which capitalists contribute nothing in the production process, yet unfairly acquire the surplus value (in the form of profits) of the products produced by the labor of workers. More perspicuously, the relation described is as follows. Capitalists employ workers for the workers' labor and pay the latter wages for the products that they produce. In turn, the capitalists sell the products and make profits. But, then, the argument goes, the workers are being cheated (or exploited) in the first place, since the surplus value of the products that is claimed by capitalists actually belongs to the workers. An underlying assumption of this view is that it is the workers and the workers alone produce the products. Therefore it is the workers and the workers alone who should acquire the full value (including the surplus value) of the products. In claiming the surplus value of products, then, capitalists are exploiting the workers.

Roemer has contested this account of exploitation saying that it is too restrictive. For example, a worker who volunteers her or his labor for some (perhaps charitable) end would be considered exploited on this account. Yet, common sense does not consider such volunteerism exploitation. And it can scarcely be said that, given a state-mandated policy in which taxes are levied on the employed to support the unemployed and the infirm, the latter are exploiting the former. The fact is, says Roemer, that the unemployed and the infirm are worse off under such a policy than they would be *had they been employed and healthy, respectively.* The upshot of Roemer's argument is that there are worst injustices than capitalist exploitation of labor in the sense in which such exploitation has been conceived. One such injustice is the denial of equal access to the means of production. It is on this issue that Marxian justice should focus even within a capitalistic system (Kymlicka 1990, 171–183). Considering that Black oppression is a direct consequence of a denial of equal access to the means of production in America, of which this denial is on account of race, Black liberation should thus focus on securing such access within American liberal capitalism. It is in this direction, I suggest, that West should orient his thinking in his advocacy for Black liberation and the liberation of oppressed and marginalized peoples.

It would be a most grievous mistake to construe my criticism of West's anticapitalist position either as a denial of the pernicious harm that capitalism has wrought on people of color or as a rejection of his call for accountability of the transnational conglomerates. My position, on the contrary, is that, cognizant of the fact that capitalism has ruthlessly exploited people of color, is there a way to make it amenable to revision so that it would better serve people of color, especially since it is they who have suffered the most under capitalism? Or better yet, why should people of color continue to be victims and never beneficiaries of capitalism especially when, as far as the evidence bears out, capitalism seems to hold the key to the good life—however we define the good life? My argument against West then is that, contrary to his suggestion, there is no a priori reason to believe that capitalism is incapable of reformation (or is not amenable to reformation). Indeed, if West can Christianize Marxism, as evidenced in his proposed aim of synthesizing Marxism and prophetic Christian thought, so too can we humanize capitalism. And it is for the humanization of capitalism that we should be advocating, especially in a society whose very identity is capitalism, so that the victims of capitalism, who have been largely Blacks, will become beneficiaries.

What then about West's contention that capitalism seduces its victims to subscribe to its norms, mores, and beliefs? Would not this phenomenon mean that even under a humanized capitalistic system the former victims would be transformed into oppressors since they themselves would be motivated by profit and greed? And it is precisely these that cause oppressive policies? My response to these questions is as follows. To the extent that we are dealing with human beings we cannot rule out such human proclivities. However, this is where West, as a self-styled critical organic catalyst in society, becomes highly important. He and others like him should serve as watchdogs to guard against formerly oppressed persons emulating the morally degenerate practices of the capitalist oppressors under "old-style" capitalism. West could divest the energy that he is now expending in calling for the destruction of capitalism effectively to police the conduct of the very conglomerates and corporations that now would have been humanized. In so doing, he would ensure that the practices of these humanized conglomerates and corporations, in which the worker is also an investor, would not degenerate into the morally reprehensible practices witnessed in the "old-style" capitalistic system. And he can engage this task both as a critical organic catalyst and (for what it is worth) by employing coalition politics. In short, the only insurance against human proclivities toward oppressive conduct, even within a humanized capitalistic system, is a militant watchdog mechanism that will act to constrain the conduct of the very worker-investors who now will wield and exercise power in the "new" politicoeconomic setup in society.

And last of all, even if one assumes that West is right in criticizing capitalism as he does, his proposed Marxist-informed solution of collective ownership of the means of production as a way of liberating oppressed people can scarcely be efficacious. The recent collapse of the economies of the former Eastern European countries is proof enough of this fact. These countries had all seemingly used the Marxist model in one form or another in their rejection of capitalism, and with disastrous results. Alternatively put, West's suggestion has been dealt a decisive blow by the collapse of communist and socialist economies that were infused with the spirit of Marxist theory of collective ownership. So one can conclude that West's proposed solution to the economic basis of oppression is certainly an outmoded way of thinking even as his insights from Marxist social theory are helpful to understanding the nature of Black oppression.

Finally, West presents the view that capitalism is intrinsically (i.e., logically) incompatible with liberation activities as if this were a necessary truth. Yet the evidence that he offers in support of this claim is empirical. He cites the industrial revolution in the nineteenth century both in Europe and America and European adventures into distant foreign lands that led to conquests of the inhabitants of those lands, slavery, and colonialism. All these are empirical facts. To the extent that these ventures were motivated by capitalistic endeavors, no conclusion can be drawn from them other than empirical truths about how capitalism functioned in the past and even (perhaps) up to the present. But it does not follow from all these that capitalism is logically incompatible with liberation activities, or that capitalism is necessarily (in the logical sense) exploitative, because it has been known in the past to oppose liberation activities or that it has been exploitative. If the inference in question were legitimate, then it would be logically impossible to conceive of revising or adjusting capitalism to accommodate the liberation efforts of oppressed people. And for this reason, capitalism would have to be completely destroyed and replaced by something else, possibly Marxism, as West is suggesting, if oppressed people are ever to be liberated. But no formal contradiction obtains in the idea of revising or adjusting capitalism so that it would promote liberation struggles. Besides, as I have already shown, there are indications that capitalism is undergoing some revision to accommodate worker ownership and participation in investment and management decisions. This means, in effect, that capitalism is not as it used to be during the industrial revolution or even up to the mid-twentieth century. And it follows from such changes that the antidemocratic character of capitalism is not a necessary attribute of capitalism, contrary to what West would have us believe.

If I am right in construing West's claim about capitalism and liberation struggles as a statement about the *defining attributes* of both capitalism and liberation struggles, then the inference is that the claim asserts much more than the evidence allows. The claim would be purporting to state a necessary truth, in the sense that the defining attributes of capitalism are inherently incompatible with the defining attributes of liberation struggles. And, if so, it would be logically impossible to amend or revise capitalism without destroying its identity. However, by virtue of the fact that the evidence West gives for rejecting capitalism is empirical, it is clear that he cannot therefore logically preclude the revisability of capitalism unless he wishes to sacrifice logical coherence. Finally, West's advocacy of collectivism is premised on the idea of a necessary relation between capitalism and oppression or, alternatively, a necessary incompatibility between capitalism and liberation struggles. However, because we have seen that the relation is other than he thinks, his advocacy ought therefore to be rejected, at least on logical grounds alone.

Du Bois and West: A Contrast in Marxian Motivations

Yet West is not alone among African American intellectuals who have advocated some form of Marxist strategy in their theorizations about liberating oppressed people. For example, W. E. B. Du Bois, after whom West seems to pattern himself, surrendered to Marxism in 1926 with his application for membership into the Communist Party of the United States of America.[21] Of course, there are significant differences between Du Bois and West in their respective advocacy of Marxism. Du Bois's attraction to Marxism was grounded in the belief that capitalism was incapable of reforming itself because it is motivated by selfishness. For this reason, he thought that communism was "the only way to human life." He believed that communism promises simply "to give to all men what they need and ask[s] of each the best they can contribute" (Lewis 1995, 632). Unlike West, Du Bois did not believe that capitalism logically precludes reformation. Du Bois's own belief about the incapability of capitalism to undergo self-reformation was empirically grounded in and sustained by his observation of selfishness that permeated the entire capitalistic structure and culture—entrepreneurs and workers alike. This selfishness ensured that each group exploited whatever possibilities they could. Given the intense social crises of the period—acute racism, the blatant exploitation of Black workers, and the intense animosity of White workers toward Black workers—Du Bois thus *capitulated* to a Marxist political ideology. I say "capitulated" because, hitherto, he seemed to have shown a preference, even if lukewarm, for capitalism over communism. For example, in "The Negro and Communism," he noted that even despite the fact that capitalism did exploit Black workers, Blacks did get some benefit from the capitalist system. He declared:

> American wealth [under capitalism] has helped the American Negro. .
> . . [W]ithout this help the Negro could not have attained his present
> advancement. American courts from the Supreme Court down are
> dominated by wealth and Big Business, yet they are today the Negro's
> only protection against complete disfranchisement, segregation and
> the abolition of his public schools. Higher education for Negroes is
> the gift of the Standard Oil, the Power Trust, the Steel Trust and the
> Mail Order Chain Stores, together with the aristocratic Christian
> Church; but these have given Negroes 40,000 black leaders to fight
> white folk on their own level and in their own language. Big industry
> in the last 10 years has opened occupations for a million Negro
> workers, without which we would have starved in jails and gutters.
> (ibid., 591–92)

And he asked rhetorically, "Meanwhile, what have white workers and radical reformers [of the Socialist and Communist Movements] done for Negroes?" Indeed, he pointed out that the beneficiaries of these radical movements were the White workers themselves; they received better working conditions and benefits (592). In addition, Du Bois had vigorously defended the National Association for the

Advancement of Colored People (NAACP) against attacks by the Communist Party of the United States of America, over the arrest of eight Black youths in Scottsboro, Alabama, on alleged charges of raping two White women. The Communist Party had alleged that the NAACP had allied with the capitalists and so was willing to sacrifice the eight youths to the capitalist system by failing to ensure proper legal representation for the youths (590–591).[22] Du Bois denounced the Communist Party, saying that they were "neither wise nor intelligent," and that they had engaged in "deliberate lying and deception" (585–586).

So why did Du Bois give in to Marxism? I submit that Du Bois capitulated to Marxism because of his disenchantment with certain nefarious practices within capitalism and not because of capitalism per se. In particular, he came to realize that Blacks were increasingly worse off under capitalism *especially because of the racism of White workers*. White workers deliberately created strategic obstacles to prevent Black workers being admitted into unions, and this White worker antagonism toward Black workers served the White workers. Besides, the capitalist investors took full advantage of the situation.[23] This state of affairs prompted Du Bois to say, in "The Negro and Communism,"

> Throughout the history of the Negro in America, white labor has
> been the black man's enemy, his oppressor, his red murderer. Mobs,
> riots and the discrimination of trade unions have been used to kill,
> harass and starve black men. White labor disfranchised Negro labor
> in the South, is keeping them out of jobs and decent living quarters in
> the North, and is curtailing their education and social and civil privi-
> leges throughout the nation. White laborers have formed the back-
> bone of the Ku Klux Klan and have furnished hands and ropes to
> lynch 3,560 Negroes since 1882. (ibid., 589)

The situation Du Bois describes in this passage is a rollback of the limited "civil and social privileges" that Blacks had won at the time, a situation analogous to a contemporary rollback of the few gains Blacks have won as a result of the Civil Rights protests of the 1960s.

Against this background, one should construe Du Bois's earlier attack of the Communist Party over the Scottsboro incident as grounded in an implicit expectation (or hope) that, in time, capitalism would provide some emancipatory possibilities for Blacks. (The attack was also on what Du Bois considered the political opportunism of the Communist Party for attempting to exploit the incident for its own purposes. At the time the Communist Party was striving to establish a foothold in the American political soil.) Thus, even as Du Bois acknowledged the selfishness that motivated capitalism and believed that Black liberation would require "a wholesale emancipation from the grip of the white exploiters without," rather than simply from "an internal readjustment and ousting of [their] exploiters" (ibid., 587), he did not call for a complete destruction of the capitalist order as such. It would seem that he believed that Black liberation could still be attained within the capitalistic system. Thus he endeavored to argue for Black liberation without necessarily committing himself, at least at this point, to a rejection of capitalism. The realization, however, that the White worker turned out to be the most hostile enemy of the Black worker under capitalism seemed to have extinguished any hope that he may have entertained about the emancipatory possibilities of capitalism.[24] In short, the intense racist climate created and sustained by White workers militated against any emancipatory possibilities Du Bois could have envisioned under capitalism. And since the racism promoted the interest of the White workers, as it was no doubt beneficial to the capitalists, he concluded therefore that there was no hope of reforming capitalism unless racism was eliminated. But the elimination of racism was impossible; racism was entrenched in the society. Thus, a new political order was needed. For Du Bois, Marxism turned out to be that order; it was the last and only alternative.

Granted my analysis, it is not so much then that Du Bois believed that capitalism is logically incompatible with emancipatory possibilities as that he was disenchanted with the racism that the White workers manifested toward the Black workers, racism that seemed to serve both White workers and the capitalist investors. It is for this reason, I believe, that he concluded that capitalism could not be self-reforming. But the "could not" is certainly *not* of the logical type that seems to inform West's thinking. Germane to this point is Shamoon Zamir's observation that even as Du Bois held what were then radical views on the issue of race in advocating racial justice and racial equality—unlike Booker T. Washington—his radicalism "did

not take the form of anticapitalist political and economic programs."[25] Zamir is correct, I think, in noting Du Bois' "conservatism," along with others, during the aftermath of the failure of
Reconstruction in 1877. "Conservatism" in this context means that
Du Bois maintained "a fairly uncritical acceptance of the economic
and social status quo" even as he was virulently opposed to racial
inequities (Zamir 1995, 10). Of course, Du Bois would later establish a contingent causal relation between racial injustice and capitalism, the result of which we find in the passage I have already quoted
as part of his capitulation to communism. But this all the more
shows that, unlike West, Du Bois did not consider capitalism as
intrinsically incompatible with liberation endeavors.

Theorizing Oppression

I have presupposed the concept of oppression throughout my discussion, but especially in my rejection of West's reductivist analysis
that translates oppression into economic domination and decision-
making control of capitalists. A brief statement about the concept
therefore is in order if only to show why such a reductivist account
fails.

To begin, oppression exhibits two distinctive but interrelated features. First, in social contexts it applies essentially to social groups
and derivatively to individual members of social groups. And second,
it is a malleable or plastic concept. Concerning the first characteristic, I mean that the term "oppression" designates a subordinate social
positioning of groups in society, by virtue of which positioning the
subordinate groups may be subject to a variety of denigrating and
sometimes dehumanizing treatment by the dominant group(s). The
notion of social positioning is important because it explains the kind
of experiences that groups are likely to have. In other words, since
groups are variously situated, the treatment of subordinate groups,
and hence the experiences of such groups, reflect and are a function
of the social position those groups occupy in society. As an illustration, Blacks and other non-Whites, women, lower-class Whites, gays,
and lesbians all experience oppression in society in the sense that, as
groups, they are positioned as subordinate to the dominant group(s);
consequently, they are marginalized.[26] (It happens that the dominant
group in contemporary Western societies consists of middle-class,

heterosexual, White males.) But the specific kinds of experiences that result from each subordinate group's own oppression clearly vary. Consider women. Their experiences of sexual harassment in the workplace and institutional obstacles to gaining promotion beyond certain managerial levels, both because of gender, are forms of oppression that men do not normally have. (This phenomenon in respect to women is often referred to as "the glass ceiling syndrome.") Similarly, some Blacks and lower-class Whites experience economic exploitation and powerlessness that other Blacks and Whites do not experience. And lower-class Whites, despite the fact that they usually are oppressed economically, enjoy racial privileging and the attendant benefits of such privileging while their Black counterparts experience racial denigration and concomitant social inequity. Still, all of these groups are oppressed. It follows from the distinct set of experiences of each group that there is no one particular kind of experience that constitutes *the* oppressive experience of all social groups. By extension, there is no one particular meaning that can be given to the term "oppression" save in a very general sense (Young 1990, 40).

Of course, that oppression manifests itself in a variety of ways does not preclude groups having similar kinds of experiences. For example, person A may be rejected for a job because of her age and person B because of her race. Both individuals are rejected because of their membership certain subordinate groups. Without a doubt their experiences, qua group members, in terms of the feelings of rejection and humiliation, are similar. Nevertheless, as I will show presently, their oppression cannot be reduced to the experiencing of these feelings. On one reductivist model, oppression would seem to exist if and only if a person experiences feelings of rejection or humiliation. Thus, where an individual does not experience these feelings, the individual not having encountered a situation in which (say) she or he is discriminated against, she or he is not oppressed. Yet this view is manifestly false, for, analogously, it would follow that an individual's failure to see that she or he is the object of ridicule because of her or his buffoonery entails that she or he is not being ridiculed. On the contrary, it is an individual's social location as a member of a subordinate social group that makes her or him an oppressed member of society. It is in this sense that an individual is oppressed even though she or he has not yet had any denigrating experience attendant to her or his oppression. By extension, even if arguably, a social group in principle can be oppressed by virtue of its subordinate social positioning without any of its members having had any denigrating or dehumanizing experience.

True, there is another sense of oppression in which a person may be dominated by another and so is rendered powerless even to make decisions about her or his life. This is the subjective (or personal), nonstructural sense, and it is usually exhibited in, but not limited to, domestic relationships such as between spouses and also between partners in relationships. Cognizant of this sense of oppression, however, it is with the structural sense I shall be concerned here. This is because it is this sense of oppression that is germane to sociopolitical discourses concerning groups. It is this sense that Young effectively captures in her conception of oppression as a social group designator. Young correctly notes that social group membership is a brute fact of individual existence precisely because the individual is born into a group. This means that the group is both ontologically and socially prior to the individual in that it preexists the individual (ibid., 44–45). Accordingly, oppression is first and foremost always of social groups and derivatively of individual members of social groups. Or, alternatively, it is to the extent that individuals are representatives of social groups that they are oppressed.

This brings me to the second characteristic I claimed for oppression, namely, that it is a malleable concept. By this I mean that oppression can take on a variety of forms and thus can manifest itself in a variety of ways and differently to different groups. In this respect, racial oppression is distinct from but contingently related to economic oppression. The same can be said of gender oppression. For the purpose of this study, the malleability of the concept makes clear why any reductivist account is subject to severe constraints. For example, it now can be seen why West's dissolution of Black oppression into a general economic oppression is misleading at best. Also, we now can appreciate fully why the Marxist system West favors is still susceptible to oppression in matters of decision-making even if one assumed that it could succeed in overcoming economic oppression. More generally, overcoming one form of oppression does not necessarily entail overcoming other forms of oppression.

To sum up, there are at least two distinctive characteristics of oppression. First, oppression is a group designator in social contexts; thus consciousness of one's oppression is not a condition of the existence of that oppression. The oppression still may exist even if an individual or a group has not experienced it. And second, oppression is a malleable or plastic concept whose extension encompasses a variety of disparate if sometimes resembling experiences.

Conclusion

At the heart of the discussion I have undertaken in this chapter is the issue how, if at all, on West's view, justice can be attained for Blacks and other oppressed groups in a liberal capitalistic society. This question is central to African American critical thought. But it is also central to an ongoing debate in contemporary discussions of social justice between liberal theorists such as John Rawls, Ronald Dworkin, and Will Kymlicka, on the one hand, and Marxist theorists such as John Roemer, Kai Nielson, and West, on the other. The liberal position is that there should be equality of access to the means of production in society. Or, better still, there should not be any impediments in the way of persons or groups in their quest for access to resources in society. In this regard, liberals advocate a system of justice based on fairness, in the sense of equal access to the resources in society, that upholds private ownership of the means of production. Some Marxists too, like Roemer, endorse the idea of justice and argue similarly that justice can be effected only if equal access to the means of production is available to everyone in society. It is significant, however, that the views of both liberals and Marxists on the issue of attaining justice in society seem to converge. In my view, since Black oppression is a direct result of a denial of access to the means of production in the society, and I take this denial to be a function of racism, I have therefore argued, contra West, that we should seek social justice for Blacks and other oppressed peoples within the current liberal capitalistic system. Among other things, I have tried to show that Black liberation should consist in ensuring for Blacks equal and unimpeded access to the resources of the society. My position derives its credibility partly from the fact that it is compatible with the revised Marxian view and the standard liberal capitalist view and partly because in its own right it exhibits certain limitations of West's crypto-Marxian position. The upshot of my argument against West is twofold. First, even as his crypto-Marxian position is an amalgamation of the virtues of Black prophetic Christianity and traditional Marxist social theory, it cannot escape certain conceptual and empirical difficulties. Second, West need not call for the abolition of private ownership of the means of production and institute a collectivist system to achieve Black liberation. On the contrary, as I have argued, Black liberation (and the liberation of oppressed people) can be effected through reformatory and transformatory praxis within liberal capitalism.

Yet the quest for social justice within liberal capitalism, even for the various groups involved, is not without difficulties. One such difficulty appears in the relation between Blacks and Jews, and it is this issue I now will address.

CHAPTER FOUR

Black-Jewish Conflict and Dialogue

Introduction

> Black anti-Semitism and Jewish antiblack racism are real, and both
> are as profoundly American as cherry pie. (1994, 104)

The declining nature of the Black-Jewish relationship in contemporary America has been a central topic in the discussion of social justice for Blacks and people of color in America. This is because of the well-known (even if at times grudgingly acknowledged) historical alliance between Blacks and Jews to challenge oppression and advance the cause of social justice in the United States. This alliance itself is a product of a fundamental historical accident constituted by a mutual and similar experience of suffering between the two groups. For example, historically both groups have been victims of the worst form of oppression and degradation experienced by humanity: slavery, dispersal, and dehumanization. Going as far back as biblical times (Exodus), Jews experienced slavery and oppression at the hands of the pharaohs, and in more recent times they have experienced the Nazi holocaust. Blacks experienced four centuries of slavery and oppression as a result of the White supremacist ideology that gained ascendancy in 1492.[1] And even in contemporary America the lived reality of Blacks is social death. This similarity in their experiences of degradation is the basis for a mutual quest for group survival by Blacks and Jews. And it is this quest that in turn necessitated both groups to form an alliance to target racism, anti-Semitism, and oppression (1994, 106).[2] Yet this alliance has ruptured lately, as is clear from the nature of the discussion among scholars.[3] The question then is how did this state of affairs come about?[4]

Cornel West takes up this issue both in a variety of avenues but most prominently in *Race Matters, Jews and Blacks,* and *Struggles.* The general thrust of West's position is that the rupture in the relation between Blacks and Jews is owing to a misperception by each group of the other, a misperception about each group's social location in the larger society. Blacks perceive Jews as Whites in a society that privileges whiteness and denigrates blackness. Thus, in their view, it is whiteness that accounts for Jewish success. On the other hand, Jews perceive Blacks as depending on society instead of on themselves for social uplift. Thus, it is Black lack of effort that explains Black social failure. In the belief that each group misperceives and thus misrepresents the situation of the other, West therefore proposes that their mutual misperceptions be corrected; otherwise the moral legitimacy of their individual quests for social justice, particularly the quest of Blacks, will be undermined.

But there is an imbalance in West's treatment of the two perspectives. West provides a detailed and penetrating analysis of Black misperception of Jews, and hence of Black anti-Semitism, but he does not provide an explicit complementary analysis of Jewish misperception of Blacks and, consequently, of Jewish anti-Black racism. Besides, some scholars have contended that the Black-Jewish issue goes beyond a mutual misperception and misrepresentation by both groups. Jane Anna Gordon, for example, maintains that, against the backdrop of a mutual racially inscribed misperception by each group of the other, one of the most influential items that precipitated the disintegration of the Black-Jewish relationship was socioeconomic. Specifically, it was a clash of socioeconomic interests between the two groups in New York City over community control of the local school board in Ocean Hill-Brownsville. According to Jane Gordon, this clash became embedded in the racial dynamics of the society as a conflict between Whites and Blacks, and that in turn was transcribed into charges of Black anti-Semitism and countercharges of Jewish anti-Black racism (J. Gordon 2001, 1 and 2; see also L. Gordon 1997a, ch. 5, esp. 98–99). Gordon's view suggests that

West's diagnosis of the problem is inadequate. In light of this issue, then, and to represent West's position effectively, I shall first reconstruct West's view of Jewish misperception of Blacks, and hence what constitutes Jewish anti-Black racism, from his observations about conservative Jewish positions on social issues affecting Blacks. Second, I shall use Jane Gordon's discussion to supplement West's diagnosis of the problem, and then go on to discuss West's proposed solution of dialogue as remedy.

Black Misperception and Misrepresentation of Jews

In his account of Black misperception of Jews, West calls attention to Black failure to recognize and acknowledge the perpetual Jewish preoccupation with group survival as a function (or consequence) of historical accidents going as far back as medieval and modern Europe (1994, 104). Specifically, he cites Jewish expulsion from European countries, from England in 1290 to Kishnev in 1903 (104), and says that this European expulsion itself was the result of a profound hatred of Jews. This hatred was motivated by certain myths held about Jews. First is the Christian myth of Jews as Christ-killers. Jews were deemed to have committed theocide in crucifying Christ. Second is the social myth of Jews as callous, avaricious, and selfish; these traits are said to be manifested in the economic sphere. (One need only recall Shylock in Shakespeare's *The Merchant of Venice*.) Jews are believed to conspire among themselves to dominate and control the economic sphere. For West, Blacks subscribe to these myths and fail to grasp the causal role of the aforementioned European expulsion of Jews in the Jewish preoccupation with self-reliance and group survival. Both of these factors have led to a profound misperception of Jews. And this misperception underpins Black anti-Semitism.

West identifies three distinctive items around which Black anti-Semitism revolve: (1) Blacks' view of Jews as a variety (or species) of White in a color-conscious society; (2) a mentality of envy and resentment by one underdog of another underdog that succeeds; and (3) Jewish abrogation of a certain moral imperative that all oppressed groups are expected to follow. I shall elaborate each of these points in turn.

First, Blacks view Jews as a *group of Whites* that, like any other group of Whites, is destined to succeed in America precisely because of America's endemic color prescription. The color prescription guarantees success to Whites of any kind and relative failure to Blacks of any kind. West claims that recent Jewish immigrants to America (1881–1924) have been largely successful because "[t]hey brought a strong heritage that put a premium on what had ensured their survival and identity—institutional autonomy, rabbinical learning and business zeal" (ibid., 105). However, Blacks attribute this success to racial privileging of Jews as a variety of Whites in a color-conscious society. Thus, in the minds of some Blacks, even though Christian America does betray symptoms of anti-Semitism, as it often has, those symptoms yield to the color prescription (Lerner and West, 66–70).

For some Blacks, then, one consequence of Jewish success in America is that Jews have not only ceased to be an oppressed group, but also, and more importantly, that they have been integrated (or assimilated) into the dominant oppressing group. Thus, even despite the fact that there were times when both Jews and Blacks united to agitate for social justice in America, some Blacks now view the Jewish integration into White America as a betrayal of those past alliances. This perception (or misperception) of Jews is the cause of both the "top-down" and "bottom-up" anti-Semitism of which Gates and West speak, respectively.[5]

Second, the idea of the underdog mentality is that an underdog that seems to be mired in relative failure, especially due to institutional obstacles that are strategically put in place to ensure failure, tends to be envious and resentful of another underdog that is relatively successful. According to West, such an underdog mentality is integral to Black anti-Semitism. Jewish people have been largely successful in American society despite strong anti-Semitic sentiments. This being the case, Blacks (and others) posit myths about Jews to explain Jewish success. For example, there are claims about Jewish deliberate seclusion from the larger society and about Jews as a well-organized social group and thus of a Jewish conspiracy to dominate and control the institutions of power in the society. In all of this, says West, there is no reference to hard work and discipline of Jewish people or of their determination and desire to be educated *in order to* enter the American mainstream.

According to West, a third item, the supposed violation of a moral imperative, is integral to Black anti-Semitism. The idea here, in brief, is that among oppressed groups and peoples there is an imperative of empathy and understanding of the predicament of any oppressed group. Blacks consider Jews violators of this moral imperative because of what they deem Jewish American uncritical support of Israeli oppressive treatment of Palestinians in the West Bank and Gaza Strip, as well as Israeli government collaboration with the apartheid regime of South Africa in the 1980s under the administration of President Ronald Reagan. The allegation is that, insofar as there was a time when Jewish people suffered degradation, vilification, and dehumanization, they ought to know better than to visit or support oppressive treatment of others. In this regard, Jewish American acquiescence to the oppressive practices of Israel and their moral endorsement of the apartheid government of South Africa are worrisome to some Blacks. Such attitudes remind them of a similar support that Jewish American conservatives lent to challenges of affirmative action and related equity programs intended to help Blacks enter the American mainstream. (I return to this point later.) In the minds of some Blacks, these forms of behavior by Jews bespeak at the very least Jewish moral indifference to the plight of other oppressed people and at the worst manifest Jewish selfishness. And this perception of Jews occasions Black anti-Semitic sentiments.[6]

Michael Lerner (in Lerner and West 1995) has expanded this point about alleged Jewish selfishness (ch. 4; see also ch. 7). Lerner acknowledges the existence of some measure of selfishness in the Jewish community but attributes such selfishness to two dominant causally related factors: (1) a backlash against Black anti-Semitism commensurate with an ascendancy of Jewish neoconservatism and (2) a general ethos of selfishness in the American society, especially in the socioeconomic sphere.

For Lerner, there is a perception in the Jewish community that Blacks have not appreciated the disproportionate support Jews have given to the Black quest for social justice. Citing Jewish involvement in the Civil Rights movement, Lerner says that Jewish students who had gone to the South and worked with Blacks were later betrayed by Black Power advocates, the latter accusing the students of "attempting to dominate and manipulate Black organizations."

Furthermore, the Black Power advocates made the students feel as though "all they had offered was worthless" (ibid., 86). This accusation and rejection of the Jewish support "had a powerfully debilitating impact on Jewish liberalism and universalism that gave tremendous credibility and power to the Jewish neocons[ervatives]" (86). Indeed, Lerner continues, the very Jewish liberals who had been highly critical of the Jewish community for not doing enough in support of Blacks were now being devastated by the same Black movement (86). This rejection of Jewish liberalism empowered the Jewish neoconservatives, who then used it to consolidate their position that Jewish people should confine themselves to Jewish interests and let all others alone.

Beyond the rejection of Jewish liberal support in the 1960s, Lerner claims further that most Blacks, including Black intellectuals, generally have not acknowledged Jewish support for Black causes. In response to a denial by West, who cites various political and social leaders who have acknowledged Jewish support, Lerner says:

> Sure, those Blacks who seek Jewish economic or political support acknowledge the role, *if pressed*. But from most Blacks, including most Black intellectuals, Jews rarely get a feeling that we are recognized for the disproportionate support we've given to causes close to the heart of the Black community. Instead, we sense a special hostility coming at us from Black intellectuals and professionals who seem most interested in making . . . critiques of Israel. (ibid., emphasis added)

Added to all this is an undercurrent of Black anti-Semitism, says Lerner, which Jews found most shocking (136; cp. 141–142). Black anti-Semitism "has been critical" in occasioning a lot of Jews to adopt a conservative outlook that focuses on Jewish self-interest" (142). And such a move in the conservative direction harmonizes with the general tendency toward conservativism in the larger society. The dominant ethos in the larger American society since the 1980s has been selfishness, especially in the socioeconomic sphere. Jewish people were generally torn between the pull of this ethos and the opposite pull exerted by their sense of social responsibility to identify with the oppressed. However, says Lerner, an upsurge of Black anti-Semitism simply provided many Jewish people a convenient excuse for tilting in favor of selfishness. Their rationale runs as follows: "Oh well, my Jewishness shouldn't count against my being Republican or my selfishness because these [Black] folks for whom I'm trying to not be selfish hate me!" (142). The upshot of this all is to say that Black misperception of Jews, together with Black anti-Semitism, is a partial cause of the rupture in the relation between Blacks and Jews.

West leaves little doubt that he considers such perception and representation of Jews by Blacks to be severely flawed. For example, he asserts that Black perception and representation of Jewish socioeconomic success are inaccurate because they "den[y] the actual history and treatment of Jews" (1994, 111). In other words, West believes that this conception of Jews fails to take into account that Jews experience variant forms of oppressive treatment from the dominant (White) social group, as do Blacks, even despite the fact many Jews are White. Yet it is precisely on such an inaccurate representation of Jews that Black anti-Semitism is founded.

Second, West dismisses as a myth the view of Jews as well organized and conspiring to dominate and control the institutions of power in the society. He notes, however, that it is this very myth about Jewish unity and organization that Black nationalists such as Louis Farrakhan of the Nation of Islam ironically invoke as a standard for Blacks to emulate in the Black quest for social justice: "Farrakhan sees Jewish unity as a model for Black unity. That perception may be romantic and idealized, but that's what he sees" (Lerner and West 1995, 108). For West, what this means, in effect, is that Blacks are trying to have it both ways: They use this myth to vilify Jews and, when convenient, appeal to it as a standard for effective political organization. This suggests a confusion in the minds of those Blacks whose characterization of Jews is based on this myth.

And third, even though he is critical of conservative Jewish support for Israeli Zionist policies under the Likud Party, West desires that such support be understood in the larger context of Jewish experience of expulsion from various European countries, the Nazi holocaust, and, consequently, Jewish anxiety over group survival.

Before turning to West's treatment of Jewish misperception of Blacks, however, it should be remarked that neither Lerner nor West has offered any adequate explanation for the alleged upsurge in

Black anti-Semitism. Of course, it cannot be denied that there are *instances* of such anti-Semitism. Louis Farrakhan exemplifies such anti-Semitism. But "upsurge" is too strong a term. Besides, one should be particularly mindful of reducing all criticisms of Jews to anti-Semitic rhetoric. The reason is that some of the very critics of Jews are themselves Jews. Of these some are White (Norman Finkelstein) and some are Black (Lewis Gordon).[7]

Jewish Misperception and Misrepresentation of Blacks

West does not provide an explicit account of Jewish misperception of Blacks to complement that which he offers of Black misperception of Jews. Yet there are elements in his discussion on the basis of which one can reconstruct his views of Jewish anti-Black racist positions. For example, in a discussion with Michael Lerner, West notes that Jews, while still claiming to support Black quests for social justice in the mid-1970s, moved from the cities to the suburbs and in so doing developed "more subtle anti-Black racism, which persists to this day" (Lerner and West 1995, 139). West asserts this view in response to a poignant and candid admission by Lerner that Jewish movement to the suburbs was partly "to escape the perceived problems brought to the neighborhoods by some of the African-Americans who were moving in" (139). The phenomenon to which Lerner is referring is what is now popularly known as "White flight" from supposed (i.e., real or imaginary) Black crime. This phenomenon reflects the perception in the dominant society of Blacks as "the problem" and the identification of blackness with criminality.[8] In short, Blacks are socially undesirable. It is precisely this phenomenon that constitutes White anti-Black racism and, a fortiori, Jewish anti-Black racism because Jews share this general *White perception* of Blacks. Indeed, Lerner is quite unambiguous in acknowledging this point, as is borne out by the following passage:

> I certainly wouldn't deny the existence of anti-Black racism in the Jewish community. Most of this is a transference of general white racism, which Jews have bought into increasingly as they've assimilated American values; some of it is based on encounters with Blacks in which either violence has been experienced, or in which Jews have not respected the values that seem to dominate in Black culture. That

culture is often a response to oppression, and Jews want to know why Blacks don't deal with oppression the way Jews did. Jews, however, never faced a breakdown in family and community in any way comparable to hundreds of years of slavery, so they don't understand why Black culture can't embody Jewish strengths. *They find the answer in American society's assertions of Black inferiority, which fits a tendency amongst Jews toward goy-bashing: putting down non-Jews as somehow less than them. . . . It is especially easily applied to Blacks because even the white goyim say this about them.* (139–140, emphases added)

Yet West does not seize upon this issue for elaboration and an in-depth treatment that would have complemented his discussion of Black anti-Semitism. Dilating on this point in the analysis of the conflict between Blacks and Jews would not have constituted anti-Semitism any more than Lerner's bemoaning of what he deems Jewish belief that Blacks did not acknowledge and appreciate Jewish involvement in the Black quest for social justice would constitute anti-Black racism. Indeed, the point about Blacks being "the problem"—seen in historical, sociological, and psychological contexts—is all the more important because it was integral to the conservative leaning of many Jews. More specifically, it was on the basis of this belief that Jewish conservatives lent their support to the call to eradicate affirmative action and other government remedial programs that were instituted to help Blacks, women, and other minorities enter the American mainstream.[9]

The call to dismantle affirmative action and related social programs originated largely from White males. They believed that such programs gave Blacks and other minorities, including women, an unfair advantage over others. The alleged unfair advantage consisted in the *presumption* that Blacks and others were less qualified than their White male counterparts for positions in government, business, and other spheres of life, yet they were awarded positions by virtue of their color or/and gender and not by virtue of merit. And any policy in recruitment, college/university admission, and government contracting that violates the fundamental principle of meritocracy that purportedly is central to American life is immoral if not illegal. Implicit in this call to eradicate affirmative action was the underlying idea that Blacks in particular lacked the ability (intelligence?) otherwise to compete fairly; hence they had to depend on government intervention. Jewish conservatives, then, in lending support to this call to eradicate affirmative action, tacitly subscribed to this myth about Black inability to compete in the absence of such a program.

In addition to supporting calls for dismantling affirmative action, conservative Jews also lent support to the idea of dismantling social policies aimed at helping the poor, those people who have been marginalized in the society. The argument advanced for dismantling such programs was grounded on a belief, albeit false, that these very marginalized people were lazy, lacked a work ethic, and were responsible for their unfortunate station in life. The belief that the less fortunate and economically disadvantaged are lazy is deemed antithetical to yet another fundamental belief in American life, namely, that anyone can succeed in America as long as she or he works hard. The corollary of this latter belief is (the myth) that personal failure is a result of an individual's failure to work hard enough. It is beside the point that the expression "failure to work hard enough" is relative at best and vague at worst. The point is that, since Blacks disproportionately comprise the disadvantaged in society, it is believed that they are disadvantaged because of their own lack of effort or desire to succeed. Accordingly, it is argued, government policies to help them and others who are disadvantaged do more harm than good, for such policies simply entrench laziness instead of motivating Blacks and other disadvantaged persons to expend effort to succeed. Therefore, all such policies, except those aimed at the indigent, should be dismantled.

How does Jewish support for eradicating these social programs translate into a misperception of Blacks and constitute anti-Black racism? Recall that the underlying idea behind the call for dismantling affirmative action was that affirmative action gave Blacks and others an unfair advantage over Whites in a society presumed meritocratic. Furthermore, as was noted, implicit in critiques of affirmative action was (and still is) the idea that Blacks are incapable of competing fairly without such a program. In supporting the call to dismantle affirmative action, therefore, Jews demonstrated an acute failure to appreciate the gravity of the structural dynamics of Black oppression, especially since such oppression is race-based. As West notes, affirmative action policies must be seen in the larger historical context as a weak response to "[t]he vicious legacy of white supremacy—institutionalized in housing, education, health care, employment and social life."[10] Put otherwise, the systemic exclusion of Blacks from the workplace and other public institutions, simply on account of race, was what motivated affirmative action policies in the first place. Thus, to construe affirmative action policies as according to Blacks special privileges by virtue of their status as victims of racial discrimination is not only manifestly false, but also is a gross and deliberate misrepresentation of such policies. Second, and more significantly, the myth about Black inability to compete fairly reflects the racist stereotype about Black intelligence (or lack thereof) relative to the White race that is endemic in Western intellectual culture.[11] It is to this stereotype therefore that Jewish conservatives knowingly or unwittingly subscribe in siding with those who advocate the dismantling of affirmative action and related policies aimed at helping Blacks and others who are disadvantaged.

Next, the argument for dismantling those social policies aimed at the poor, who happen to be disproportionately Black, on the ground that such policies encourage laziness, trades on yet another stereotype about Blacks, namely, that they have a certain predisposition to laziness. There can be no doubt that there are lazy Blacks, and not every Black person who solicits social support actually deserves such support. But the same can be said of Whites and others. Indeed, even in a racially homogenous society there are individuals who are lazy and thus are undeserving of social support. Yet laziness, stupidity (or lack of intelligence), and deception are claimed to be the inherent cognitive features of Blacks.[12] It is precisely such claims about Blacks that Jewish conservatives tacitly affirm, even if perhaps unwittingly, in their advocacy of the dismantling of the social programs in question.

It is clear from the foregoing account that the conservative Jewish position was undergirded by the very same stereotypical beliefs about Blacks that the larger society holds, beliefs that West himself discusses in the first two chapters of *Prophecy Deliverance* (1982). For this reason, there is no doubt that West is committed to the view I have reconstructed from his observations. Given this view, it seems reasonable to conclude that *one reason* for the conflict between Jews and Blacks, especially among the educated and middle-class of both groups, is the very Jewish subscription to the racial stereotypes about Blacks in the larger (White) society. Indeed, by foregrounding Jewish misperception of Blacks, and hence Jewish anti-Black racism, one can see a causality between Jewish attitudes and Black attitudes. More specifically, even if arguably, the alleged upsurge of anti-Semitism among Black intellectuals may be read as a *reaction to* Jewish (overt or covert) anti-Black racism. And such a reaction simply invokes some of the very myths and stereotypes about Jews that are given currency in the larger society.

No doubt West is as perturbed by the anti-Semitic views of Black intellectuals as he is of Jewish anti-Black racism. By focusing on the perspective of each group he provides an insight into the nature of the conflict, especially between the well educated of both groups. His considered judgment is that both groups have allowed themselves to fall prey to certain stereotypes about each other. In other words, we have here a state of affairs that is best captured by Lerner's term "comparative victimology" (Lerner and West 1995, 73). Both Jews and Blacks are victims of a society that puts a premium on racist prac-tices and beliefs and in which individual self-worth is a function of the social group to which a person belongs, with social groups arranged hierarchically. Thus, each group, to advance its members, denigrates the other by drawing upon the stereotypes about the other. And pre-cisely because stereotypes are scarcely accurate representations of their subjects, both groups therefore find themselves in conflict because of a mutual misperception of each other. Of significance, for West, is that each group *misrepresents* the other and so their mutual criticisms of each other simply translate into naked "tribal" self-inter-est. The danger with such a self-interested viewpoint, however, is that it argues against the moral legitimacy of any demands for social jus-tice that either group will make. This, I submit, is the import of West's observation that the issue at stake "is not simply black-Jewish rela-tions, but, more importantly, the *moral content* of Jewish and black identities and of their political consequences" (1994, 108, emphasis in text). This issue is especially critical for Blacks, who are the most vilified, degraded, and dehumanized social group in American society. It is in this respect that West proposes a correction of each group's perception of the other as a first step to resolving the conflict. He believes that such a correction can be effected through a dialogue between the two groups, dialogue of the kind he and Michael Lerner undertake, that will highlight the moral content of the respective identities of Blacks and Jews.

Supplementing West's Diagnosis: One Substantive Issue between Blacks and Jews that Drew Upon Known Stereotypes

In her study, Jane Anna Gordon (2001) identifies one specific issue that she considers essential to the disintegration of the relation between Blacks and Jews. This was a clash of socioeconomic (or class) interests between the two groups over the management of local school boards in the New York City school system. In particular, the conflict was between a predominantly Jewish teachers' union, the United Federation of Teachers (UFT), and the local community of Ocean Hill-Brownsville over community control of the local school board. According to Gordon, Ocean Hill-Brownsville sought community control over its local school board for two reasons. First, members of the local community believed that they were more attuned to the needs of the local schools and so had a vested interest in the schools because, among other things, they lived in the community and their children were the ones attending the schools. Second, the members of the local community wanted "to rid their schools of racism, which they believed was perpetrated primarily through the control of their schools by outsiders" (95). For the community advocates, if their local community had some measure of control over the recruitment and retention of school personnel, the curriculum, school morale, and the budget, then such control would affect positively the quality of the education their children received.

Opposed to this position was the United Federation of Teachers. The UFT viewed community control as a decentralization of the school board and hence an erosion of its own power and authority. Or, better still, the UFT viewed community control as a very powerful and real threat both to the gains it had won for its members in terms of salaries, job security, and benefits and to its own very political clout and even relevance. Thus, from the perspective of the UFT, local demands for community control over local school boards had to be opposed and stopped at all costs.

Essentially, then, the conflict was between poor Blacks, Puerto Ricans, and Latinos/Latinas, which comprised the community of Ocean Hill-Brownsville, on the one hand, and lower-middle-class White Jewish teachers and administrators under the UFT banner, on the other hand. The former demanded decision-making control of their local schools to ensure that their children would receive the kind and quality of education that would liberate them from the shackles of the underclass and guarantee them some measure of upward social and economic mobility in the future. The lower-middle-class White Jewish teachers, on the other hand, saw such control as a threat to their hard-won lower-middle-class status in the society, one they had acquired as a result of UFT political and related activities.

It is to be remarked that the parties to this conflict were recent (or relatively new) immigrants to the Jewish and Black communities. In particular, these were immigrants from Eastern Europe and the Caribbean, respectively. These new immigrants were not linked to and by the "historical" alliance between African Americans and Jews prior to and during the 1960s, the period of the Civil Rights movement. Moreover, the new members of the respective groups very quickly became integrated into the pervasive conflict-oriented *racial* dynamics of the larger society. Added to the complexity of the situation was the fact that Blacks and Jews were (and are) differently situated in the socioeconomic hierarchy, with Jews at the top and Blacks at the bottom. (For more on this issue and in a related context see L. Gordon 1997a in note 7 in this chapter.) Thus, what was in fact a social (read educational and economic) conflict that, admittedly, reflected the racial and class dynamic of the larger society, was translated into an ethnic conflict between Blacks and Jews with charges of Black anti-Semitism and Jewish anti-Black racism. In particular, the UFT characterized advocates of community control as a violent Black Power movement, and then recast the Ocean Hill-Brownsville demand for community control over local schools as a violent anti-Semitic initiative by the Black Power movement to root Jews out of the local school system (J. Gordon 2001, 73–74). As Jane Gordon states,

> When the UFT printed 500,000 copies of a series of photocopied anti-Semitic pamphlets as examples of the board's views, of "what [it] was up against," the local [governing] board grew outraged. Numerous

> community efforts to denounce their content proved fruitless. The
> [local] governing board could not shake the public opinion that they
> were nationalistic and Jew-hating. . . . Jonathan Kaufman saw charges
> of anti-Semitism as little more than a labor strategy. (101)

Of course, all this is not to deny that there were instances of Black anti-Semitism or Jewish anti-Black racism (ibid., 108). However, as Jane Gordon notes, the charge of Black anti-Semitism was deliberately orchestrated by the predominantly Jewish UFT, a move by the UFT that "changed the tenor of the debate over the schools dramatically."[13] And to conclude, Gordon calls attention to the fact that "many historians and residents in New York City at the time recall the event as representative of the deteriorating relations between blacks and Jews more than they do as a conflict over schooling" (101). To sum up, the Ocean Hill-Brownsville conflict was not only influential in the disintegration of Black-Jewish relations, but it also drew upon and exploited the well-known stereotypes of each group by the other. And in so doing, the conflict provided a concrete instance around which each group projected its misperception and misrepresentation of the other. What then is the solution?

Dialogue (or Conversation), Perception, and Cognitive Belief

West proposes dialogue (or conversation) as a solution to the conflict between Blacks and Jews. To begin, there are two levels to his conception of dialogue: a self-regarding level and an other-regarding level. On the self-regarding level, dialogue is self-critical. Specifically, it examines one's perception of oneself and of others—in this case each of the groups in question—and the beliefs attendant to those perceptions. Through dialogue in this sense one submits for rational scrutiny those precritical perceptions and beliefs that one has come to hold about oneself and others and one undertakes to thrash them out. The goal of dialogue here is to challenge oneself to face one's prejudices and fears so as to facilitate self-improvement in the sense of self-knowledge.

In the other-regarding level, dialogue is a critical intersubjective exchange between oneself and another (seen as groups). On this level, the parties to the dialogue encounter each other, confront each other, and examine the perceptions and beliefs held by each about the other.

The end of such dialogue is to arrive at a mutual understanding of each other wherein such understanding will facilitate a change in the perception that each one has of the other. To change the perception is to *correct* the misperception that each has of the other prior to the dialogic encounter, a misperception shaped largely by stereotypes, and to replace it with a perception that accurately represents the reality of each group. Obviously, dialogue in the other-regarding sense presupposes and is enriched by dialogue in the self-regarding sense because an honest exchange with another about one's fears *about the other* presupposes introspection in order to determine and come to terms with one's prejudices about oneself and the other.

The concept of dialogue as a transformative agent to alter perceptions and hence the attendant cognitive states of individuals (singularly or collectively) has a historical antecedent in Western thought going as far back as Plato. Through a systematic exchange between Platonic Socrates and his interlocutors we often witness an examination of thesis and counterthesis (the method known as *elenchus*). The result of such examination is a gradual but systematic epistemic progression from a state of ignorance to a state of knowledge, the latter consisting in an intellectual grasping of those first principles of knowledge that are Platonic Forms or Essences. Indeed, for Plato, the purpose of dialogue (or conversation) is to change the view of the individual on three levels. First, on the epistemic level, it is to occasion enlightenment where hitherto there was ignorance. Second, on the ontological level, it is to ascend from a world of nonbeing (or unreality) to that of being (or reality). And third, on the moral and hence practical level, it is to occasion and inculcate virtue in the individual, consequent upon the individual's attainment of a state of knowledge, and to hold vice at bay, the latter of which Plato considers a product of ignorance. This practical level is significant for Plato because virtue is not simply a condition of the individual soul but also, and more importantly, a condition that ultimately finds expression in individual actions. And it is precisely at the level of conduct that virtue is most visible in terms of its effect both on the individual possessor and on the recipients of the individual's actions. It is for this reason, therefore, that *turning the soul around* through instruction (read dialogue or conversation) is paramount in Platonic ethics (Plato 1992, 518 c–d).

Contemporary philosophers such as Jurgen Habermas and Iris Marion Young, in varying ways, have extolled the virtues of dialogue to transcend discrete social units and to build larger communities of interwoven interests.[14] Habermas (1984/1987), for example, characterizes his position as the theory of communicative action. The central idea in the theory is that the end of communicative action is mutual understanding and agreement between the parties in a dialogic situation, wherein such understanding and agreement are a sine qua non for cooperation. Indeed, says Habermas, "It is constitutive for communicative action that participants carry out their plans cooperatively in action situation defined in common" (2:126–127). Throughout his discussion Habermas' emphasis is on three terms: mutual understanding, agreement, and cooperation. As he says elsewhere, in contrasting communicative action from the teleologically driven action advanced by Max Weber,

> I shall speak of *communicative* action whenever the actions of the agents involved are coordinated not through egocentric calculations of success but through acts of reaching understanding. In communicative action participants are not primarily oriented to their own individual successes; they pursue their individual goals under the condition that they can harmonize their plans of action on the basis of common situation definitions: In this respect the negotiation of definitions of the situation is an essential element of the interpretive accomplishments required for communicative action. (1:285–286; emphasis in the original)

It is in a vein similar to Plato, Habermas, Young, and other social and political theorists, therefore, that one should understand West's appeal to (the power of) dialogue and conversation to mend the rift between Blacks and Jews.

How will dialogue or conversation effect the perceptual and cognitive change West anticipates? For West, dialogue will enable each group to abandon its narrow egocentric focus in virtue of which it limits its concern to its group-interest to the exclusion of *other* (group) interests. Because the egocentric perspective pits all against all, or group interest against other interests, it therefore leaves each individual group in an extremely vulnerable and precarious situation against the backdrop of a common enemy, viz., White supremacy and attendant structures. Since it is White supremacist thinking, manifested through various structures of power, that accounts for the disparity in the lived realities of groups—in the present case between urban Blacks and suburban Whites—victims of *different forms* of White supremacist thinking therefore would best serve their varied but interconnected interests by perceiving each other as moral equals, at least in terms of their equal vulnerability to suffer harm in a White supremacist climate. This perception in turn would occasion among them mutual succor and empathy. From the vantage point of moral equals, the particularities of each group's immediate anxieties can then be addressed in a mutually supportive way, that is, with each group assisting the other. In short, dialogue will enable each individual group to transcend its immediate group interest and include other (group) interests.

To illustrate, urban Black life is rife with certain immediate anxieties, such as poverty, deprivation, decay, and despair. These anxieties are seized upon and exploited by some who allege Jewish anti-Black racism as *the* cause of the prevailing condition. To stem the tide of Black anti-Semitism among the affected members of this group requires, therefore, that the very lived condition of the urban Blacks be addressed with empathy and understanding. This calls for ameliorating the immediate economic and social concerns of the affected group with urgency. A condition of addressing these concerns is that the members of the group in question be valued first and foremost as moral subjects like oneself. To perceive the individuals as moral entities at all is to recognize and affirm, among other things, that the bleak existential realities to which they are subjected on a daily basis violate them as human beings. It is to affirm, in other words, that no moral entity ought to live under those deplorable conditions that constitute the lived reality of urban Blacks. In this respect, a Jewish person's perception and appreciation of the plight of the urban Black, together with her or his moral acknowledgment of the latter, would impose a moral obligation on her or him, *qua human being*, to help address the latter's predicament. The point here, alternatively put, is that a thorough and accurate understanding of the realities of the existential constraint on urban Black life would necessitate a perceptual and cognitive change in the Jewish perceiver. And this change in turn would activate a sense of moral obligation in the Jewish perceiver toward the Other, who hitherto, she or he had misperceived and consequently vilified. The Jewish person's empathy and resultant action in turn would occasion a reciprocal perceptual and cognitive change in the urban Black, who hitherto had misperceived and hence vilified Jews as uncaring, selfish, and the cause of the sordid condition of Black urban life.

It does not matter at this point how, on West's view, the dialogue itself is to be effected between Blacks and Jews. (I take up this issue later.) What matters is that he considers dialogue as significant in bringing about a perceptual and cognitive change in both parties. I take the kind of perceptual and cognitive change suggested as a result of dialogue and the mutual understanding established as the crux of West's meaning in the assertion that dialogue will have ethical implications for Jewish and Black identities (1994, 109). In other words, for West, dialogue will serve not only to replace egoistic impulses with other-interested motivations and mutual caring of each for the other— ("I am my brother's keeper")—but, more importantly, it will serve to elicit the most fundamental moral impulse in each of us, namely, compassion. To be Jewish or Black *in ethical terms* is, in short, to be able to show compassion for the dejected and despised or, more generally, the oppressed in society. Such compassion has political consequences in moving the individual beyond her or his immediate self-interests to engage the sociopolitical and ethical concerns of the larger society of which she or he is a part. It is the political consequences of the ethics of compassion that West (and Lerner) will later characterize as the "politics of meaning" (Lerner and West 1995, 258–73).

Conceptual Problems Surrounding Leadership and Dialogue

Yet, for all its seeming attractiveness, West's proposed solution of dialogue as a healing device to resolve the conflict between Blacks and Jews is beset with several conceptual difficulties. These difficulties begin to appear when one considers the question: "How will dialogue be implemented?" West suggests "an emergency meeting of various progressive leaders and progressive intellectuals" of the Jewish and Black communities in order to exchange ideas and "to launch a strategy for serious cooperation." And he continues,

> One dimension would be to create links between the grassroots mem-
> bers of neighborhood organizations, and get them involved in dia-
> logue. Dialogue is a form of struggle: it's not just chitchat. Create a
> dialogue that focuses not just on the vulnerability of both groups, but
> on these larger issues of justice, democracy, and the crisis in our own
> communities. Then try to hammer some programs that relate to the
> everyday lives of these groups. It could be tutoring, it could be strug-
> gling against tenant abuse—it could be a whole lot of things. We have
> to put this on the agenda because we're concerned not solely about
> the self-interest of the respective groups but more about the future of
> this country. (ibid., 266–267)

Very good. But consider first the notion of an emergency meeting of Black and Jewish progressive leaders. Who are these leaders in
the Black and Jewish communities? By what criterion does one distinguish between progressive and nonprogressive (read reactionary
or conservative) leaders? And, most importantly, who decides on the
qualification for inclusion in the emergency meeting? These questions are significant because they call attention to the fact that the
concept of leadership is left vague or undefined in West's discussion
of healing. One can very easily envision a state of affairs in which
some individual, X, is contacted to attend an emergency meeting of
the kind West proposes on the basis that she or he leads a large and
affluent church in a metropolitan area. However, another individual,
Y, who is involved in grassroots organization to uplift rural (or even
urban) Blacks is ignored possibly because of certain kinds of views
that she or he holds. Y, nevertheless, considers herself or himself progressive and so believes that she or he ought to have been invited.
Feeling rebuffed, Y challenges the very idea of the meeting as illegit-
imate and unrepresentative.

It will not do to respond, as perhaps West might, that such an
aggrieved individual can simply be included as a leader. Such a
response has the dangerous slippery slope effect of entailing that anyone who considers himself or herself a leader and who therefore
questions the legitimacy and representativeness of the meeting on
similar grounds automatically will qualify for inclusion as a progressive leader. After all, leadership would now seem to be in the eye of
the beholder! That this method of resolving the issue is terribly bad

becomes clearer if we consider that it would permit anybody, including hate-mongers or individuals whose views may be deemed reactionary, to qualify *as a progressive leader*.[15] At the same time, West would have no logical grounds to exclude such individuals. This is just one consequence that follows upon the indeterminacy of the concept of progressive leadership in West's discussion.

Difficulties over representative and progressive leadership are not limited to the Black community. Michael Lerner charges that in the Jewish community wealthy (and invariably conservative) Jews have used their resources to dominate and thus appropriate Jewish "voice" in the sense of claiming to represent all Jews.[16] Examples of Jewish organizations that Lerner says are controlled by the few wealthy Jews include the American Jewish Committee, the American Jewish Congress, the Conference of Presidents of Major Jewish Organizations, the Anti-Defamation League, and the UJA/Federations (ibid., 225–227). So, here again, questions about the criterion for deciding progressive leadership and about group representation apply. The dominant conservative groups would simply masquerade as progressive liberals and claim a place at the meeting to the exclusion of the "authentic" progressive liberals. This kind of politics of inappropriate representation is possible because of the limiting concept of leadership in West's discussion (Lerner and West, 227).

And this brings me to a second difficulty, namely, that the concept of leadership that West advances is just too restrictive in focusing only on those deemed "progressive." Not very much will be gained in resolving the conflict between Blacks and Jews as long as West's focus is only on the so-called progressive leaders. The reason is that the progressive leaders are like the proverbial choir to whom preaching is not really needed. Indeed, by West's own account, they are already doing in different ways the very kinds of things that need to be done to mend the situation.[17] If anything, therefore, it is the nonprogressive leaders and their following who need the psychic conversion that dialogue is supposed to bring about. They, more so than the progressive group, are vital to any form of dialogue that is to be promulgated to address the mutual concerns of Blacks and Jews. For this reason, West would therefore have to expand his concept of leadership to include the Leonard Jeffrieses, the Louis Farrakhans, and the Khalid Muhammads, despite the views they hold.

Finally, there is an equally important difficulty with West's notion of convening an emergency meeting. The very notion implies some kind of a proto-Marxian vanguard or cadre of Platonic philosopher kings and queens that constitutes a driving force to move the Black and Jewish communities toward healing. Consider some of the phrases West uses in talking about what needs to be done to mend the rift between Blacks and Jews: "we need to call an emergency meeting"; "to launch a strategy"; "to create links between grassroot members of neighborhood organizations, *and get them involved* in dialogue" (emphasis added). The phraseology here suggests that this enlightened group, whether Platonic or Marxian, will summon the two "tribes" and create a dialogue between them *for their own good*. After all, it is the moral legitimacy of their respective demands for social justice that is at stake, *and they do not seem to know this very important fact!* Thus they should be made to see it, again, for their own very good. For this reason, the dialogue, under the guidance or supervision of the enlightened leadership, will focus not narrowly on the respective vulnerabilities of each "tribe," but, more importantly, on the "larger issues of justice, democracy and the crisis in our communities" (ibid., 266).

Granted my reading of West, issues of democracy and accountability of the enlightened leadership immediately arise. For example, how, if at all, will this enlightened leadership be made accountable to the grassroots? What significant value will the leadership place on the viewpoints of grassroots individuals? What relevant role does the grassroots have in the selection of the enlightened leadership? To appreciate the force of these questions, consider that for both Plato and Marx the masses have to be instructed and directed for their own good, notwithstanding Marx's remark about the dictatorship of the proletariat. This shows that neither Plato nor Marx really valued the views of the masses *about the general (read theoretical) concept of societal good*. True, West does not hold such a position. On the contrary, he explicitly ascribes a role to the masses in saying that individuals at the grassroots level should be encouraged to get involved in dialogue. Moreover, he continues, the issues that affect their daily lives—which they know best—must be put on the agenda (ibid., 267). Even so, he betrays a measure of intellectual leadership elitism and condescension to the masses much like Plato, if not like Marx, in a way that leaves one wondering how amenable his elite group would be to the ideas of the masses, at least in terms of vision, and thus how democratic and accountable this group would be to the masses on issues such as what constitutes the general good. It is this idea of the general good that we find crystallized on specific items such as democracy and social justice. I raise this issue of democracy and accountability because one constantly hears from West about "what we need to do for them" The "we" here, I submit, are the enlightened few (including West himself?), at least in the manner of Plato.

Of course, there is nothing wrong with intellectual leadership elitism if one believes with Plato and Marx that some people just have to be led and directed for their own good. However, West's explicit call for accountability, for example of preacher to laity or leader to followers, is a repudiation of such an elitist position (see 1982, 18.) This is all the more so because he recognizes that such elitism is invariably at odds with democracy and accountability, particularly to the very group that is being directed for its own good. Nevertheless, he seems to gloss over this fact as he advocates convening an emergency meeting between Jewish and Black progressive leaders. He fails to see that the issue of democracy and accountability applies as much in the initial stage, when crucial decisions are the absolute prerogative of the (interim?) leadership group, as in the later stages in the activities of the entire Jewish and Black groups.

The point of the foregoing criticism of West is that the very notion of a proto-Marxian vanguard or Platonic group of enlightened leadership that seems present in his discussion is logically incompatible with both his constant demand for democracy and accountability and his very repudiation of the Marxian notion of a vanguard. Lewis Gordon has noted that it is the demand for democracy and accountability that distinguishes West's brand of Marxism from other forms of the doctrine. Thus, for Gordon, West's variant of Marxism is left-wing (read radical).[18] I do not dispute this reading of West. Yet, for the reason I have given, the concept of a proto-Marxian vanguard, reified in the Communist Party, or a Platonic enlightened leadership, or even Du Boisean Talented Tenth, seems to rear its head in West's discussion even despite his explicit pronouncements otherwise. To avoid this difficulty, therefore, West would have to devise a way of implementing an emergency meeting between Blacks and Jews without implying, even if unwittingly, the notion of such a vanguard or an elite enlightened leadership as I have alleged, and with all the consequences that follow.

The issues on which I have focused thus far in West's discussion are not just irritating underbrush that should be cleared before dialogue can occur between Blacks and Jews. They are actually important conceptual matters about leadership itself, the elucidation of which is a prerequisite for any meaningful engagement of both the subject and content of dialogue. I turn now to the concept of dialogue.

One reason West gives for the use of dialogue is that dialogue functions like a bridge that must be traversed by the conflicting parties to enable each side to peer into the domain of the other. To traverse this bridge is to exchange ideas and information via the medium of language. And to peer into the domain of the other side is to perceive and thus to understand the reality of the other side. Or, better yet, it is to facilitate a perceptual and cognitive transformation on each side of the conflict—what West calls an "intellectual change and existential transformation" (1999b, 534). It is in this way that dialogue is supposed to rectify the mutual misperceptions of each side prior to the dialogic encounter.

As I indicated earlier, the central question around which dialogue should revolve, for West, is: What does it mean to be Jewish or Black in ethical terms? This question is about the moral import of Jewish and Black identities inscribed in a sociopolitical context. Since the conflict between Blacks and Jews occurs largely in the sociopolitical sphere, its resolution, in West's view, must appeal to certain basic principles of morality that apply to each group as also to the entire human species. The moral principle is empathy, compassion, or Humean sympathy. West construes the operation of this principle along the following lines: If it is recognized that, for instance, Jewishness or Blackness entails empathizing with the oppressed, then this recognition of Jewish or Black identity would automatically obligate Jewish and Black people to function together in the sociopolitical sphere to alleviate their mutual oppression. After all, they are both the most despised, degraded, and oppressed people in the world. Their mutual survival requires therefore that they coalesce morally and politically to challenge the cause and structures of their common oppression. And this coalition is rooted in empathy. That this motivation is behind West's advocacy of dialogue is clear from the following passage:

> My own investment in black-Jewish alliances is not simply a political effort to buttress progressive forces in American society. It also is a moral endeavor that exemplifies ways in which the most hated group in European history and the most hated group in U.S. history can coalesce in the name of precious democratic ideals—ideals that serve as the sole countervailing force to hatred, fear and greed. (ibid., 534)

Thus he characterizes dialogue as "the go-cart of compassion" (534).

West is under no illusion that dialogue can be unpleasant. Quite the contrary, he expects dialogue to be charged and even highly unpleasant. Accordingly, he speaks of the willingness of both parties to be open and "vulnerable enough—hence trusting enough—to be questioned in a transformative mode." And he argues against what he calls "dialogical dogmatism," which he defines as "a form of intellectual exclusion that chooses interlocutors with whom one is comfortable." Against this form of dialogue West advocates one that "transgress[es] the 'respectable' bounds of dialogical dogmatists . . . [one that] is the lifeblood of radical democracy and political break-throughs" (ibid., 534).

Yet, granting the verities of dialogue as proclaimed, serious doubts can be raised about the efficacy of speech in resolving the Black-Jewish conflict.[19] Dialogue (or communicative action) of the kind proposed by West and even Habermas presupposes, indeed requires, a situation in which the parties to the dialogue are social equals. In such scenarios dialogue undoubtedly works. However, the situation between Jews and Blacks is not of this kind. Consider again the Ocean Hill-Brownsville incident. We see from this incident that Jews are not as oppressed as Blacks and people of color generally. Thus, this incident simply enacts and reflects America's racial politics and the hierarchical social locations of groups, with Whites at the top and people of color at the bottom and the former oppressing the latter. Second, and to reinforce this point, I have already noted that each group perceives itself and the other group through racialized lenses. For different reasons, each group perceives itself as socially unequal to the other. This is the essence of Jewish anti-Black racism and Black anti-Semitism, the latter of which may be construed as a *reaction* to White racism. But this perception itself is merely a reflection of the concrete social realities of the two groups relative to the dominant (White) group. As Cheryl Greenberg (1999) correctly notes,

> The two communities [Black and Jewish] . . . enjoyed a different relationship with the dominant culture. Most Jews were white people, and although anti-Semitism was real, race was the deeper rift in American society. White ethnic groups have shifted from ethnic to white over time since most rewards and opportunity in America were apportioned not by ethnicity or religion but by race, and Jews were no exception to this pattern. Jews were no more eager to embrace the cause of a pariah people [namely, Blacks] than any other white community. (155)

The racialized lenses through which Blacks and Jews view each other (and themselves), insofar as those lenses reflect a deeper reality about the larger American society, impose severe constraints on dialogue between the two groups. Indeed, it is precisely the different social locations of Jews and Blacks and the perspectives those locations occasion that underlie both the Ocean Hill-Brownsville conflict and the Crown Heights conflict over the accidental killing of Gavin Cato, a seven-year old Black boy, by a Hasidic Jewish motorist.[20] The latter incident in turn gave rise to subsequent Black revenge in the stabbing death of Yankel Rosenbaum, a twenty-nine-year old Hasidic Jewish scholar from Australia. In other words, both the Ocean Hill-Brownsville and the Crown Heights incidents instantiate the perception and mutual recognition of the distinct social locations of Jews and Blacks in a society that has reified races as distinct ontological categories in a hierarchical order. Granted the reality of races as distinct ontological categories, and given that this reality underwrites the perspectives of Blacks and Jews, there is no doubt that unless these ontological categories are directly assailed there will be very little chance for resolving the conflict between Blacks and Jews. What this means, in effect, is that, insofar as Blacks and Jews perceive each other as social unequals, wherein the perception is veridical because it is grounded in the ontological categories of race that encumber the entire society, West, Lerner and others, notwithstanding their good intentions, will continue to entertain the false belief that dialogue will mend the rift between Blacks and Jews. True, dialogue may be a good starting point. However, it will not get far inasmuch as the conflict between Blacks and Jews is rooted in a deeper structure that transcends but at the same time envelops both groups. At the risk of overstatement, my point, in short, is that race has a primordial status in the conflict between Blacks and Jews, and localized discussion between the two groups will not resolve the issue. In light of this view, it would seem that a better solution is an all-out assault on the superstructure of race itself, better yet racism, in the larger society; thereafter the Black-Jewish conflict stands a chance of being mediated through dialogue.

Conclusion

I have been arguing that West's proposal for a resolution of the Black-Jewish conflict is woefully inadequate because it fails to target the racial superstructure in which the conflict and related social injustices are anchored. As I have shown, West's call for dialogue is motivated by the belief that dialogue will effect a perceptual and cognitive transformation on both Jews and Blacks so that each side would see the other differently and accurately. An accurate perception (or representation of the other), he believes, would occasion a psychic change that would translate into a change in attitude both in oneself and the other. Both parties would therefore very easily see the need to resuscitate their faltering alliance against oppression. I have tried to show, however, that West's position is seriously mistaken in that it is predicated on the idea of the conflicting parties viewing each other as social equals. But since Blacks and Jews are not social equals, it is impossible for dialogue of the kind West and Lerner (and perhaps even Habermas) speak of even to get started in any meaningful way.

The inadequacy of West's proposal suggests an inability or reluctance to provide a penetrating and incisive analysis of the root cause of the conflict itself. It is just not enough to say that White supremacy is the cause of all forms of oppression; it has to be acknowledged also that Jewish anti-Black racism is a spinoff of White supremacy, and this makes it *the* source of the specific conflict. After all, Jewish anti-Black racism is predicated on the same kinds of beliefs and attitudes embedded in and espoused by White supremacist thinking. West therefore has to come to terms with the realization that the Black-Jewish conflict is nothing but a playing out of a scene (or even an act) in the quintessential drama of race relations in the society at large. As such, the nature of the conflict precludes dialogue as remedy. It matters not that the dialogue is supposed to focus on issues of identity or, that is, of what it means to be Black or Jewish in ethical terms. Such a discussion is ancillary to the more fundamental question: Are Blacks and Jews socially (read racially) equal in the society? If not, how can all social groups, regardless of race, ethnicity, and the like, *be* equal? These questions are significant because they direct attention to the fact that any attempt to resolve the Black-Jewish conflict should focus and target primarily the racial structure and hierarchy that dominate and govern social group interaction in the society as a whole. Only thereafter will issues of democracy and social justice in a pluralistic society become legitimate subjects for discussion. Even so, one attempt of the society to address the issue of social justice is by implementing an affirmative action policy. I now will examine West's position on this policy.

CHAPTER FIVE

Affirmative Action and Proto-Marxism

Introduction

No examination of the issue of social justice would be complete without a discussion of affirmative action. The reason is that, even as its adequacy is still being debated, the current race- and gender-based affirmative action was the first systematic response to Black demands for social justice.[1] In *Race Matters, Jews and Blacks,* and *The Cornel West Reader,* West takes up the subject of affirmative action. In *The Cornel West Reader,* for example, he characterizes affirmative action as a significant but weak response to Black demands for social justice (1995b, 495).[2] According to West, affirmative action is significant because it was the first formal policy response of the society to the systemic exclusionary and discriminatory practices against Blacks. Such practices existed in a variety of spheres and were manifested in a number of ways, such as in employment, housing, healthcare, and political disfranchisement. But affirmative action is weak, contends West, because it was a concession extracted from the powerful political, business, and educational establishment through pressure from organized citizens and angry unorganized citizens, the latter of whom vented their anger in street disturbances. And so, as a concession, it offers much less than it otherwise could to address the issue of social justice with fairness and equity. Thus, says West, it is "imperfect" (495). To address this alleged imperfection West advances a class-based alternative affirmative action proposal.

It is not my aim to examine either the adequacy (or otherwise) of affirmative action, its intricacies, or even its historical evolution. Nor do I intend even to discuss the vagueness (or indeterminacy) of the term "affirmative action" and hence the problem of interpreting the specific set of issues it supposedly designates.[3] Assuming a working notion of affirmative action as a federally mandated policy to ensure employment and related social opportunities for qualified Blacks and women in both the public and private sectors, my proposed aim is specifically to examine West's declared preference for class-based affirmative action over the current race- and gender-based policy (1994, 95).[4] This issue is important because West is aware of the race and gender considerations that led to affirmative action in the first place. Thus it is curious that he should advocate a policy that focuses on class rather than race in the context of social justice as it relates to Blacks. To phrase the issue differently and with emphasis on the Black (in the very extended sense of non-White) experience of social *injustice*, what advantage, if any, does West's proposed class-based alternative affirmative action proposal have over the current race- and gender-based policy in meeting Black demands for social justice? Moreover, even granting any advantages to his proposal, is West's alternative position compatible with Black demands for social justice? It is with these questions that I shall be concerned in this chapter. Specifically, I shall show that West's proposal is consistent with his humanistic endeavors. To that extent it is more advantageous to the current policy because it is more inclusive than the latter. However, and particularly because of this advantage, it is out of step with the specific challenges that historically have circumscribed Black (and women's) demands for social justice and to which race- and gender-based affirmative action is thus a response. Thus, his proposal fails as a remedy to the specific forms of social injustice that affect Blacks and women.

Historicizing Race-Based Affirmative Action Policy

In his review of the current affirmative action policy, West reminds us of America's endemic color prescription of privileging Whites over Blacks in all aspects of social life but particularly in the socioeconomic sphere. This racial privileging influenced the distribution of wealth, power, and income in the society, especially since it deliberately "denied opportunities to most 'qualified' Black people" (ibid., 93). It was to the socioeconomic inequality suffered by Blacks, says West, an inequality that derived from racial considerations that excluded Blacks from the socioeconomic mainstream, that American progressives responded in their advocacy for a more equitable and fair distributive system. This response was affirmative action.

But West characterizes affirmative action as a compromise solution to Black demands for social justice. Specifically, it was a compromise between the big corporations and government on the one hand—that is the very custodians of the socioeconomic status quo—and Blacks on the other, the victims of the inequalities wrought by the policies of these same institutions. For West, however, such a compromise did not go far enough. In his view, substantive redistributive measures should make opportunities available to all those in the economic and social periphery. And this would include Blacks and non-Blacks. He suggests that such measures should involve "more federal support to small farmers, or more FHA (Federal Housing Association) mortgage loans to urban dwellers as well as suburban home buyers" (ibid., 94).

West realizes, however, that advocates of social change were up against powerful sociopolitical and economic interests that favored the status quo; thus it was not possible for them to obtain such substantive redistributive measures as he has outlined. As he correctly notes, advocates of social change therefore had to settle for whatever small concessions they could extract from "the care-takers of American prosperity" (ibid., 94), cognizant that all such concessions were reluctantly made. To that end, he continues, those advocates relied upon and utilized the legal institutions to press for the implementation of the concessions that they had wrested from the corporations and government.

West finds it significant that various American governments had adopted a variety of de facto affirmative action measures in previous times to assist other groups. Examples of such measures are loans to select immigrant groups, subsidies to certain farmers, FHA mortgage loans aimed at specific (types of) home buyers, G.I. Bill benefits to American veterans, and the like. What this shows, says West, is that the concept of affirmative action was not new to the American sociopolitical and intellectual landscape. Against this background, then, he finds it puzzling, and rightly so, that there was virulent opposition to affirmative action as a remedial policy implemented in the 1960s to enable Blacks and women to gain a foothold in the American mainstream. But why such opposition?

Although West does not explore this issue, it is well known that the main reason for the opposition was that affirmative action came to be identified in the American psyche, albeit wrongly, with *racial preferencing of Blacks over Whites*. Unfortunately, even West is guilty of this misidentification, as is clear from his remark that "recent efforts [through affirmative action] to broaden access to America's prosperity [by including African Americans] have been based on *preferential policies*" (ibid., 94; emphasis added).[5] This (mis)identification of affirmative action with preferential treatment has provided a platform from which critics of the policy have attacked the policy as unfair. As West is aware, the standard argument against affirmative action is that affirmative action is morally wrong and socially unjust because it supposedly violates the principle of individual merit that is (presumed) central to American life.[6] More particularly, critics argue that affirmative action violates the American ethos of meritocracy at least insofar as Black employability is concerned. They contend that Blacks fail to meet the principle of merit that governs socioeconomic life *because they are less qualified than Whites,* yet private employers and other institutions that receive federal money have been mandated to give them preference in hiring and government contracting over qualified and competent Whites.[7]

Obviously, this view of affirmative action presumes that a White person who is rejected for a position in favor of a Black person is more qualified for the position than the Black. Or, alternatively, a Black person who is hired for a position is less qualified for the position in the first place, so that she or he is deemed to have won the position at the expense of her or his White counterpart. It is precisely this presumption of superior White qualification and inferior Black qualification that informs Robert Fullinwider's working definition of the term "preferential hiring." In his critique of affirmative action, Fullinwider states that "*a black is preferentially hired over a white when the black, because he is black, is chosen over at least one better qualified white, where being black is not a job-related qualifica-*

tion" (1980, 17; emphasis in the original). Fullinwider repeats this definition in a variety of ways throughout the book. For example, he writes: "By definition, preferential hiring involves lesser qualified persons being chosen over better qualified persons, the selection being predicated on a factor (race) that is not job-related" (86; cp. 72–73).[8]

I shall characterize all positions similar to Fullinwider's as the *normative though banal, self-serving, and wrongheaded concept of affirmative action*. Interestingly, it is this sense of affirmative action that has gained currency and that largely has influenced the debate on the alleged social undesirability and moral repugnance of the policy. To repeat, the normative but banal, self-serving, and wrongheaded sense of affirmative action essentially represents the policy as being opposed to qualification and merit. West and others, then, by acquiescing to the characterization of affirmative action as preferential treatment, have empowered and enamoured critics of the policy to decry the policy as anything but fair and thus to give it a pejorative meaning. Of course, given the pejorative formulation, affirmative action would appear palpably unfair and morally outrageous and so would deserve to be condemned and opposed. One can even presume that Blacks, too, the supposed beneficiaries of the policy, would oppose the policy; for after all they, more than any one else, know firsthand what it means to be victims of discrimination. Thus they would be in the forefront of any movement to oppose affirmative action insofar as it advocates *discriminatory, preferential and nonmeritorious hiring*.

Yet precisely because the very supposed beneficiaries of affirmative action conceivably could mount a virulent opposition to the policy is reason enough to believe that the policy, construed as mandating the hiring of less qualified and less competent Blacks over qualified and competent Whites, is suspect. And it is for this reason I think that defenders of the policy ought to have exercised considerable caution in characterizing the policy as preferential treatment. West's failure to see that critics of affirmative action have subverted the very meaning of "affirmative action," and his own very glaring use of the term to mean preferential treatment, paradoxically leaves unassailed the very erroneous basis on which critics attack the policy as unfair, morally outrageous, and socially undesirable.[9] In other words, given the pejorative sense of affirmative action by opponents such as Fullinwider, West's identification of affirmative action with preferential treatment a fortiori argues against his very advocacy for social justice insofar as it is grounded on some conception or other of affirmative action. Because I consider this an egregious error on West's part he cannot be absolved from criticism, especially since he is fully aware of both the historical circumstances that gave rise to the policy of affirmative action and some of the intricacies of the policy.

West's Alternative Class-Based Affirmative Action Proposal

Both the aforementioned pejorative characterization of affirmative action and the opposition it has engendered are not the reason, however, that West rejects the policy in favor of the class-based alternative that he proposes. West's preference for a class-based affirmative action policy derives instead from his belief that the custodians of America's socioeconomic prosperity, viz., big corporations and big government, are indiscriminate in their choices of the victims that are sacrificed on the altar of the free market. For West, the sacrificial victims, regardless of race, are those on the periphery of the economy— the "have-nots and [the] have-too-littles," as he describes them (1994, 94). In other words, although this group happens to be predominantly Black, in the extended sense of all non-Whites, it includes lower-class Whites, too. In West's view, since socioeconomic inequality cuts across racial lines and yet is the cause of the very existence and nature of the lower class in the society, any substantive remedial policy therefore has to address the issue of class disparities in the entire society. It is because West thinks affirmative action, as a remedy to racial and gender socioeconomic inequalities, does not address the larger issue of class disparities in the society as a whole that it is inadequate.

This does not mean that West disputes the importance of the current race- and gender-based policy. On the contrary, he acknowledges that the current policy, even with its limitations, is highly useful because it affords minorities and women some measure of access to the mainstream of the society. He points out that the current policy is able to achieve this goal because it is backed by legal sanctions that require compliance from otherwise reluctant public and private sectors. Nevertheless, he insists, the role of the current policy is negative because *it is limited only to ensuring the abatement of discriminatory practices against minorities and women* (ibid., 95). But this means that the policy leaves intact the very corporate and government structures, dominated by upper- and middle-class White males, around which revolve power, wealth, privilege, and overall success in the society. West therefore contends that for affirmative action to be effective it should attack and dismantle this bastion of upper- and middle-class White male supremacy and dominance in the society. And for this purpose he thinks that a class-based alternative affirmative action policy is a better candidate than the prevailing race- and gender-based policy. Or, to put it differently, West believes that an effective remedy to social injustice should consist of adopting class-based policies, strategies, or devices that entail redistributing the resources in society. And his proposed variant of affirmative action is such a redistributive measure.

It is pertinent at this point to make at least two crucial observations about West's alternative proposal. First, West's call for a class-based affirmative action policy is consistent with his humanistic endeavors. The thrust of his humanistic endeavors, as I showed in Chapter Two, is to agitate for the politically, economically, socially, and morally dispossessed and disenfranchised in society, and thus to help ameliorate their suffering. Since this group includes diverse races and genders—after all, suffering and exploitation, especially when wrought by market forces, are indifferent to individual specificities—West's class-based affirmative action proposal is thus unequivocally more inclusive and far reaching than the current race- and gender-based policy. In this regard, at least, West's proposal admittedly has an advantage over the current policy.

Second, West's proposal for a class-based affirmative action policy is *supposedly* an extension of his professed commitment to a proto-Marxian outlook. I showed in Chapter Three that although West acknowledges that race is integral to social (in)justice, whereby a disproportionate number of Blacks are victimized in a racially stratified society, nevertheless he privileges class considerations as the major driving force behind social inequities and social injustice. By class considerations he means the ownership of capital (or the lack thereof) and how this phenomenon is central to issues of social justice. It is this position that presumably motivates his call for a class-based affirmative action policy as a solution to social inequities. With these observations in mind, I turn now to the key question with which I am concerned in this chapter: "How consistent is West's view of a class-based affirmative action proposal with Black demands for social justice?"

The Peculiarities of Black Experiences

If West is correct in his view that Black oppression is grounded more in economics than in racial considerations, then there scarcely can be a doubt that his suggestion for redistributing societal resources with a focus on class considerations is the proper remedy to Black oppression. But that West is wrong in this claim can very easily be demonstrated by a brief sketch of some of the race considerations that are pivotal to Black demands for social justice. These are considerations of race (and gender) bias in the society. This conjunctive bias is entrenched in the structures and institutions of power in the society, and thus is the cause of (and reason for) the current affirmative action policy having the defining attributes that it does. To demonstrate why affirmative action has these features I shall appropriate what I take to be a sociopsychological framework that Du Bois provides in *The Souls of Black Folk* (1989). In my view, this framework situates the lived reality of Blacks since emancipation.

To begin, the sociopsychological framework that Du Bois provides is one in which Whites perceive Blacks as "the problem" in and to the society. This perception reverberates in the opening sentences of *Souls*:

> Between me and the other world there is ever an unasked question: unasked by some through feelings of delicacy; by others through the difficulty of rightly framing it. All, nevertheless, flutter around it. They approach me in a half-hesitant sort of way, eye me curiously or compassionately, and then, instead of saying directly, How does it feel to be a problem? They say, I know an excellent colored man in my town; . . . To the real question, How does it feel to be a problem? I answer seldom a word. (ibid., 1–2)

Although this passage is autobiographical, the experience of which Du Bois speaks applies to every Black person in the society. Du Bois, and by extension every Black person, is looked upon and examined both as an anthropological curiosity in a very extended sense and as an aberration in the society that calls for an explanation. To illustrate, a Black professor new to a predominantly White college/university is looked upon skeptically both by her or his students and her or his colleagues. The unasked question of some White students is whether or not they can expect from the Black professor the kind of knowledge they would obtain from a White professor. The point here is about the presumption of knowledge and hence intellectual gain in favor of the White professor versus doubt about any intellectual gain from the Black professor. And from the point of view of some White faculty, the presumption is that the Black faculty is a race-hire, not one based on intellectual merit. In short, the burden of proof is on Blacks to validate their existence in one form or another. As Iris Marion Young (1990) states, "In daily interchange women and men of color must prove their respectability" (58). This is what it means to be Black in America.

This phenomenon of being "the problem" bespeaks a psychic and sociological divide between Blacks and Whites, a divide Du Bois captures in the concept of the veil (1989, 2). The veil is a psychological divide because it both conditions and reflects Black and White mutual perceptions of each other. And it is also a sociological divide because it represents the physical and cultural demarcation of the society along racial lines. Of significance is the debilitating effect of the phenomenon of being "the problem" on Black self-awareness and Black aspirations. According to Du Bois, the phenomenon of being "the problem" prevents African Americans from developing any "true self-consciousness" and, worse, "only lets . . . [them] see . . . [themselves] through the revelation of the other world" (3). Du Bois will go on to characterize as a state of double-consciousness the fact of Black self-perception and self-evaluation through the lenses of Whites. For Du Bois, then, the major struggle of African Americans is to overcome this state of double-consciousness. But it is instructive that this state of affairs exists in the first place only because Blacks are deemed to be "the problem" in and to the society. This is the sociopsychological framework that has circumscribed Black existence since emancipation.[10]

Du Bois picks up the thread of the discussion in the essay "Of the Dawn of Freedom." There he informs us that the "deeper question" that both precipitated the Civil War and preoccupied the posteman-cipation period was: "What shall be done with Negroes?" (ibid., 10–11). In the context in which Du Bois raised this question the immediate concern was the deplorable material conditions of the hordes of destitute slaves who had been emancipated by the war and so had become fugitives. Specifically, these fugitives lacked the basic necessities of life—food, shelter, and clothing—and were tagging along and thus swelling the ranks of the Union forces. And in response to this concern was the establishment of the Freedmen's Bureau, first, under the jurisdiction of the Department of Treasury, and later in various other forms as an autonomous or quasi-autonomous body. Benevolent societies and organizations also evolved, and they provided assistance to the destitute former slaves. And, finally, various "commercial experiments" were established to transform ex-slaves into remunerated laborers and to integrate them into civil society (12–26).

But the question of what to do with Negroes also may be con-strued in a much larger context as an inquiry into whether or not it was possible for Blacks and Whites to coexist in the society, espe-cially given that Whites considered Blacks their ontological and hence social inferior. This is an issue that Thomas Jefferson raised very pointedly in his *Notes on the State of Virginia* (1955), in the essay entitled "Laws."[11] In this essay, Jefferson examined, among other things, what he considered "a powerful obstacle" to the eman-cipation of slaves, the issue, namely, whether or not it would be socially practicable to integrate ex-slaves into the society: "It will probably be asked, Why not retain and incorporate the blacks into the state, and thus save the expense of supplying, by importation of white settlers, the vacancies they [the slaves] will leave?" (138). The reason this issue was significant is that Jefferson believed, as did other eighteenth-century intellectuals, that there are fundamental ontological differences between Blacks and Whites that are mani-fested in skin color, cognitive makeup, and aesthetic features.[12] Ontologically, to be White is, on this view, to be endowed with supe-rior cognitive (including emotional) makeup and beautiful physical features that are aesthetically pleasant. And to be Black, by contrast, is to be bereft of cognitive ability (including a complex emotional makeup) and to be physically ugly and thus aesthetically odious. Not only are these differences supposedly "fixed in nature," as Jefferson suggests (138), but, more importantly, it is because of them that Whites are ontologically superior to Blacks. Concerning the emotion of love in particular, Jefferson declares that with Blacks "love seems . . . to be more an eager desire, than a tender delicate mixture of sentiment and sensations" (139). In other words, Blacks are inherently incapable of experiencing the tender and complex emotion of love; they have only a raw sexual desire for a member of the opposite sex. And he sums up this view of Black ontological makeup saying that in general Blacks possess "more of sensation than reflection" (139).

To reinforce this claim about the ontological differences between Blacks and Whites, and hence of the natural inferiority of Blacks to Whites, Jefferson goes on to draw a contrast between the treatment of Black slaves in America with that of White slaves in the Roman Empire during the Augustan age. He calls attention to this difference in treatment to highlight what he takes to be a fundamental difference in cognitive abilities between the two groups. The condition of the Roman slave, he declares, was "more deplorable than that of the blacks on the continent of America." In particular, Roman slaves were mistreated by their masters and then were disposed of together with "old oxen, old waggons, old tools [and] old diseased servants" (ibid., 141). But Black slaves in America, he claims, "cannot enumerate this [kind of treatment] among the injuries and insults they receive" (141). Yet, notwithstanding their deplorable condition and even despite their maltreatment, continues Jefferson, Roman slaves were the "rarest artists" (142) in the Roman Empire. In addition, they excelled in science and as a result were often employed as tutors to the children of their masters (142). This state of affairs contrasts with that of Black slaves in America. Black slaves were inherently incapable of producing any work of the intellect.

If the conditions of the slavery thus described are minimally identical, in the sense of one person being owned by another and made an object of servitude, how then can one explain the supposed marked differences in the cognitive abilities of Roman slaves and American slaves? To Jefferson, the answer lies in race: Slaves in the Roman Empire were intellectually productive because "they were of the race of whites" (ibid., 142), whereas slaves in American society were cognitively unproductive precisely because they were Black.

The correlation here is between the attribute of Whiteness, intellectual endowment, and intellectual productivity, on the one hand, and, in sharp contrast, the attribute of Blackness, a congenital absence of intellectual endowment, and lack of intellectual productivity, on the other. Drawing upon these racial differences, Jefferson concludes that it is nature itself "which has produced the distinction" (142) in cognitive makeup between the races.

For Jefferson, then, the supposed ontological differences between Blacks and Whites constituted a powerful epistemological objection to the emancipation of slaves. But it was not the idea of emancipation as such that troubled Jefferson. What troubled him was the social consequence of emancipation. Among other things, emancipation might give rise to a "mixture" of the races and such a mixture would stain (read contaminate) the White blood. This fear of staining White blood was Jefferson's greatest nightmare. As he says,

> Among the Romans emancipation required but one effort. The slave, when made free, might mix with, without staining the blood of his master. But with us a second is necessary, unknown to history. When freed, he is to be removed beyond the reach of mixture. (ibid., 143)

With emancipation the society would be faced with two options: either to send emancipated slaves elsewhere and avoid "mixture" or to integrate them into the American (read White) society and be prepared to deal with "mixture." Jefferson's view in light of the supposed ontological differences between Blacks and Whites is that emancipated slaves should be sent "beyond the reach of mixture"—that is, elsewhere.

The question "What shall be done with Negroes?" to which Du Bois directs our attention was therefore as much about the immediate material condition of slaves who had been emancipated as a result of the war as it was about the issue of racial coexistence in American society. But Jefferson had already proposed an answer, namely, to exclude Blacks from the society to prevent "mixture." Obviously, that answer did not prevail. Nevertheless, the position it advocated, deriving as it did from the supposed ontological differences between the races, underlies the systemic institutional exclusion of Blacks from the socioeconomic and political milieu since emancipation. This systemic exclusion is seen more particularly in the economic sphere in which, postemancipation, the swelling ranks of Black labor were perceived as a threat to the social and economic well-being of the dominant White worker group. White workers therefore organized and took steps through labor unions and other extra-parliamentary mechanisms both to prevent Black workers from being members of labor unions and, more importantly, to ensure that Blacks were kept out of meaningful employment in the market. Put otherwise, White workers viewed Black workers as *competitors* who had to be stopped at all costs so that White workers could preserve White jobs and hence maintain White economic and social dominance. I use the expression "White jobs" deliberately because White workers were operating on the presumption of the right of ownership to jobs and hence of the right of first refusal in the job market. This phenomenon operates even at present, although it is disguised with much sophistication. As Albert Mosley puts it, "Many White males have developed expectations about the likelihood of their being selected for educational, employment, and entrepreneurial opportunities that are realistic only because of the general exclusion of women and non-Whites as competitors for such positions" (Capaldi and Mosley 1996, 26). In sum, with emancipation, White workers arrogated this presumed right, and it was on the presumption of this right that they effected overt and covert measures to inhibit Blacks from entering the economic mainstream.[13] All of this was because they perceived Blacks as "the problem" in and to society.

The Du Boisean sociopsychological framework within which I have cast the question "What shall be done with Negroes?" enables us fully to appreciate the historically sedimented truth of Du Bois' articulation of the aspiration of the African American. The aspiration is not simply to reconcile the African American's dual identities of being both African and American without sacrificing either, but more importantly, it is to be able to effect this reconciliation "without having the doors of Opportunity closed roughly in his [or her] face" (1989, 3). Having the doors of opportunity slammed shut against the faces of Blacks historically has been one of the hallmarks of the Black experience as Blacks endeavor to shape their identities and overcome the constraints imposed on them by the phenomenon of double-consciousness. In large measure, affirmative action was proposed as a response to the sociopolitical agitation motivated by the experience of systemic denial of opportunity that circumscribed the lived reality of Blacks. Or, to state the point differently, affirmative action was one attempt of the society finally to come to terms with the all-pervasive issue of Black social existence in a society steeped in anti-Black racism. And this racism manifested itself in various ways, among which was the deliberate and systemic denial of opportunities to Blacks. If Blacks were "the problem," then they were an intransigent problem that just would not go away and could not be made to disappear, as Jefferson would have liked. The problem had various dimensions: economic, political, and social. But its various dimensions crystallized into the existential. Blacks were (and continue to be) America's existential quagmire.

The Peculiarities of Women's Experiences

Variant forms of institutional practices of the kind that excluded Blacks from the social mainstream also were aimed at women and with similar results.[14] In a recent symposium at the National Cathedral School in Washington, DC, Supreme Court Justice Sandra Day O'Connor provided a litany of systemic exclusionary practices aimed at (White) women who aspired to be lawyers in the United States.[15] Among other things, O'Connor observed that in 1875, for example, the Wisconsin Supreme Court ruled that Lavinia Goodell could not be admitted to the bar because, wrote the Chief Justice, "the practice of law was unfit for the female character [and that] [t]o expose women to the brutal, repulsive, and obscene events of courtroom life, . . . would shock man's reverence for womanhood and relax the public's sense of decency" (2000, 31). Similarly, in 1869, the Illinois Supreme Court gave a ruling against another woman, Myra Bradwell, from practicing law in the state. Bradwell had studied law under her husband and had applied to be admitted to the Illinois bar. According to Justice O'Connor, the Court reasoned that "as a married woman, [Bradwell's] contracts were not binding, and contracts were the essence of an attorney-client relationship" (31). In its ruling the Court stated that "God designed the sexes to occupy different spheres of action, and that it belonged to men to make, apply and execute the laws" (31). Of note, the United States Supreme Court upheld the ruling of the Illinois Supreme Court.

The rationale for the type of practices and rulings that barred women from the public sphere may be characterized as the argument from the natural constitution of the sexes. As with the argument about the ontological differences between the races, the argument here is that women are constituted differently from men in terms of cognitive makeup and thus of the cognitive skills that are contingent upon that makeup. Proponents of this view believe that, by nature, women are compassionate, gentle, and motherly; thus their cognitive makeup capacitates them for work in the spheres of "art and religion" and not in spheres that require logical acumen. The study and practice of law, on the other hand, require reason and logic. Moreover, law calls for an adversarial temper, shrewd negotiating skill, and exposure to the unjust and immoral. Women therefore are inherently incapacitated from studying and practicing law. Given their temperament as caring, compassionate, and gentle, women's place was in the home. This view that relegates and confines women's existence to the domestic sphere is known in feminist circles as the cult of domesticity.

If the cult of domesticity was upheld legally by venerable institutions such as the Supreme Courts of states and the United States Supreme Court, there were other institutional obstacles in the way of women's entry into the public domain. These were societal stipulations in the very *requirements that governed admissibility* into the public domain. This was evident in 1879, in the case of Belva Lockwood, a New York attorney and the first woman admitted to practice law before the Supreme Court of the United States. Says Justice O'Connor, Lockwood "had to try three times to get a special bill passed in the [U.S.] Senate, changing the admission requirements" just so that she could practice law (ibid., 32).

Finally, even in those cases in which women happened to enter the public domain, they encountered a very hostile professional climate in the workplace and that quickly forced them out. For example, the first three women FBI agents were appointed in the 1920s. However, observed Justice O'Connor, "each of them was subsequently asked to and did resign when J. Edgar Hoover became Director" of the agency (ibid., 32).

What all these examples show is that women, as Blacks, were not only excluded from the public sphere, but even when some were brave enough to mount legal challenges to their exclusion and subordination they lost. The legal exclusion of women because of their gender, as was the legal exclusion of Blacks because of their race, is highly significant. The very institutions of power in the society sanctioned the oppression of women as it did the oppression of Blacks. As O'Connor goes on to note, even the ratification of the Bill of Rights in 1791 did little to change the prevailing state of affairs about the legal status or rights of women (ibid., 33). This was because the scope of the Bill was limited to the federal domain. States had jurisdiction over the political and legal rights of their citizens. And they drew largely upon British common law that "gave women few property or contractual rights" (33). It was only after the adoption of the Thirteenth, Fourteenth, and Fifteenth Amendments to the United States Constitution that women, like Blacks, were guaranteed certain individual liberties throughout the nation. These were liberties that states could not abridge.

I will conclude this section with a few remarks about my generic use of the term "women." I have used the term "women" in a blanket sense, cognizant of the discussion of the politics of representation that has informed Black feminist discourses going all the way back to Sojourner Truth, Anna Julian Cooper, and others.[16] In particular, Black feminists have raised questions about the hegemony of White women in feminist movements, especially the use of White women's experiences of gender oppression as the norm of all *women's* experiences, much as whiteness was used in enlightenment discourse as the norm for humanity. (I take up the latter issue in chapter 6.) The issue here is that White women benefit as much from the racial privileging of whiteness as do White males, and even subscribe to the racial caste system in the society, yet they universalize their experiences of gender exclusion from the public sphere as *the* experiences of all women.

Black feminist critics therefore have called attention to the fact that Black women, unlike their White counterparts, experience a twofold oppression. First, Black women experience racial oppression *because they are Black*, and so are subject to the normative gaze that transforms them, like all Blacks, into objects of denigration, vilification, hatred, and violence. Second, they experience gender oppression, because they are females in a society that is patriarchal and structured around male privileging. Because of this twin characteristic of their oppression, therefore, Black women's experiences are not only markedly different from those of White women, but also, and more importantly, their experiences are unique. And precisely because of this uniqueness, the generic term "women's experiences of oppression" is a misnomer, for it elides that uniqueness by suggesting erroneously that all women's experiences are similar.

Bearing in mind the nature and complexity of the issues of representation, (in the sense of "Whose experiences constitute women's experiences?"), I have used the term "the experiences of women" in a sense that allows for appropriate adjustments that reflect the uniqueness of Black women's experiences.

Implications for West's Proto-Marxian Outlook

The foregoing sketch of the experiences of Blacks and women amply shows that in each of the economic, political, and social spheres, both groups were systemically excluded from the institutions of power in the society through which individual self-worth is measured. The society therefore had to be forced, through protests and other measures, to accept the reality of Blacks and women as persons whose existential rights as well as basic civil rights had to be recognized. Race- and gender-based affirmative action policy, even despite its imperfections, was a recognition and acceptance of this fact. This is the reason for the race-and gender-defining attributes of the current affirmative action policy. And Cornel West is fully aware of this. So to propose as he does an alternative class-based affirmative action policy is to ignore the peculiarity of the experiences of Blacks and women that led to the current policy. In other words, West's alternative proposal is out of step with the distinct and peculiar experiences of Blacks and women, experiences that shaped the current affirmative action policy. Because of this, his proposal, notwithstanding its advantage of being more inclusive than the current policy, is at variance with the motivations behind Black and women's demands for social justice.

Besides being out of step with the experiences of Blacks and women, West's class-based proposal implies either (1) that the race and gender exclusionary practices that necessitated the current policy have been resolved and as such there is no need for affirmative action that is specific to race and gender; or (2) that race and gender concerns can be resolved through class considerations. The first alternative is clearly at odds with West's general position on oppression. His various discussions bear ample evidence that women and other minorities are still struggling against oppressive practices in the society. Thus the implication in question is purely accidental.

This leaves us with the second alternative. In light of my previous discussion (Chapter Three), it is this position that reflects and is consistent with West's proto-Marxian outlook. Yet this alternative is reductivist, simplistic, and false. As I showed in discussing West's view of social justice, oppression manifests itself in a variety of ways. These include race, ethnicity, class, gender, religion, sexual orientation, and so on. One form of oppression cannot be reduced to another, nor can the variety of ways in which oppression occurs be reduced to a single form. This is Iris Marion Young's point in the essay "The Five Faces of Oppression" to which I called attention in my examination of West's view of the Black quest for social justice (Young 1990, ch. 2). Granted my discussion, West is therefore wrong in believing that race and gender oppression can be reduced to class oppression so that a resolution of the latter is also a resolution of the former. Yet it is this simplistic and false answer to oppression that underlies his advocacy for a class-based affirmative action policy as a panacea to social injustice in its multifarious forms.

Still, some may object to the race and gender focus of affirmative action on the ground that lower-class White males also, that is, those who did not own property, were excluded by the very power structure that excluded minorities and women. Thus, the critics may say, race- and gender-based affirmative action policy historically has discriminated against lower-class White males and for that reason is unjust. But this objection fails to take into account the fact that affirmative action is a remedial measure of the society specifically targeting a structural problem of racial and gender oppression. Saying that race and gender oppression is structural entails that the oppression is embedded in the very institutional structure and apparatus of power in the society. It follows from this view that, although a particular individual or group of White males may not consciously and directly have taken any specific action that targets Blacks and women as such, yet, by virtue of the membership of such males into the dominant social group around which revolves power in the society and that oppresses Blacks and women, they therefore are participants in the entire oppressive system. At the very least, they enjoy some of the benefits of a conjunctive racial and gender privileging enjoyed by members of their kind, that is, those who similarly are both White and male within the societal structure, and who are vested with decision-making power and authority. And it is precisely these benefits enjoyed by lower-class White males, even if on a trickle-down basis, that are denied Blacks and women. Thus, race- and gender-based affirmative action cannot be an injustice against them. Indeed, the claim that the current affirmative action is unjust toward lower-class White males implies that lower-class White males are innocent victims of the policy. But, if my argument thus far is sound, both this claim and its implication are anything but correct. A victim is a person who is made to suffer undeservedly, and hence unjustly, for an action the she or he did not commit or for a practice in which she or he did not participate either directly or indirectly. But it is precisely this claim that I have challenged as false. The issue of suffering or victimhood, let alone one that is undeserved, does not even apply and does not even make sense in this context.

But suppose, for the sake of argument, one grants that lower-class White males were (and continue to be) excluded from the power structure that excluded (and continues to exclude) minorities and women from the social mainstream. Still, it does not follow that they are (and have been) oppressed *in the same way* as Blacks and women. Historically, lower-class White males may not have belonged to the property-owning class, but in principle, because of their race, they were admissible into this class *if they fulfilled certain other requirements* (in this case class). To illustrate, if a White male member of the lower class happened to acquire property he automatically became a member of the economic class and so was accorded the relevant rights and privileges deemed appropriate to his membership. But the same could not be said of women and Blacks. They could not even in principle be eligible for entry into the mainstream. By law women, because of their gender, were disallowed the right to own property or even to be admitted into certain professions, and by law Blacks, by virtue of their race, were themselves property prior to emancipation. (And a property is not of the kind that could own property any more than one color can characterize another!) To be sure, such policies do not exist at present. However, varying oppressive practices exist in more subtle, nefarious, and invidious forms. One such form is popularly known as the "glass ceiling syndrome." This is when an establishment has recruited a minority or woman but also has adopted an unwritten policy that limits the individual's professional ascent in the establishment. Another example of a contemporary exclusionary practice is when a business or educational establishment claims to diversify the workplace or student body by recruiting minorities and women but unofficially imposes a limit on the number of minorities and women it is willing to recruit.

Besides, as I have already noted, after Black emancipation from slavery and during Reconstruction, lower-class White males benefited as much from the very White racial- and male-gender-biased superstructure that discriminated against Blacks and women as their middle-class counterparts who created and maintained White male dominance in the society. Recall the deceptive and nefarious practices of labor unions, in complicity with capital owners, to exclude Blacks from the social mainstream. Thus, there scarcely can be a doubt that lower-class White males were just as involved in the oppression of Blacks and women as their middle-class counterparts.

Because, then, lower-class White males were (and in my view continue to be) active participants in the oppression of Blacks and women, contrary to how they usually are presented, they therefore are not victims of affirmative action in any intelligible sense even despite their *lower* class status. In other words, the attempt to remedy the injustice that Blacks and women have suffered over the years does not imply any kind of victimization of lower-class White males in any manner whatsoever. I take this to be the thrust of some defenses of the current affirmative action such as Boxill's.

Finally, since it is in virtue of their *class membership* that lower-class White males are deemed oppressed, qua lower class, affirmative action is therefore wholly irrelevant to their oppression or its amelioration. Again, affirmative action was formulated to remedy the systemic and institutional exclusion of Blacks and women from the socioeconomic mainstream *because of their race and gender*. As I have argued, historically, lower-class White males always have been part of that mainstream. Their race and gender ensured them a place there. Because their oppression is not of the kind that women and

Blacks have continually faced in society, it is not clear how affirmative action victimizes them—not unless it is assumed that they have the right of first refusal to jobs, college admission, and the like. Thus, it is very misleading to suggest, as does the objection, that affirmative action promotes social justice for Blacks and women at the expense of lower-class White males who themselves are victims of oppression. Such a view reduces all forms of oppression to the economic, with the consequence that a resolution of oppressive practices against a particular set of victims is ipso facto discriminatory against victims of *another* set of oppressive practices. But this consequence is false precisely because the antecedent condition on which it is grounded assumes wrongly that the experiences of the different sets of victims of oppression are identical. Granted my discussion, race and gender oppression is very different from class oppression. So too are the experiences of the victims. And so too must be the amelioration of the problem(s).

The significance of the peculiarity of the experiences of African Americans, in particular, going as far back as slavery is at the heart of Bill Lawson's essay "Moral Discourse and Slavery."[17] Lawson calls attention to the impoverishment of the English language in lacking a specific term that designates and captures the uniqueness of African American experience of oppression going as far back as slavery. Lawson has in mind the equivalent of a term such as "The Nazi Holocaust" that captures the peculiar experiences of Jews in Nazi Germany during World War II. For Lawson, such a term would be significant in giving expression to the uniqueness of the oppressive experiences of African Americans and to articulating an argument with moral suasion that will evoke a Humean sympathetic appreciation for African American advocacy of remedial programs to offset the legacy of slavery. Lawson characterizes this linguistic void as a lexical/functional gap in the English language and goes on to argue that it is this void that explains societal failure to appreciate (both intellectually and emotively) the gravity of the legacy of slavery on the descendants of former slaves. Consequently, society at large fails to grasp the necessity for social remedies to enable the victims of the legacy of slavery to overcome the psychological and social constraints imposed on them by the very institutional structure of the society over a long period of time. Moreover, says Lawson, it is this failure that motivates opposition to remedial programs such as affirmative action that were intended to redress the legacy of past inequities on African Americans. Lawson's point, in other words, is that society at large is not evil or mean; rather, society has failed to understand, both intellectually and emotively, the impact of slavery on African Americans precisely because of the lexical/functional gap in language. Thus, if this gap is filled by some term that is adequate to the task, the ordinary individual would empathize with the victims of that legacy and so would support programs aimed at redressing such a grave moral issue.

Lawson's position undoubtedly presupposes the existence of good faith in and by the dominant society at large. And some may wonder about the reliability of such a presupposition, considering the frequency and intensity with which some members of the dominant society have mounted legal challenges, sometimes successfully, to affirmative action, one of the hard-fought gains of the 1960s. Thus, critics may say that if we used the most simplistic form of inductive reasoning, we should be led to believe otherwise than Lawson is suggesting. In short, we have strong evidential basis to believe that such good faith as is presupposed by Lawson will not be forthcoming from the dominant society.[18]

Even as I sympathize with this skeptical view, I am inclined to adopt the principle of charity, nonetheless, and to agree with Lawson on this issue if only because language serves a variety of uses in addition to stating or reporting facts, a point well noted by Bishop George Berkeley.[19] As Berkeley aptly puts it, language can be used for, among other things, "the raising of some passion, the exciting to or deterring from an action, [and] the putting the mind in some particular disposition; to which the former [i.e., the mind] is in many ways subservient" (1965, sect. 20). Indeed, the emotive use of language is perhaps the most powerful in conveying human experiences and in eliciting from others a sympathetic reaction. Thus, a battery of terms may be needed both to undo the anti-Black racism that has permeated the language in which Blacks have been (mis)represented and to undo the damaging effect of such representation on the psyche of Blacks. But most importantly, such a vocabulary will have the emotive force of occasioning sympathy in others hitherto opposed to remedial measures such as affirmative action aimed at Blacks because it will adequately and succinctly capture the peculiarity of the situation of Blacks in the society.

However one may elect to receive Lawson's point, it does highlight the fact that social issues, especially those concerned with the distribution of societal benefits and burdens and with an eye to moral equity, are not formulated in the abstract. The formulation of policies that deal with such issues, especially in the context of competing interests, requires that one attends to and shows an appreciation for experiences that are unique to groups (or individuals). It is against the backdrop of such understanding that one should approach the subject of affirmative action and any other distributive measures. And I have focused on the specific issue of the unique experiences of African Americans and to some extent women to show that those experiences clearly argue against West's class-based affirmative action proposal as a remedy to social injustice. To be sure, West's proposal, as I have indicated, is consistent with his professed humanism. However, it elides the peculiar experiences of the very people whose victimization by oppressive practices constitutes the cornerstone of the current affirmative action policy. And this is precisely the reason I believe his class-based proposal is out of step with Black (and women's) demands for social justice. To repeat, it was (and is) because of race, not class, that Blacks were (and continue to be) excluded from the socioeconomic and political mainstream of society. Accordingly, it was to this phenomenon of institutionalized racial exclusion, at least insofar as Blacks were concerned, that affirmative action was addressed.

It may perhaps be suggested in West's favor that the reason he advances a class-based position is that he wishes to have extended to the growing Black underclass those benefits that middle-class Blacks have enjoyed under affirmative action. The current affirmative action policy has benefited middle-class Blacks who had been poised to enter college and the workplace but who, because of their race, were institutionally excluded. With the walls of exclusion legally down because of race- and gender-based affirmative action, the entry of this group into the socioeconomic milieu has been relatively smooth. However, this has left out a substantial number of Blacks who have not had the advantages of education and economic wherewithal to enter the social mainstream. Since it is by virtue of their class that this group has been left out of the socioeconomic mainstream, the argument might continue, an affirmative action policy with a focus on class will be much more germane to ameliorating the dismal condition of this group than does the current policy. Thus West is quite right in proposing as remedy to this situation the alternative type of affirmative action policy that he does.

There is certainly some validity to the argument that the current affirmative action policy has not benefited the Black underclass. But the argument begs the question that it is by virtue of their class that the Black underclass is left out of the social mainstream. One question to ask is: "Why is it that underclass Blacks lack the educational, social, and economic opportunities that otherwise should enable them to enter the mainstream of the society?" It is surely circular to answer that it is their class membership that prevents them from having the necessary opportunities for entry into the mainstream. Such an answer is tantamount to the tautology that it is their underclass status that makes this group an underclass. We already know that an underclass by definition is a group that is outside of the social and economic mainstream of society. So, to tell us that it is their underclass status that keeps the Black underclass out of the social mainstream is both trivial and unhelpful.

Perhaps a more fruitful answer is that it is because of their race that the Black underclass is shut out of the social mainstream and hence that prevents them from gaining any benefits of the current affirmative action policy. To show that this answer is not farfetched, consider again my argument in support of the claim that affirmative action has been deliberately (and sometimes accidentally) misconstrued as preferential treatment of unqualified Blacks over qualified Whites. If in light of this argument affirmative action is problematic even for middle-class Blacks who are minimally qualified for positions—for this is the basis of virulent anti-affirmative action campaigns—then it stands to reason that those Blacks who are *unqualified* because of lack of education and skills do not stand a chance of having the benefits of affirmative action extended to them. And they are the Black underclass. But the reason the members of this class are denied educational and other opportunities that otherwise should capacitate them for entry into the social mainstream is simply and unequivocally their race. The issue here is racial unprivileging of Blacks and racial privileging of Whites. By this I mean the denial of opportunities for upward social mobility to Blacks *because they are Black*, in contrast to the availability of such opportunities to Whites *because they are White*. It is this phenomenon that explains the disproportionate number of Blacks that comprise the underclass even as the overall population of Blacks is only 12.3 percent of the entire society.[20]

My contention, in short, is that in a society in which the distribution of societal benefits and burdens is highly racialized, the size of the Black underclass is disproportionate relative to the size of the overall Black population precisely because of the racialization of the very distribution process itself. Thus, the key societal problem is not affirmative action but the very racialized attitudes that infect the entire distribution process, including the distribution of opportunity for entry into the social mainstream. Indeed, it was the policies that were shaped by these racial (and gender) attitudes that in turn necessitated race- and gender-based affirmative action as a corrective measure. Given the prevalence of these attitudes and the social injustice they still engender, it is race- and gender-based affirmative action, not one that is class-based, that will provide effective remedy. Thus, West's proposal misses the cause of the inequities in the society and so fails as a solution to the problem of social injustice.

Conclusion

In this chapter I have advanced a critique of West's view of a class-based affirmative action policy as a solution to social injustice. West's alternative proposal is an extension of his professed proto-Marxian outlook. However, I have shown that this outlook is problematic because of, among other things, its narrow, reductivist conception of oppression. On this account, West presents race and gender oppression as consequences of the maldistribution of societal resources when in fact it is the cause of the very inequities in question at least insofar as Blacks and women are concerned. And because of this approach he mistakenly thinks that a class-based affirmative action policy is an effective remedy to social inequities. I have challenged this position by showing that it fails to respond to the historical conditions in which the lived realities of Blacks and women have been circumscribed. I have argued that these conditions were (and are) the proximate cause of affirmative action. West's proposal, on the other hand, is a response to a belief that he has of an egalitarian world in which all of humanity is to live happily. While that belief may be important to West because it upholds his professed humanism, I have argued nonetheless that it is wholly irrelevant to the oppression of Blacks and women in society.

It would be entirely missing the point to argue that the current affirmative action policy has drawbacks, hence any other policy is preferable. The point is about an issue of social justice the grounds of which are *the peculiar experiences of a select group of people*. The nature of these experiences precludes West's brand of affirmative action as remedy. This, I submit, is a major constraint on his proto-Marxian outlook on affirmative action. Better still, I have defended the current race: and gender-based affirmative action policy over West's proposed class-based alternative. I have grounded my argument on the premise that there is an entrenched White male supremacy in the society, of which West if fully aware but which he overlooks in his discussion of affirmative action. It is therefore fitting that I amplify this premise, especially as the issue it raises pertains to Blacks and the subject of social justice.

CHAPTER SIX

Modernity, Philosophy, and Race(ism)

Introduction

Those who are familiar with the philosophical writings of West are aware of the centrality of modernity to his thought, especially in his advocacy of social justice.[1] Although modernity is the period between 1688 and 1789, its significance can be traced all the way back to Columbus' adventure into the New World in 1492. This is because Columbus' sojourn inaugurated European expansionism and the denigration and oppression of people of color both through African slavery and, later, colonialism.[2] What does not fully emerge in West's discussion, however, is a sufficiently detailed account and penetrating analysis of the central role of modern philosophical icons such as John Locke, David Hume, Immanuel Kant, and Georg Wilhelm Frederick Hegel in shaping the discourse on race and the oppression of people of color. To provide a historical context for the oppression of people of color, in the sense of slavery and colonialism, and hence a context for our concern with righting those wrongs, requires more than a general account of the intellectual climate upon which such oppression was founded. It requires also giving prominence to those philosophers whose views helped in no small measure to shape the discussion of the issues that subsequently got translated into the public policies that affected people of color. In my view, West does not give as much prominence as he might otherwise to those philosophers; as such, he fails to bring out the implications of their

views for the oppression of people of color and thus for contemporary discussions of social justice.[3]

I find this inadequacy in West's historicism troublesome for two
reasons. First, as a philosopher whose focus is on modernity, West is
aware that the discipline of philosophy, to adapt an expression of
Kant, is the queen of the humanistic studies in the sense that philosophy, through its practitioners, helps to influence public policy.[4] It is
incumbent therefore on any scholar, but especially a philosopher,
who undertakes to historicize those factors that helped to create and
sustain the oppression of people of color to examine the role of
philosophers in particular in the entire phenomenon. Such an examination, when carefully undertaken, will exhibit at least the inconsistency between the high ideals professed by some of our iconic
philosophers, especially in the area of morals, and their practice.
Second, if West had given more attention than he does to the role of
modern philosophers in the oppression of people of color, he would
have shown that his ethical concern with social justice is a direct and
targeted response to an epoch that was strongly influenced by those
philosophers.

My proposed aim in this chapter, therefore, is to augment West's
discussion of modernity by foregrounding the views of some of the
key philosophers in question on the subject of race and hence discussions of the oppression of people of color. Such a historical sketch
will serve to reinforce my claim about the ethical basis of West's concern with social justice. Of course, to those already familiar with the
subject nothing that I may say here, especially in the first two sections, is particularly new.[5] Still, in elaborating the views of some
modern philosophers on the subject of race, I will have shown that
those philosophers may have significantly influenced the climate
against which Black demands for social justice are to be seen than
often is acknowledged. In this regard, I simply will have added my
voice to an ongoing discussion on the subject.

From Raciology to Racism and White Supremacy: A Survey

In the context of the history of Western philosophy, modernity rep-
resents the period between the sixteenth and eighteenth centuries in
Europe, the period generally referred to as the Age of Reason or the
Age of Enlightenment. During this period human reason supposedly

reigned supreme in that human beings deployed their reason to examine and unravel the data of sense in a bid to acquire knowledge of their immediate environment, viz. the universe. Thus we learn of, among other things, the great scientific revolution ushered in by such intellectual giants as Francis Bacon (1561–1626); Sir Isaac Newton (1642–1727), the great English mathematician and physicist; Johannes Kepler (1571–1630), the German astronomer and physicist; and many others. As Crane Brinton states, "The enlightenment man tended toward a simple view that the agent of progress is the increasingly effective application of Reason to the control of the physical and cultural environment."[6] In philosophy, the concern of the period was largely epistemological, or the quest for knowledge. We hear of René Descartes' search for certainty in innate ideas of the mind and of a similar but empiricist quest by John Locke in positing atomistic sensation upon which to ground all knowledge claims.

One subject also of putative and intense scientific curiosity during this period was (what is now called) raciology. This is the systematic study, characterization, and classification of the varieties of man. In speaking of *man* instead of *human* I wish to signal that this distinction turned out to be significant for the phenomenon of trans-Atlantic slavery than has been recognized by philosophers and therefore should not be minimized or overlooked in discussions of the intellectual climate of the period under consideration. I shall elaborate the distinction and bring out its implications for the issue of social justice later. For the present, it is only pertinent to observe that raciology commenced as a scientific inquiry. It was premised on the supposed observable physical differences among the varieties of man, and on the basis of those differences racial categories were created. Thus, among the various categorizations of man in "The God-Given Order of Nature" by the Swedish Carl von Linneaus, we find the following:[7]

1. Wild man. Characteristics: four-footed, mute and hairy.
2. American (i.e. Native American). Characteristic: copper-colored, choleric, erect. Hair: black, straight, thick; nostrils: wide; face: harsh; beard: scanty; obstinate, content, free; Paints himself with fine red lines; Regulated by customs.
3. European. Fair, sanguine, brawny. Hair: yellow, brown, flow-

ing; eyes blue; gentle, acute, inventive. Covered with clothes
vestments. Governed by laws.
4. Black. Phlegmatic, relaxed. Hair: black, frizzled; skin silky;
nose flat; lips tumid; crafty, indolent, negligent. Anoints himself
with grease. Governed by caprice. (Eze 1997b, 13)

Linneaus' larger aim in this work is to classify the varieties of
natural objects that fall under human scientific observation. In this
vein, he distinguishes four types of natural objects: minerals, vegeta-
bles, animals, and then man. My concern, however, is with his elaboration of the varieties of man. On one level, Linneaus seems to be
providing a lexicon of the various categories of man in terms of each
group's putative physical characteristics. On another level, however,
Linneaus begins to forge an association for each group between the
physical and the mental/psychological, as is evident in the adjectives
that he uses to *describe* the groups. For example, he characterizes
Blacks as "governed by caprice" and adds that Blacks are crafty,
indolent, and negligent. This characterization is in contrast to
Europeans whom he says are "governed by laws," sanguine, gentle,
acute, and inventive. A cursory glance at these characterizations
reveals Linneaus' use of value-laden expressions (or value judgments)
such as "crafty," "indolent," and "negligent" for Blacks and "sanguine," "gentle," "acute," and "inventive" for Europeans. Evidently,
these value judgments are subjective (or else cultural). Yet Linneaus
presents them as if they were objective facts of nature that science
has revealed.

Linneaus' classification and characterization are significant for
two reasons. First, they are supposed to reflect the God-given order
of nature. In other words, the very hierarchical arrangement of the
beings in question was supposed to have been ordained by God.
Second, Linneaus' task supposedly was descriptive, for it was putatively scientific. And all that science does is describe what is. Thus
Linneaus, qua scientist, was a revealer of that which God supposedly
has inscribed in nature.

Following in the footsteps of Linneaus is Georges-Louis Leclerc
(also known as Count de Buffon), who theorizes about the geographical and cultural distribution of mankind. Drawing upon the
classification Linneaus provided, Leclerc advanced the view that all

men originated from one and the same stock and that they migrated to various parts of the world. Thereupon, he says, geographical and climatic conditions, together with dietary habits, occasioned differences that then manifest themselves physically, and thus intellectually.

As with Linneaus, we find in Leclerc a radical distinction between European man, on the one hand, and non-Europeans (or "savages"), on the other. For Leclerc, the distinction was between the civilized and the uncivilized, wherein to be civilized implies having a certain kind of intellectual and physical endowment and to be uncivilized implies a congenital absence or deprivation of those endowments. Thus, in terms of intellectual endowments, Leclerc declares that the chief characteristic of "savages" is that "they never think." That is, they are incapable of thinking and are inherently stupid and ignorant; hence they lack arts and industry (ibid., 17–18). And in terms of the physical, he declares that "savages" "live miserably [and] are ugly and ill-made" (27). Of course, their manner of existence, for Leclerc, is a function of climate, geography, and dietary habits. Geographically, savages live in either of two extreme climates: too hot or too cold. But either way, the result is the same: stupidity (intellectually) and ugliness or physical deformity (physical). The nature of the non-European and the manner of his or her existence is in sharp contrast with that of the European, of which Leclerc says the following:

> The most temperate climate lies between the 40th and 50th degree of
> latitude, and it produces the most handsome and beautiful men. It is
> from this climate that the ideas of the genuine colour of mankind,
> and of the various degrees of beauty, ought to be derived. The two
> [other] extremes are equally remote from truth and from beauty. The
> civilized countries situated under this zone, are Georgia, Circassia,
> the Ukraine, Turkey in Europe, Hungary, the south of Germany, Italy,
> Switzerland, France, and the northern part of Spain. The natives of
> these territories are the most handsome and most beautiful people in
> the world. (26)

Bearing in mind the foregoing distinction between Europeans and non-Europeans, let us return to the concept of raciology with which I started. In the sense in which I defined that term, namely, as the systematic study, characterization, and classification of varieties of man, there is nothing wrong with raciology as a scientific inquiry. After all, science brings to our attention things hitherto hidden and unknown. In this sense, science simply discovers brute facts in nature. Moreover, as an empirical discipline, science does not make (or better still, ought not to make) any value judgments about the things it supposedly reveals. Accordingly, if raciology is a science, as was professed by its practitioners, then it simply should reveal brute facts about the supposed physical differences among entities of a particular kind. But it is precisely because raciology, through its practitioners, imputes psychological characteristics to groups based on what it deems the physical; makes normative and aesthetic judgments about groups based on the practitioners' judgments about those groups' physical characteristics; and, most importantly, creates a hierarchy of the groups—a hierarchy grounded on a supposed correlation between the psychological, normative, and physical—that it ceases to be a scientific enterprise and becomes instead a racist and White supremacist *ideology*. It is the fundamentals of such an ideology that are explicitly affirmed in Linneaus' and Leclerc's elaboration of the varieties of man and in the latter's explanation of the diversity of races. Still, it may be asked, why is this discussion of raciology relevant to the study of modern philosophy and especially to the issue of social justice?

Modern Philosophy and the Sanctification of White Supremacy

Raciology elaborates varieties of man, but it was the philosophers of the period who then proceeded to make use of some of the central ideas found in raciology to distinguish between the concepts *man* and *human* (or person) and to give that distinction social significance. The distinction between *man* and *person* first appeared in Book II, Chapter 27, of John Locke's *An Essay Concerning Human Understanding*, the discussion of the problem of personal identity.[8] Simply stated, the problem of personal identity is of specifying the conditions for reidentifying an entity as one and the same over a period of time cognizant that the entity has undergone change. In the philosophical literature this problem is known as accounting for identity through change. For Locke, this was a metaphysical enterprise, but it was significant for its axiological consequences. Locke wanted to answer this question to address an issue of social and ethereal justice, namely, the conditions for ascribing rewards and punishment to *persons* both here and in the hereafter. He thus begins by distinguishing between the application of the concepts *man* and *person,* restricting the term 'man' to the physical form of an entity and the term 'person' to that which is incorporeal, called the soul. Moreover, the soul is characterized by consciousness in the sense of reason and reflection; hence, it is rational.

More perspicuously, for Locke the referent of the term "man" is the collection of those physical features that characterize body *but which are organized in a particular way, specifically in terms of shape.* Thus, he says, "whoever should see a creature of his own shape or make, though it had no more reason all its life than a cat or a parrot, would call him still a *man*; or whoever should hear a cat or parrot discourse, reason, and philosophize, would call or think it nothing but a *cat* or a *parrot*" (1894, II, 445–446, emphases in the original). On the other hand, the referent of the term 'person' is *an incorporeal self-conscious entity that is endowed with reason and reflection.* Or, as Locke states, a person is a

thinking intelligent being, that has reason and reflection, and can consider itself as itself, the same thinking thing, in different times and places; which it does only by that consciousness which is inseparable from thinking and . . . essential to it. (II, 448–449)

This definition of the term 'person' is significant because it limits the term 'person' to an entity capable of reasoning and affirming self-identity. Indeed, Locke will go on to tell us that the term 'person' is "forensic," meaning that it is used in the context of "appropriating actions and their merit," and thus to designate "only intelligent agents, capable of a law, and happiness, and misery" (ibid., II, 466–467). The upshot of this distinction between the terms 'man' and 'person' is that, for Locke, questions about identity are to be answered differently in respect of the kind of entity with which we are dealing at any one time. Because the terms 'man' and 'person' designate two different *kinds of entities,* questions about the identity of man are to be answered differently from questions about the identity of person. Given this view, Locke answers the question about the conditions for ascribing identity through change to *persons,* saying that it is self-consciousness over time (known in the literature as the memory criterion) that should be used.

It is not obvious that Locke drew the distinction between man and person with the express aim of categorizing people of color, but particularly Blacks, as men but not as persons (or humans).[9] However, whether by coincidence or not, it is curious that this distinction appears again in Kant's writing (see note 8) and became significant for rationalizing the enslavement of Africans. Indeed, it is particularly instructive that Hegel later will use self-consciousness as the defining psychological feature that distinguishes humans from animals, but particularly humans from "animal man," as he goes on to call Africans. My contention, then, is that Locke drew a distinction that turned out to be pivotal to the characterization of Africans (and generally Blacks) as less than human or persons especially by later philosophers such as Hume, Kant, and Hegel, but particularly for the institution of chattel slavery. A brief discussion therefore is in order about the views of Hume, Kant, and Hegel on the subject of race, especially their views about Blacks. Concerning Hume and Kant, in particular, it is noteworthy, to begin, that on issues of epistemology, ethics, and even political philosophy, these two philosophers are diametrically opposed to each other.[10] However, there is no opposition between them on the subject of the supposed racial superiority of Whites and racial inferiority of Blacks. On this matter they were in agreement, with Kant endorsing the view of Hume. This agreement itself is quite telling. I shall begin with Hume's view.

Hume's explicit and unambiguously racist view of Blacks is presented in his essay "Of National Characters." His principal concern in this essay is to elaborate upon and account for the variety of character features (or manners) of different nations. Hume, characterizing himself as the empirical scientist of morals, comparable to Isaac Newton in the natural sciences, claims to observe that the Swiss, for example, are reputed to be more honest than the Irish, that the French display more gaiety and wit than the Spanish, and so on.[11] Hume then attributes national characters to what he describes as moral causes, namely, sociopolitical, economic, and other relevant factors, and he rejects the view that physical causes, as expounded by Leclerc and others, are causally efficacious in the formation of national characters. It is in this context that he proceeds to record in a footnote, as an afterthought, his famous (or notorious) observation about the Negro and all other species of men (i.e., non-Europeans):

> I am apt to suspect the negroes and in general all other species of men (for there are four or five different kinds) to be naturally inferior to the whites. There never was a civilized nation of any other complexion than white, nor even any individual eminent either in action or speculation. No ingenious manufactures amongst them, no arts, no sciences. On the other hand, the most rude and barbarous of the whites, such as the ancient Germans, the present Tartars, have still something eminent about them, in their valour, form of government, or some other particular. Such a uniform and constant difference could not happen, in so many countries and ages if nature had not made an original distinction between these breeds of men. Not to mention our colonies, there are negroe slaves dispersed all over Europe, of whom none ever discovered any symptoms of ingenuity; though low people without education will start up amongst us and distinguish themselves in every profession. In Jamaica, indeed, they talk of one negroe as a man of parts and learning; but it is likely he is admired for slender accomplishments, like a parrot who speaks a few words plainly. (quote in Eze 1997b, 33)

Unlike Leclerc, who attributes the diversity of the races, and therefore what he deems the putative physical and psychological differences of the varieties of man, to geographical, climatic, and dietary causes, Hume claims that racial diversity and its supposed correlative psychological differences are the original stamps of nature. Whereas Leclerc has espoused a White supremacist ideology as a contingent outcome of other contingent facts, such as geographical location, climatic factors, and dietary habits, Hume has now made a bold leap to affirm that the supposed psychophysical correlation is an inviolable law of nature. The hierarchical ordering of the races is now complete and fully established, at least with a philosophical stamp of approval, with the White explicitly declared "superior" and the rest, but especially the Black, as "inferior."

There can be no doubt that Hume's remark is well thought out and not a momentary aberration. He insists on this issue in accommodating, if only mildly, a query from James Beattie (1735–1803), his most formidable critic. Beattie had provided counterexamples to

Hume's assertion that all other (read non-European) nations or peoples lacked arts or sciences by citing the well-known empires of Peru and Mexico, and of the manufactures and arts of Africans and Native Americans. As Beattie puts it,

> The empires of Peru and Mexico could not have been governed, nor the metropolis of the latter built after so singular a manner, in the middle of a lake, without men eminent both for action and speculation. Every body has heard of the magnificence, good government, and ingenuity, of the ancient Peruvians. The Africans and [Native] Americans are known to have many ingenious manufactures and arts among them, which even Europeans would find it no easy matter to imitate. (ibid., 35)

And most importantly, Beattie goes on to generalize his critical observation about the intellectual current of the time, saying that it "seem[ed] to be a fundamental maxim with many of our critics and philosophers . . . [t]hat every practice and sentiment is barbarous which is not according to the usages of modern Europe" (36). In other words, Beattie is charging his contemporaries with what we now describe as Eurocentricism.

Hume's reaction to Beattie's objection and criticism is particularly noteworthy. In a later revision of the essay "Of National Characters," Hume makes a negligible modification to the sentence, "There never was a civilized nation of any other complexion than white . . ." by replacing the word "never" with the phrase "scarcely ever," so that the revised sentence reads: "There scarcely ever was a civilized nation of that complexion [i.e., Black], nor even of individual eminent in action or speculation" (ibid., 37). In other words, Hume is unimpressed by Beattie's counterexamples. What this shows is that Hume is unrelenting in his view of the racial superiority of Whites and the inferiority of Blacks even when confronted with evidence that should lead him to the contrary view. In short, he is being dogmatic in his validation or endorsement of the racial hierarchy created by raciology.

Interestingly, Kant later draws upon Hume's remarks about the supposed natural inferiority of Blacks and the superiority of Whites to dismiss as "stupid" a view of a Black man on the sole ground that the view's proponent was Black. The view in question, we are told, was supposedly about the different ways Black men and White men treated women. The Black man, a carpenter, is reported to have said to a Catholic Priest, Father Labat, "'You whites are indeed fools, for first you make great concessions to your wives, and afterward you complain when they drive you mad'" (ibid., 57). It is not significant for the present that we consider the sexism of the view. What is significant is Kant's response. At first, Kant seemed to give some credibility to the view, saying, "there was something to be considered" in the view. Then, with the realization that the view's proponent was Black, he immediately added "but . . . this fellow was quite black from head to foot, a clear *proof* that what he said was stupid" (57; emphasis added).

But Kant's dismissal is not just a casual statement. It is a "proof," a deduction, the force of which comes out most poignantly through a syllogistic formulation:

Take anything, x, in the universe; if x is both Black and man, then x is stupid.

(This individual) a is both Black and man.

Therefore (this individual) a is stupid.

Thus formulated, Kant's "proof" will have deductively, if trivially, established the stupidity of the Black man in question, for in the major premise of the argument the conjunctive properties of being black and being man are synonymous with (the property of) being stupid. Thus the relation between the antecedent and the consequent clauses is one of entailment. From this premise, then, and the minor premise that affirms the instantiation of the conjunctive properties claimed, the conclusion of the argument thus necessarily follows. But the "proof" is not just about the congenital cognitive deprivation of the Black man in question. It is true of every Black person by virtue of the universal scope of the major premise. Thus the Black carpenter simply instantiates *in concreto* the "truth" in the claim of the major premise.

It may be asked, however, on what basis Kant affirms the synonymy between blackness and stupidity, or, more generally, between skin color and cognitive features (of lack thereof). The answer, according to Emmanuel Eze, is found in Kant's lectures on practical anthropology and geography.[12] Practical anthropology, for Kant, studies the "inner" (read psychological and moral) features of an entity and (physical) geography studies the "outer" (read physical) features of the entity in respect to both its location in space and its subjection to the deterministic laws of nature. Practical anthropology conceives of the individual as a rational self-conscious entity, namely, one that establishes its own identity through time and is endowed with a rational will in virtue of which it conceives of itself as a moral entity capable of enacting moral laws and initiating choices and actions. It is in terms of these twin cognitive features of rational self-consciousness and a rational will that human moral agency is established. As we know from reading Kant's ethics, a moral agent is autonomous precisely because the will of such an entity is *the* source of morality, its motivational force not deriving from and hence not subject to external factors. Thus, such a will is self-determined. Kant, then, says Eze, consistent with the prevailing raciologist doctrine, takes whiteness to be nature's external stamp (or manifestation in the phenomenal world) of both the existence of rational self-consciousness and a rational will and blackness as the absence (or negation) of these twin cognitive characteristics.

But Kant does not construe the identification of skin color and cognitive features or their absence (formulated as a relation of synonymy in the syllogism above) simply as an empirical fact. For if the relation were empirically grounded, then it would be logically possible to discover (empirically) an instance of whiteness *and* cognitive deprivation and an instance of blackness and cognitive presence. And it is exactly such empirical oddities that he wishes to preclude. Rather, Kant takes the identity (or synonymy) to be metaphysically grounded as an a priori principle of thought in much the same way that he considers the principle of causation an a priori principle of reason. In other words, in the same way that there cannot be an exception in experience to the principle of causation—since the very possibility of experience presupposes the causal principle—so can there be no exception to the identity of blackness and cognitive deprivation or whiteness and cognitive presence. On this view, then, Kant's dismissal of the view of the Black man as stupid, meaning unintelligent, which follows his approving citation of Hume's challenge, is a much more forceful argument for Hume's position than

Hume himself offered because it is metaphysically grounded.[13] It is that argument I provided (or reconstructed) in the earlier syllogism.

Kant's view in the foregoing account may be astonishing, but it is not the most striking of his racism. Kant's most striking racist views are found in his articulation of the concepts of the beautiful and the sublime in his valuation system. For Kant, the beautiful and the sublime are feelings through which humans experience and express moral and aesthetic sensibilities. Through the feeling of the beautiful humans experience joy and through the feeling of the sublime they experience awe and reverence. These feelings are part of the ontological makeup or psychological fabric of humans, *as is the capacity to reason in accordance with laws*.[14] While for Kant aesthetic and moral sensibilities are present in one form or another in Europeans, they are however either substantially diminished or completely absent in non-Europeans. For example, Kant characterizes the (diminished) moral and aesthetic sensibilities of East (Asian) Indians as "a dominating taste of the grotesque." And he declares that their religion "consists of grotesqueries. Idols of monstrous form, . . . unnatural atonements of the fakirs (heathen mendicant friars) and so forth are in this taste" (ibid., 55). One would have thought that the very fact of a religious outlook at all, notwithstanding how it is expressed, is evidence of the presence of the feeling of the sublime (awe and reverence) in East Indians. But Kant does not think so, although he does so consider the religious practices of Europeans.

Kant's views are even more outrageous in respect to Negroes (i.e., Africans) and Native Americans. He says that these groups have not a tincture of moral and aesthetic sensibilities. "The Negroes of Africa," he declares, "have by nature no feeling that rises above the trifling" (ibid., 55). They have a religion, but it is a "religion of fetishes . . . possibly a sort of idolatry that sinks as deeply into the trifling as appears to be possible to human nature" (55–56).[15] Kant makes similar remarks about Native Americans (56).

When finally we turn to the writings of Hegel, we see that modern (or "enlightenment") philosophy reaches its crescendo in both the sanctification of racism and the unsanitized proclamation of White supremacy. Not only does Hegel establish a cultural divide between Europe and the rest of the world, especially sub-Saharan

Africa, but he also explains this divide both in terms of geographical location and a fundamental difference in nature between the European and the sub-Saharan African. Geographically, the axis of historical movement, he says, is the Mediterranean Sea (ibid., 121). And it is the Mediterranean that connects Europe with northern Africa. For Hegel, Europe is synonymous with (the source of) the great events that shape world history. However, the European is able to shape world history not simply because of the geographical location of the European continent relative to the Mediterranean, but, more importantly, *because the European is endowed with self-consciousness in which consists humanness or personhood.* Hegel takes self-consciousness to be the manifestation of Spirit (i.e., the divine mind) *in concreto.* Self-consciousness entails the awareness of oneself as inherently free—that is, as an agent that can affirm its self-identity and its capability of effecting change. This *awareness of oneself* as a free agent capable of originating change by means of one's voluntary actions is the ultimate constituent of one's humanness. Thus, for Hegel, there is a mutual entailment between freedom and self-consciousness. Or, more perspicuously in respect to White supremacist thinking, freedom (in the sense of agency), self-consciousness, and humanness are logically interrelated concepts that are concretely instantiated in the European.

The antithesis of the European is the sub-Saharan African. Indeed, Hegel says of sub-Saharan Africa both that it is not a part of world history and that it is not animated by the Idea of Spirit (i.e., of the divine mind). The "Idea of the spirit," he notes, "displays itself in reality as a series of external forms" (ibid., 110), that is, those events that shape world history. The Negro African, then, is not in reality of the kind that can be part of world history because he or she is devoid of self-consciousness or the distinctive attribute in virtue of which a particular type of thing, namely, humans, is an agent of change. Instead, the Negro African is *man as inscribed in nature.* In this condition, the African is "unfree and natural"; is at one with nature; and is a "creature of the senses" rather than a creature of the reason (110). This distinction between man and person loudly echoes that noted earlier in Locke's discussion of the concept of a person. In any case, Hegel takes lack of self-consciousness to be the natural condition of the African.

The significance of saying that the Negro African is not self-conscious is that the African has no concept of "any substantial and objective existence." In other words, he or she has no idea of anything that transcends his or her subjective existence. The kinds of things Hegel has in mind are God, the state, justice, and the like (ibid., 127). In light of this claim, Hegel thus declares that "man as we find him in Africa has not progressed beyond his immediate existence." And by this Hegel means that the African has not emerged into a human being, for to emerge into a human being is, he says, to conceive of oneself "in opposition to nature" (127). All of these considerations lead Hegel to conclude:

> All our observations of African man show him as living in a state of savagery and barbarism, and he remains in this state to the present day. The Negro is an example of animal man in all his savagery and lawlessness, and if we wish to understand him at all, we must put aside all our European attitudes. We must not think of a spiritual God or of moral laws; to comprehend him correctly, we must abstract from all reverence and morality, and from everything which we call feeling. All this is foreign to man in his immediate existence, *and nothing consonant with humanity is to be found in his character.* (127–28, emphases added)

The distinction between man and person that we first saw in Locke's discussion will have proven more useful now than Locke possibly could have anticipated or envisioned. This distinction enables Hegel to provide a retrospective justification of the enslavement and conquest of Africans, for European colonialism, and hence for the exploitation and oppression of people of color. After all, Blacks are not humans or persons; they are "animal man." Thus there cannot be any moral transgressions against them. As we saw in the preceding chapter, the issue of whether or not Blacks are humans was uppermost in Thomas Jefferson's mind when he contemplated both the prospects of emancipation of Blacks from American chattel slavery and, more importantly, of the social consequences of emancipation.

Significance of the Foregoing for Morality and Public Policy

The focus on the views of some of the key "enlightenment" philosophers, although brief and sketchy, is significant because it reveals a lineage (or continuity) in their thinking on the issue of the supposed racial inferiority of Africans and superiority of Europeans. The positions on race advanced by those philosophers deserve serious attention above all else because those positions supposedly were grounded in the metaphysical views they held.

Consider again the distinction between *man* and *person* that Locke advanced as a prelude to his discussion of personal identity. Since the essence of a person (or human being) is rationality, Africans are not considered humans given the general belief that Africans are not endowed with the rational faculty. Moreover, since self-consciousness is peculiar to persons qua rational beings, and it is in virtue of self-consciousness both that self-identity is established and that moral predicates are ascribable to or withheld from an entity, it follows that Africans are not moral entities because they are not self-conscious beings. Another way of expressing this point is to say that Africans have no concept of self-identity and a fortiori are ontologically incapable of conceiving themselves (or anything for that matter) as agents. Indeed, the implication of ascribing self-identity at all is that one can conceive of oneself as an agent. But it is precisely this conception of the *self-as-agent* that Africans supposedly lack. And the reason Africans lack such a conception is that they are deprived of the cognitive capacity both to acquire the concept of self-as-agent and to recognize its presence in the mind. (One is left to wonder, however, whether Locke takes the concept of self-as-agent to be innate even despite his virulent opposition to innate principles in Book One of the *Essay*.)

It follows from the foregoing view that, given Locke's distinction between the concept of a man and that of a person, together with the general current of raciology, Africans are not of the kind to whom moral predicates are ascribable. (Recall Locke's assertion that the term 'person' is forensic.) Instead, they are nonmoral entities like chairs, tables, and any other object. Africans, in short, are *things*. Significantly, this conception of Africans as things (or objects) was at the heart of chattel slavery. It does not matter that Africans have the physical makeup of man as did Europeans. The important point is that they lack self-consciousness, the distinctive characteristic that is required, according to the philosophers, to be designated human or person. Hegel puts it best in declaring that Africans have yet to emerge into human beings. But until such time when Africans do "emerge," they should be considered "animal man" (ibid., 127).

One consequence of characterizing Africans as "animal man" is that Africans cannot but *actually* live in a state of nature, perhaps in the crudest Hobbesian sense in which there are no possessions, no laws, and hence no rights, no justice, and so on. Indeed, these concepts simply do not apply.[16] The application of axiological concepts such as *law, government, property, rights, rewards, punishment, duty, obligation, good, bad, right* and *wrong,* and so on presupposes the existence of civil (as opposed to "natural") society. Only humans live in civil society, not animals and animal man. The latter exist in a state of nature. And it is for this reason that animals can be hunted down for their coat and even their flesh and can be subjugated through domestication. For the same reason, it seems, Africans (or animal man) can be enslaved either through kidnappings or through well-orchestrated "intertribal" wars comparable to cock fights. Apropos is Hegel's advice to Europeans to expunge all their sensibilities of God, justice, morals, and the like in their dealings with Africans. Little wonder that Hegel thought that colonialism would be good for the "savages." Perhaps he meant that colonialism might facilitate the "emergence" of Africans from the state of animal man to that of human. Nothing more therefore needs be said about Hegel.

Locke's concept of a state of nature of course is radically different from Hobbes's. But even so, as I will show presently, Africans do not fare any better—*as persons*—in a Lockean state of nature. On the contrary, they fare much worse than is often recognized. I shall begin by noting some important differences between Locke's concept of a state of nature and Hobbes'. According to Locke, all persons, qua rational beings, live in a state of nature prior to becoming members of civil society.[17] Unlike Hobbes, however, each individual is a free and independent being, fending for himself or herself and *possessing and exercising a natural right to life, liberty, and estate.* Locke characterizes this condition of existence as "a state of perfect freedom [in which men] . . . order their actions, and dispose of their possessions *and persons* as they think fit . . . without asking leave or depending upon the will of any other man" (1952, II. 4, emphasis added). It is also a state of "perfect equality, where naturally there is no superiority or jurisdiction of one over another" (II. 7).

In Hobbes's state of nature, by contrast, individual vulnerability to suffer harm is what characterizes existence, and it is the inherent fear of suffering harm and even death that compels humans to form political society. Moreover, life in a Hobbesian state of nature is extremely precarious because at any given moment the individual could be overrun. Not so, however, in Locke's. Even though all persons live in a state of nature, the original condition of existence prior to civil society, they are each under the governance of a law of nature. And this law prescribes that, in light of the natural equality of all as free and independent beings, "no one [therefore] ought to harm another in his [her] life, health, liberty or possessions" (ibid., II. 6).

Finally, a significant difference between Hobbes's state of nature and Locke's pertains to the notion of possession. For Hobbes, there is no ownership of anything in a state of nature, "no *Mine* and *Thine* distinct*," as Hobbes puts it, meaning that the concept of property just does not apply.[18] For Locke, by contrast, the individual has a natural right to his or her estate or possessions in a state of nature. And the principal estate, possession, or property to which each individual has a natural right is his or her "person." As Locke states, "every man [woman] has a 'property' in his [her] own 'person.' This nobody has a right to but himself [herself]" (ibid., V. 27).

Qualitatively, then, life in a Lockean state of nature is far superior and preferable to life in a Hobbesian state of nature, especially because of Locke's conception of rights in a state of nature and of individual subjection to a law of nature. Given Locke's concept of natural rights, therefore, it might appear that Africans, Native Americans, and Europeans all enjoy this bounty from nature, at least in Locke's view. But I think that this appearance is misleading and should be resisted because, on closer examination, Locke's theory would not apply to Africans. First, the possessors of natural rights are *rational self-conscious beings*. Since Locke has identified such beings as persons, and given that raciology has declared that Africans are bereft of reason and rationality, it would seem to follow that Locke's theory of natural rights is inapplicable to Africans. Besides, Locke does not say anything, at least explicitly, that suggests that he considers Africans as persons and hence as objects of natural rights. His very silence on this issue is quite telling, especially because he was fully aware of the African slavery and also of the raciologist doctrine.[19]

Second, in Locke's state of nature, reason is the faculty through which persons *recognize* both the existence of the law of nature and their subjection to it. But, again, recall that Africans supposedly are devoid of the rational faculty. This means not only that Africans are congenitally incapable of recognizing the law but also, and more importantly, that it does not even make sense to speak of the application of the (concept of) law to them. Only entities capable of recognizing the law, or who have the potential to recognize the law, in principle can be subject to it. This excludes Africans, given the view of raciology. Assuming that I am right, it immediately follows that, ontologically, Africans cannot be candidates for the ascription of natural rights in a Lockean sense any more than can trees and stones.

Third, through raciology and modern philosophy, Africans have been presented as a different *species*.[20] This position, together with Locke's restriction of the concept of natural rights to persons, entails that Africans are not (and cannot be) candidates for those rights. And there is no evidence that Locke's concept of natural rights admits of a transspecies application. It is instructive that, in Locke's view, violation of a person's natural rights in a state of nature warrants punishment of the transgressor (ibid., II. 7–12). It follows from such a view that only moral entities can be victims or transgressors in a moral sense, and hence can be subject to punishment or reward. Yet, for the reasons already given, these moral concepts would not apply to Africans.

The issue I am raising about the moral status of Africans (or its lack thereof) has important consequences for Locke's view of slavery. It is often overlooked that Locke's discussion of slavery is set within a *moral* context. Locke regards slavery as a form of *just punishment* exacted by a "lawful conqueror" against a captive who has "by his fault forfeited his own life by some act that deserves death" (ibid., IV. 15). In other words, slavery presupposes some grave wrongdoing in the first place, one that warrants the death of the perpetrator of the wrongdoing. The crucial concepts here are *punishment, lawfulness, fault, desert,* and *forfeiture*. These concepts apply only in a social (read moral) context. Thus, Locke, in speaking of slavery, has in mind slavery as a form of punishment for a moral infraction. The moral crime of the wrongdoer presumably is his or her opposition, perhaps, to being conquered in the first place. (Notice that the enslaved *person* is a captive of war.) What is significant, for Locke's purpose, is that the conqueror may choose to delay the death of his captive and instead retain the captive indefinitely in servitude. In this condition of servitude, the conqueror may choose to do whatever he deems fit with the captive, for he has "absolute, arbitrary and despotical power" over the latter (ibid., IV. 15–16). The only way the enslaved captive can put an end to his servitude and subordinate status, says Locke, is that, finding that "the hardship of his slavery outweigh[s] the value of his life, . . . [he resists] the will of his master to draw upon himself the death he desires" (ibid., IV. 15–16).

It is tempting to conclude from the situation of slavery thus described that Locke had in mind African slavery. After all, it may be said, African slavery was in existence at the time, so surely Locke must have been rationalizing such a morally abhorrent practice by inscribing it in a moral context. But I think that we should resist such a temptation. Given my claim that Africans are not persons even in Locke's state of nature, with the consequence that axiological concepts are inapplicable to them, it is doubtful that Locke had any thoughts about Africans in his discussion of slavery. The reason is that, for him, the objects of slavery are moral entities. Specifically, they are groups of *persons* engaged in a war and in which the stronger defeats the weaker and hence takes the weaker as captives. If I am right that, given the current of the time, Locke's concept of a person precludes Africans, then we should see his justification of slavery differently. Either it was aimed at the domestic institution and practice in Europe or it was aimed at justifying his "waste land" theory of property acquisition that involved the conquest of Native Americans and the seizure and development of their land.[21]

The position I am advancing, then, is that Locke's failure to condemn the African slave trade is far from accidental. It is a consequence of his disregard for Africans as humans or (persons). I confess that my contention is speculative and conjectural. But there is strong basis for such speculation and conjecture given the strong connection between Locke's epistemological and practical concerns. More particularly, since Locke's disquisition on personal identity and the concept of a person is aimed at resolving an axiological issue of ascribing rewards and punishment, such conjectural remarks as I have advanced about his silence on African slavery are therefore warranted. To repeat, my position is that Locke need not justify or condemn African slavery given the parameters of his discussion of slavery. At the same time, African slavery turned out to be most beneficial to his (and European) economic interests. He thus can have no moral qualms about the institution and practice of slavery when applied to Africans.

It is instructive that the issue concerning Locke and African slavery has puzzled scholars with little sign of a resolution. For example, Jennifer Welchman has contended that Locke justified African slavery but that such justification is consistent with his thesis that slavery is a just consequence of war and is punishment for a moral violation in a state of nature.[22] Harry Bracken has repudiated Locke's view of slavery as racist because it justified African slavery at all.[23] Bracken's argument is grounded on the distinction between primary and secondary qualities that Locke draws in *Essay* (II, VIII, 7–24). Bracken reminds us of Locke's claim that we do not know the real constitution of any given substance, the real power in the object that supposedly operates through the primary qualities and produces in percipients any of the *ideas* of the properties supposedly possessed by the object. What this means is that we are completely ignorant of the essences of things, including minds. Indeed, Locke remarked that even in our individual subjective cases we do not know the nature of the substance in us that thinks. All we know is that thinking takes place in us. And thinking is a quality (or attribute) that, like all other qualities, resides in substance. Since then we do not know the nature of the substance in us in which thinking inheres, Locke reasons, we therefore have no logical basis to preclude the possibility of matter being characterized by a substance that thinks.

Bracken construes Locke's discussion of primary and secondary qualities as a denial of real essences of things, including minds, and says that Locke's view leaves us only with nominal essences to make attributions such as cat, man, dog, and so on. And the construction and ascription of nominal essences are grounded on features such as color, smell, race, religion, sex, and the like—those characteristics that Locke himself had classified as accidental or secondary qualities of objects. But Locke, says Bracken, "does *not* want to treat these things as accidental" (1984, 42; emphasis in text). This is because it is on account of them that we can distinguish the various kinds of things we encounter and categorize or rank them into sorts. (See also Section III of Bernasconi 1992, 293–318.) Given the primacy of these features in Locke's system, therefore, together with Locke's antiessentialism, concludes Bracken, Locke's empiricist position very easily provides a basis for racism of the kind consistent with raciology.

Finally, Robert Bernasconi poses a question about the ontological status of Africans in Locke's social theory and of the bearing of this issue on Locke's silence on African slavery (ibid., 299 and 311; cp. 298). Bernasconi's concern derives from several correct observations he makes about Locke's views. First, he notes that there are certain "marked divergencies between the slavery Locke justified and the slavery that Locke invested in" (297). Unfortunately, Bernasconi does not pursue this distinction in detail, especially to connect it to what he correctly observes to be Locke's silence on the African slave trade. Second, Bernasconi notes that Locke nowhere mentions African slavery in his political writings. This failure is significant, especially because at the time Locke was secretary to the Council of Trade and Plantations, and, says Bernasconi, "would have known more about the internal workings of the slave trade more than many of his contemporaries" (295). But, continues Bernasconi,

> [t]here is no record that Locke ever entertained any doubts about the practice of African slavery. He owned two parcels of shares in the Royal African Company, and, at the age of 37, he had a hand in writing the Constitution of Carolina. . .The document included the clause, "Every freeman of Carolina shall have absolute power and authority over his negro (*sic*) slaves, of what opinion or religion so ever." Locke thereby helped frame one of the most extreme legitimations of the slaveholders' power over their slaves. The phrase "absolute power" was later employed by Locke in his discussions of slavery in the *Two Treatises of Government*. (295–296)

In consequence, Bernasconi notices a contradiction between the views Locke expresses in the *Two Treatises on Government* (about the inalienable rights of persons) and the *Fundamental Constitutions of Carolina* (about slaveholders having absolute power and authority over their Negro slaves.) It is this contradiction that motivates his concern about the ontological status of Africans in Locke's social ontology.[24]

Given such divergent perspectives, my position is therefore as much a suggestion as any other. However, I believe that the evidence favors my view because it apparently dissipates the palpable inconsistency that would follow upon Locke's ascribing personhood to Africans and at the same time tacitly or otherwise endorsing their enslavement, *especially since Africans were not at war with the Europeans*. Jennifer Welchman's attempt to reconcile what she supposes Locke's justification of the African slavery with the "just punishment" theory thus simply does not make sense. According to Welchman, Africans themselves were engaged in intertribal warfare and that was an abridgement of the Law of Nature. Thus, Europeans could visit punishment in the form of slavery to the perpetrators of crimes committed in a state of nature. This state of affairs is permissible under Locke's conception of a state of nature. As she says,

> [I]t would be sufficient cause to enslave a man in sub-Saharan Africa if he was known to have threatened at least one person or if he had tolerated or concurred in one such assault. It would not be necessary that the captor be the person attacked, nor would it be necessary that the captive remain in his captor's hands. Being property [a condition he attains as a result of his infraction], the captive might be sold, bartered, or given to whom ever his captor pleased—even Europeans. (1995, 79)

First, it never occurred to Welchman that African existence in a state of nature *as a brute fact* was a European invention that curiously coincided with European economic interests. Second, although it is true that Locke, Hobbes, Hume, and others theorized about the origin of civil society from an antecedent state of affairs that they each characterized as a state of nature, they never considered a state of nature as an empirical phenomenon. Instead, they conceived of it simply as a philosophical fiction, a logical starting point for their theorizings. Hume says as much in the *Treatise*.[25] So it is farfetched to posit such a notion just to make intelligible the enslavement of Africans within the parameters of Locke's discussion of slavery. The intelligibility that Welchman seeks is purchased at too costly a price.

I agree that Locke's view of slavery is consistent with his tacit endorsement of African slavery, but not for the reason Welchman gives. I take Locke's view to be consistent only because Locke does not consider Africans as humans and as such his theory of slavery does not apply to Africans. It is for this reason, I submit, that Locke does not have any compunction about the enslavement of Africans any more than he would about (say) the enslavement of animals. Indeed, on my account, it is even doubtful that the term 'slavery' as applied to Africans has the same import for Locke as it would when applied to persons. So, on this basis, I think Harry Bracken too is mistaken in thinking that Locke justified African slavery. And Bernasconi's concern is effectively addressed, for there is no contradiction after all between Locke's views in the *Second Treatise on Government* and the *Fundamental Constitutions of the Carolinas*. Furthermore, if it did not occur to Locke to justify African slavery, as Bernasconi speculates, then it was only because Locke did not think of Africans as human. As such, he did not consider it morally necessary to justify or even rationalize their (mis)treatment any more than one would think it a moral imperative to justify or at least rationalize one's mistreatment of animals.

Whether or not the position I have advanced withstands scrutiny will depend upon a more extensive and penetrating analysis of the relation between Locke's epistemological disquisitions and his practical concerns, which must await future research. Meanwhile, I can only conjecture, based on the limited evidence I have adduced, that although African slavery fell outside the parameters of Locke's discussion of slavery, it nonetheless proved very useful for Locke's and generally European economic enterprises. In this connection, Locke's silence on African slavery invites further speculation about possible decisions he may have made in his role as administrator in the English government. We know that Locke was secretary to the Council on Trade and Plantations in the British Administration.[26] This was an office that was entrusted with the task of ensuring the well-being of British colonial interests. According to Maurice Cranston, the Council was a "fact-finding, not an executive body, *and its secretary was for this reason a more important man than any of the councillors*" (1957, 153). Moreover, says Cranston, Locke was a very efficient secretary (153). Given that the Colonial Office was entrusted with the ultimate responsibility of procuring wealth for the metropolis, one is left to wonder what policy decisions Locke may have made that concerned African slaves. Such speculation is not unfounded when one considers Locke's role in the drafting of the constitution of South Carolina, especially when we also recall that he held shares in the Royal Africa Company, which was involved in the African slavery. Again, in light of this factor, should we then construe Locke's silence on African slavery as accidental?

Considerations similar to those that I have advanced against Locke, with appropriate modifications, apply to Hume and Kant. In the moral sphere, at least, there can be no doubt that Hume's moral ontology excludes Africans. First, the moral sentiments that Hume thinks peculiarly characterize humans and in virtue of which humans are moral entities and so can experience and express moral approbation and disapprobation would not apply to Africans.[27] Second, according to Hume, the activation of the moral sentiments in consciousness requires a complex excogitative and ratiocinative activity of cognitive reason. Recall, however, that Africans supposedly are devoid of the rational faculty. Thus, even if the moral sentiments were part of their ontological fabric, the lack of the rational faculty to activate those sentiments would mean that Africans would be incapable of experiencing and therefore expressing moral approbation and disapprobation.

On practical (read sociopolitical) issues, Hume also, as Locke, was an administrator in the British government. Specifically, he was secretary to the British Embassy in France in 1765, and in 1767 he became undersecretary in the Northern Department. This office was largely concerned with colonial affairs.[28] What role, if any, did Hume's view of Blacks have on his administrative functions in respect of British foreign and colonial policies, especially as concerns the Other? Richard Popkin has noted that Hume's view on race was central in American debates about slavery in the eighteenth century and that Hume, "was used as an authoritative supporter of slavery in an anonymous work, *Personal Slavery Established, by the Suffrages of Custom and Right reason.*"[29] Thus, it is fair to inquire about possible connections between Hume's "theoretical" disquisition on race and his practical/administrative activity as public official.

Finally we turn to Kant. As with Hume, Kant's view about the congenital *deprivation* of Blacks, cognitively and emotionally, obviously precludes Blacks as moral entities in his system. This is because a condition of being a moral entity in Kant's system is that a thing should be endowed with the cognitive faculty that capacitates it for *recognizing* the moral law. It follows therefore from the putative cognitive deficiency of Blacks, an ontological fact, that Blacks are precluded from being moral entities in Kant's system. Put otherwise, given their supposed cognitive deprivation, Blacks are absolutely incapable of formulating the categorical imperative and therefore the imperative does not apply to them.[30] This reading of Kant's view draws support from one of Kant's various formulations of the categorical imperative in the *Groundwork*: "Act in such a way that you always treat humanity, whether in your own person or in the person of any other, never simply as a means, but always at the same time as an end" (1964, 96, emphases deleted). This formulation is the conclusion to Kant's explication of the idea that the objects of morality, namely, rational beings, are always ends in themselves and therefore at all times should be treated as such. As Kant states, "man, and in general every rational being, *exists* as an end in himself, *not merely as a means* for arbitrary use by this or that will: he must in all his actions, whether they are directed to himself or to other rational beings, always be viewed *at the same time as an end*" (95; emphases in the original). On the subsequent page, Kant proceeds to identify rational beings as "*persons*," and adds that it is the distinctive attribute of personhood that "marks them [i.e., persons] out as ends in themselves" (96; emphasis in text). Saying that persons are ends in themselves means not only that persons "ought not to be used merely as a means," but also, says Kant, that persons are "object[s] of reverence" (96).

Given Kant's view of the objects of morality and also his deprecating remarks about Blacks, it is clear that Blacks are not ends in themselves, and hence not objects of reverence. And the reason they are none of these things is that they are not persons or humans, notwithstanding Kant's remarks to the contrary. Kant claims that although Negroes and Whites are of different races, they "are not different species of humans" (quoted in Eze 1997b, 40). But if this claim were true, then the categorical imperative should apply to Blacks as it does to Whites. I have raised doubts about the applica-

bility of the categorical imperative to Blacks within the context of
Kant's discussion. Thus, at the very least, Kant is inconsistent.
Indeed, the severity and gravity of Kant's anti-Black racism comes
out very clearly in the context of his grandiose moral pronouncements about how persons, qua rational beings, ought to treat each
other. Because then these pronouncements do not apply to Blacks,
for Blacks are not members of Kant's moral ontology, Kant could
offer prescriptions on how to brutalize Blacks.[31] African American
and Afro-Caribbean experiences of the brutality and inhumanity of
slavery bear witness to the success and effectiveness of Kant's views.

To sum up, the thrust of my discussion thus far is best captured
by the following generalized remarks of Ella Shohat and Robert
Stam:

> For many European philosophers, Black intelligence was perpetually
> on trial. Non-Europeans were called on to prove, for example by
> writing, what other races were granted as a birthright: their intelli-
> gence and humanity. The point is not that philosophers like Hume or
> Kant were *only* racists, or that they had nothing of value to say; but
> rather that racism, like sexism, came from the very heights of philo-
> sophical modernity.[32]

Implications of "Enlightenment" Philosophy for West's Concern with Social Justice

My discussion of modern philosophy on the specific subject of race
is significant for West's engagement with social justice because it
inscribes the issue West raises within a philosophical context. In particular, it highlights the contribution of key modern Western philosophers to hegemonic White supremacist intellectual practices that
assault the cognitive (intellectual and moral) as well as aesthetic features of Blacks in particular and people of color in general. Since
Black oppression derives from such assaults, in the form of supposed
"truths" about Blacks, the present study thus provides a backdrop
for understanding West's concern with White supremacy as *the* cause
of Black oppression in contemporary society, and hence his preoccupation with social justice. After all, we are still living the legacy of
the "enlightenment" discourse on race and its attendant practices.
White supremacist ethos and the simultaneous denigration of Blacks,

in particular, permeate the social and institutional structures within which the lived reality of Blacks is circumscribed. If my reading of West as a humanist is correct, it is against those structures in society that his advocacy for social justice is aimed.

To be sure, West sometimes seems to vacillate between the view of the preeminence of White supremacy as the chief cause of Black oppression and the claim that all forms of oppression derive from lack of ownership of capital. And his Marxian inclination more often than not leads him to favor the latter. However, I have repeatedly contested this view. My position gains added support from West's very own assertions about the role and significance of White supremacist practices in the oppression of people of color. His assertions about White supremacy would seem to suggest that Black oppression derives in the main from the pervasive, subtle, and structural, even if less formal, hierarchization of races in the society at large. And the present social arrangement of the races that is played out in terms of White privileging and Black subordination is the legacy of raciology and White supremacy as validated by iconic "enlightenment" philosophers. West does recognize this phenomenon, but he fails to give prominence to the pivotal role of celebrated "enlightenment" philosophers in sanctioning White supremacy and hence in shaping public policies that are virulent, rancorous and unsanitized forms of anti-Black racism. It is the prominence that West fails to give to the views of enlightenment philosophers in his articulation of the White supremacist thinking and culture within which to situate Black oppression that I have provided in this chapter. In so doing, we come full circle to the intellectual foundations upon which the present social dynamics are grounded, namely, White supremacist thinking and practices that are the target of West's concern with social justice.

West, Public Intellectualism, and the Harvard Controversy

The Politics of Scholarship

Having just examined the scholarship of Cornel West, with special attention to his discussion of social justice, it is rather ironic that I now should be remarking on appraising his scholarship *as a public intellectual.* Yet such comments as I am about to make are necessary in light of recent events at Harvard University.

According to various press reports, there is a feud between West and Harvard president Lawrence Summers, over the nature of West's recent scholarship. Specifically, Summers is alleged to have summoned West to his office and chastised West for West's "non-traditional scholarly pursuits which have included a rap CD (*Sketches of My Culture*) and West's association with a possible presidential run by the Rev. Al Sharpton."[1] Daniel Golden of the *Wall Street Journal* noted, however, that Summers chastised West for "pursuing outside interests rather than scholarship."[2] And reporting supposedly the same meeting between West and Summers, the *Chronicle of Higher Education* claims that Summers told West "to get busy on a major scholarly work and spoke of taming grade inflation."[3]

We have here three different versions of a "private meeting" between Summers and West (Wilson and Smallwood 2002, A8), that somehow was made public. But the fact that the meeting was private at all makes it all the more difficult to ascertain the facts of the matter. What is indisputable, however, is that the meeting has given rise

to a rift between the two men, and by extension between Summers
and Harvard's Afro-American Studies department. And although
Summers is reported to have characterized the matter simply as a
"misunderstanding," West is said to be alleging that he has been disrespected, "dishonored," and "devalued" (A8). It is reasonable to
conclude from West's own characterization of his *feelings* about the
nature of the meeting that he must have taken a dim view of
Summers' remarks about his scholarship, since the meeting was
indeed about his recent forays as a public intellectual. Of greater significance in all this is that the conflict is said to have "raised concerns
about academic freedom and affirmative action" (A8). For others,
the conflict derives simply from Summers' "efforts to tighten scholarly standards [at Harvard] and rein in the Afro-American studies
department" (A8). Yet, others who have traditionally been highly
critical of West and the Harvard Afro-American Studies department
have taken full advantage of the conflict to intensify their criticisms.[4]

The *Chronicle* has cast the issue in terms of (1) the propriety (or
lack thereof) of a president to comment on the scholarly output of a
tenured faculty and (2) the role of public intellectuals in the academy.
But I think this formulation of the issue is correct only in respect of
(2) and not of (1). In other words, I do not consider it an issue that
a president can evaluate the scholarship of a faculty. Quite the contrary, it is within the right of a university/college president to evaluate the credentials, including the scholarship, of faculty. That
presidents often do not exercise that right to the hilt is beside the
point. The fact is that they can choose to exercise it and in so doing
they are functioning within the parameters of the governance system
of the academy. Moreover, the exercise of that right is all the more
warranted when the faculty is a university professor, such as West,
and is directly answerable to none but the president.

Some critical questions that arise, however, when a president
elects to exercise her or his right to evaluate a university professor
are as follows: What criteria does she or he use to evaluate the faculty? Suppose the president is not an expert in the faculty's field, and
so becomes dependent on the judgments of others, through a peer
review system, to make her or his evaluation—how does she or he
select the peer reviewers? What input, if any, does the faculty member have in the selection process?

The pertinent issue, then, concerning presidential evaluation of the scholarship of a faculty member is the mechanism that she or he employs in the evaluation. It is not an issue about the right to evaluate a faculty member, as some might be tempted to think. The matter of evaluative mechanism becomes all the more significant when the faculty member whose scholarship is under scrutiny is a public intellectual, such as West. And here the relevant question is: What constitutes the scholarship of such an individual? Concerning West, in particular, how should one construe his political involvement and social activism, the latter manifested in various ways *including* the production of a rap CD, given his self-definition as a public intellectual? These are the questions that are implied in and by the *Chronicle's* formulation of the issue in terms of the role of public intellectuals in the academy. And it is to these questions I now turn.

Public Intellectualism as Legitimate Scholarship

To begin, consider that a public intellectual is, by definition, one whose scholarship is oriented toward analyzing and resolving some concrete sociopolitical reality that pertains to the public at large. Such a scholar is engaged not only in esoteric thinking. Rather, she or he conceives of scholarship instrumentally, in the sense of being aimed at addressing concrete practical issues in society, so that even her or his esoteric thinking has practical utility. It is in this light we see scholars like Emerson, Dewey, Martin Luther King Jr., Jefferson, Locke, and those other "enlightenment" thinkers whose views on raciology and society I examined earlier.[5] Does West fit in this category?

The answer is absolutely, decisively, and incontrovertibly yes. At the risk of overstatement and overgeneralization, this has been the central focus of my analysis of West's philosophical engagement throughout this work. In particular, we saw this in my application of West's doctrine of prophetic pragmatism to his claim about the nihilistic threat to Black America. It is such practical application of theoretic disquisition that again informs his—in my view mistaken —Christo-Marxian, anticapitalist prescription for social justice, and much more. And we again saw that West's sociopolitical engagement is informed by a humanistic endeavor in which West sees the individual as pitted against certain oppressive societal forces that stifle existential freedom and thus from which the individual is to be liberated. These forces may be economic, political, religious, intellectual, and even cultural. Thus the evidence is overwhelming in favor of West's pragmatic scholarship. And it is in this light that we should view his recent forays into politics and music. That is, West's ventures into politics and music-making are ways to put into practice the viewpoints that he advances as a public intellectual and as a humanistic scholar. And he does this by affiliating with individuals and institutions that are linked *directly* to the public and that he believes can give concrete meaning to those views. Indeed, it is the goal of a public intellectual to deploy ideas to transform society. Both West's involvement with the presidential aspiration of the Rev. Al Sharpton and his use of popular culture through rap music to reach a mass audience are consistent with this goal. These are transformative practices.

If I am right in so construing West's recent forays into politics and music as emblematic of his public intellectualism, then I do not think that President Summers has the latitude to dismiss or disregard West's excursion into those practical areas as pseudoscholarship. At most, what he can do is to weight them relative to other (read "traditional" and esoteric) scholarly enterprises. And it may well be that this is what he has done, and that the weighting is not favorable in West's estimation. That is, Summers has given a low value to such activities relative to "traditional" scholarship, and West considers such weighting demeaning or an affront to his overall scholarship.

This way of construing the problem draws support from the very manner in which some of the major newspapers have reported the incident. Recall that the *Chicago Tribune* reported that West was chastised for his "non-traditional *scholarly* pursuits" (emphasis added), and gave as examples West's involvement with Al Sharpton and the rap CD. The *Chronicle* says that Summers admonished West "to get busy on a *major* scholarly work" (emphasis added), thereby implying that West's recent scholarly work has been minor. Only the *Wall Street Journal* claimed that Summers admonished West for pursuing outside interests *rather than* scholarship. Of course, it is possible that the *Wall Street Journal* may be right and that Summers disregards West's *seemingly extracurricular* activities as scholarly. But, then, because the discussion between West and Summers was private, there is no way of adjudicating the matter. So it is safe to assume that Summers does consider West's sociopolitical involvement as scholarship, albeit nontraditional, and thus has evaluated it as he thinks fit.

Such characterizations of scholarship into so-called traditional and nontraditional, and the evaluation attendant thereto, have given rise to certain kinds of questions in the academy: First, who decides what is scholarship? Second, what is the end (or goal) of scholarship? And third, how does one evaluate ideas and points of view that, although of an academic nature, are not presented through traditional academic media such as books, monographs, and journal essays? The issue here, in short, is about the politics of scholarship within the academy. I cannot thoroughly examine such problematic issues here. Indeed, they deserve to be treated very seriously and in more depth than I can in these few pages. However, I will offer some tentative suggestions that indicate the direction of my thinking on such matters and hence, in my view, how to evaluate the scholarship of West as a public intellectual.

Traditional Scholarship and Insurgency Politics

The academy, like all social institutions, undergoes change. But it does so most reluctantly and with more resistance than many. Indeed, it tries to protect and preserve an arcane culture, much in the manner of medieval scholars who, through their institutions, desperately resisted scientific explanations of natural phenomena. Medieval scholars were the custodians of "truth," and so would brook no challenge to their sanctified authority. It is in a similar vein that the contemporary academy is resistant to change.

Traditionally, except for the sciences, art, music, and drama, scholarship has been limited to an analysis of ideas found only in print or in any other written form. It makes no difference that such scholarship has little relevance to addressing matters pertaining to the human condition, or only does so remotely. It may be acceptable if scholarship had such social consequence, but it need not necessarily be so aimed. Thus, the relation between traditional scholarship and society as such is merely contingent. Such scholarship is thought to have authority both because of its esoteric nature and because it is limited to its initiates (or members). Initiates are exclusively those who happen to have successfully gone through the rituals of prescribed intellectual engagement and thus can appreciate the esoteric subject matters(s). And those members turn out to be the custodians of the intellectual culture. They decide what constitutes scholarship and who are its practitioners. Any form of intellectual activity that deviates from the "norms" that they have prescribed is therefore nonscholarly or at best only marginally scholarly.

However, contemporary social movements, especially those of marginalized groups, through insurgency politics, have been challenging both this narrow view of scholarship and the culture that sustains it. Since exclusionary practices are largely the result of ignorance and bigotry, marginalized groups began to demand that the experiences of their members be represented in academic studies. Thus we have the inauguration of Black studies, women's studies, and gay and lesbian studies, to name a few, as well as the emergence of professional organizations representing those groups whose experiences are to be included in academic studies. The obvious goal of such studies is to effect social transformation in making academic studies meaningful to the society. And since the 1960s, the academy has reluctantly accommodated these new areas of scholarship. That is, the academy has recognized as legitimate the *content* of such studies.

But another area of academic frontier war concerns the very medium through which putative scholarly ideas can be presented and transmitted. In other words, should a putative scholarly text include music such as rap CDs, film, sports, and the like? Does not such a conception of text conflict with the sense in which the academy traditionally has understood the meaning of "text"? Furthermore, how is such "text" in the nontraditional sense to be evaluated? It is in the larger context of these questions that we should see the conflict between Summers and West, with Summers representing the "traditional" view of scholarship and West the nontraditional, "insurgency/instrumentalist" view. But, in essence, this is an ideological conflict, and it is not new to the academy.

Now, while West's use of the medium of rap music is consistent with his pragmatic and humanistic view of scholarship, it is not clear to me that he would wish his involvement in politics to be construed as scholarly. The latter is nothing short of social activism, and such activism is clearly not identical with scholarship. The Rev. Jesse

Jackson, Al Sharpton, and others are social activists, but they are not scholars. Of course, social activism may result from, and concretely express, one's scholarly endeavor, and this is what I think is true of West's social activism. But social activism is not scholarship, and I do not think that either West or Summers wishes to claim that it is.

Unlike his political involvement and other forms of social activism, however, West's use of rap music as a scholarly medium is defensible. I say this because both the content of his rap CD and the efficacy of a musical medium as scholarship can be evaluated. Indeed, it has been claimed that the CD, *Sketches of My Culture*, is a "series of academic lectures" that West has put into musical form to reach a wider audience.[6] And a scholar such as Joanne Detore-Nakamura said she had "eagerly awaited the CD for use in . . . [her] classroom" as part of her pedagogy.[7] Thus, if West conceives of himself as a teacher-scholar, which, by all indications he does, and so is concerned as much about pedagogy as about "traditional" scholarship, then there is no argument that he would take umbrage at any aspersion at his scholarly endeavors and approach. And such umbrage would be justifiable.

Moreover, it was by virtue of his scholarship, both traditional and nontraditional, that Harvard recruited West from Princeton in 1994 in the first place.[8] And West has consistently maintained that intellectual pursuits should have practical (read social) relevance. Recall his indictment of Black intellectuals, saying that they are useless to the community. This is why he is a self-styled pragmatist much in the manner of Dewey. Thus, to question or even unfavorably weight his scholarship as Summers is alleged (or perceived) to have done is to challenge the very essence of West's conception of his vocation as a scholar. Little wonder that he says that he feels devalued, dishonored, and disrespected. By contrast, Summers may conceive of scholarship in the "traditional" sense, and so is unwilling to accommodate any other sense of scholarship.

Resolution: Redefining Scholarship

What conclusions then can one draw from the Harvard controversy? First, that the conflict simply epitomizes a major ideological conflict about the very concept of scholarship, text, and related matters in the academy, in light of various forms of insurgency politics, all of which view the aim of scholarship as social transformation. Because this issue has reared its head in the walls of Harvard, the academy as a whole will now be forced to take a very serious look at it.

Second, in my view the academy will have to recognize the value of scholarship that is aimed at social transformation and to devise appropriate mechanism to evaluate such scholarship. It is precisely because there is no appropriate mechanism to evaluate such scholarship that people like West and Summers may be at cross-purposes on such a matter. And the lack of a mechanism to evaluate so-called nontraditional scholarship is that the academy is reluctant to recognize such scholarship in the first place. But the academy no longer can afford to ignore the issue. It will have to address it.

Finally, concerning the specific issue between Summers and West, I will venture to suggest that West undoubtedly has the edge. The reason is that West has decisively and overwhelmingly established himself as both a "traditional" and "nontraditional" scholar. Concerning the former, one needs only to consider such books as *The Ethical Dimensions of Marxist Thought, The American Evasion of Philosophy,* and *Post-Analytic Philosophy,* among others, to show that he need not justify himself as a scholar in any way whatsoever. In other words, if the measure of scholarship is esoteric material, then he has an abundance to validate himself.

On the other hand, need scholarship be esoteric? This is the kind of question to which West is responding in his conception of himself as public intellectual. Given his conception of scholarship as instrumental to social transformation qua pragmatist, existentialist, and humanist, West thus selects what he deems an appropriate medium to convey his scholarly ideas. The academy may be reluctant to consider such medium as scholarly, but the matter is debatable. And the conflict between West and Summers may well have instantiated that debate. But, in my view, West's scholarship as a public intellectual has a very favorable rating.

NOTES

Introduction

1. The only extended studies on West's philosophy thus far are Mark David Wood, *Cornel West and the Politics of Prophetic Pragmatism* (Urbana and Chicago: The University of Illinois Press, 2000), and George Yancy (ed.), *Cornel West: A Critical Reader* (Malden, MA, and Oxford, England: Blackwell Publishers, 2001). But these do not make social justice their primary focus.

2. See Plato, *Republic,* 2nd ed., ed. G. M. A. Grube, rev. C. D. C. Reeve (Indianapolis and Cambridge, England: Hackett Publishing, 1992); and Aristotle, *Nicomachean Ethics,* in *The Basic Works of Aristotle,* ed. Richard McKeon (New York: Random House, 1941).

3. John Rawls, *A Theory of Justice* (Cambridge, MA: Harvard University Press, 1971), pp. 3–21; cp. 60–65.

4. See, for example, the following essays by Marx: "Alienated labor," "Private Property and Communism," and "The Communist Manifesto," in *Karl Marx: Selected Writings*, ed. Lawrence H. Simon (Indianapolis and Cambridge, England: Hackett Publishing, 1994).

5. Peter Osborne (ed.), *A Critical Sense: Interviews with Intellectuals* (London and New York: Routledge, 1996), p. 128.

6. See George Yancy (ed.), *African-American Philosophers: 17 Conversations* (New York: Routledge, 1998), pp. 32–33.

7. Cornel West, *Prophecy Deliverance! An Afro-American Revolutionary*

Christianity (Philadelphia: The Westminster Press, 1982); and *The American Evasion of Philosophy: A Genealogy of Pragmatism* (Madison: The University of Wisconsin Press, 1989).

8. Cornel West, *The Ethical Dimensions of Marxist Thought* (New York: Monthly Review Press, 1991).

9. See, for example, the following essays by G. E. Moore: "A Defense of Common Sense" and "Proof of an External World," both in *Contemporary Analytic and Linguistic Philosophies*, ed. E. D. Klemke (New York: Prometheus Books, 1983); and "Some Judgments of Perception," in *Perception, Sensing and Knowing*, ed. Robert J. Swartz (Berkeley, Los Angeles, and London: The University of California Press, 1965), ch. 1.

Chapter I

1. For discussions of Cornel West's conception of his pragmatism, among other things, and West's replies to his critics, see, for example, the following essays in the American Philosophical Association's *Newsletters on the Black Experience, Computer Use, Feminism, Law, Medicine & Teaching*, vol. 90, no. 3, (fall 1991); Konstantin Kolenda, "The (Cornel) West-Ward Vision for American Philosophy;" Elizabeth V. Spelman, "Theodicy, Tragedy and Prophecy: Comments on Cornel West's *The American Evasion of Philosophy*"; Robert S. Corrington, "The Emancipation of American Philosophy"; and Robert Gooding-Williams, "Evading Narrative Myth, Evading Prophetic Pragmatism: A Review of Cornel West's *The American Evasion of Philosophy*." An expanded version of Gooding-Williams' essay has been published in *The Massachusetts Review* (winter 1991–1992): 517–542.

2. Besides these two philosophical movements, which reigned in Europe in the seventeenth and eighteenth centuries, nineteenth-century Hegelian idealism in Germany also spilled over into England and engaged philosophers such as F. H. Bradley and J. E. McTaggart. In America, a leading proponent of idealism was Josiah Royce. Essentially, idealism is concerned with giving an account of the nature of reality.

3. Richard J. Bernstein, "John Dewey," in *Encyclopedia of Philosophy*, ed. Paul Edwards (New York and London: Macmillan, 1967; rpt. 1972), Vols.1–2.

4. For example, in his contribution to the *Inlander*, a Michigan student

magazine, Dewey speaks derisively of the academy and academicians as follows (quoted in West, *The American Evasion of Philosophy* [Madison: The University of Wisconsin Press, 1989], p. 82):

> The monastic cell has become a professional lecture hall; an endless mass of "authorities" has taken the place of Aristotle. *Jahresberichte*, monographs, journals without end occupy the void left by the commentators upon Aristotle. If the older Scholastic spent his laborious time in erasing the writing from old manuscripts in order to indite thereon something of his own, the new scholastic has also his palimpsest. He criticizes the criticisms with which some other Scholastic has criticized other criticisms, and the writing upon writings goes on till the substructure of reality is long obscured.

5. West's sympathy with Dewey, on a generous reading, could be seen in the context of his own political strategy of forming alliances and coalitions to address social issues. But on a less than generous reading, West's defense of Dewey may be construed as a defense of his own attempt to draw upon (sometimes) antithetical positions to resolve problems in the society—e.g., the Black underclass issue—with the consequence that such an attempt creates a dilemma that he cannot resolve. I take up this issue later in this chapter in my discussion of West's proposed solution to the afflictions of the Black underclass.

6. Elsewhere, West describes prophetic pragmatism as an attempt to revise "Emerson's concerns with power, provocation, and personality in light of Dewey's stress on historical consciousness and Du Bois' focus on the plight of the wretched of the earth" (*Evasion*, p. 212).

7. Cornel West, *Race Matters* (New York: Vintage Books, 1994).

8. West's characterization of the problem confronting Black youths, especially in the urban centers, as nihilistic has been challenged by Eric Lott in "Cornel West in the Hour of Chaos: Culture and Politics in Race Matters," *Social Text* (fall 1994): 39–50.

9. Immanuel Kant, *Groundwork of the Metaphysic of Morals*, ed. H. J. Paton (New York: Harper and Row, 1964), p. 96.

10. I take up the subject of affirmative action in chapter 5.

11. Cornel West, "Philosophy and the Urban Underclass," in *The Underclass Question*, ed. Bill E. Lawson (Philadelphia: Temple University, 1992), p. 196.

12. Cornel West, *Prophetic Fragments* (Trenton, NJ: New Jersey: Africa World Press, 1988), p. 42, emphasis added.

Chapter 2

1. Cornel West, *Keeping Faith* (New York and London: Routledge, 1993), p. 71.

2. For accounts of humanism, see the following: Paul Kurtz, "What Is Humanism?" in *Moral Problems in Contemporary Society*, ed. Paul Kurtz (Englewood Cliffs, NJ: Prentice Hall, 1969), pp. 1–14; Corliss Lamont, *The Philosophy of Humanism*, 7th ed. (New York: Continuum Publishing, 1990); Nicola Abbagnano, "Humanism," in *The Encyclopedia of Philosophy*, Vols. 3–4, ed. Paul Edwards; and F. C. S. Schiller, "The Definition of Pragmatism and Humanism," in his *Studies in Humanism* (Freeport, NY: Books for Libraries Press, 1907; rpt. 1967). My account of humanism as a philosophical position is based largely on Kurtz's discussion.

3. Kurtz (1969) goes on to sum up humanism as "an attempt to enoble and enrich human life, whether in individual terms as each human being satisfies his [her] ideals and dreams, or in social terms, where we seek to develop rules and norms of justice" (5).

4. See Cornel West, "Prophetic Theology," in *The Kairos Covenant*, ed. Willis H. Logan (New York: Friendship Press, 1988), 115. It is to be remarked that West characterizes the essays that comprise *Prophetic Fragments* (Trenton, NJ: Africa World Press, 1988) as his "response to one basic question: How does a present-day Christian think about and act on enhancing the plight of the poor, the predicament of the powerless, and the quality of life for all in a prophetic manner?" (xi).

5. West points out that the new cultural worker is not necessarily a marginalized member of society. On the contrary, she or he may be among the very privileged elite either by birth or by some other kind of social phenomenon. Yet, even despite the privilege that she or he enjoys, such a worker, through a Humean sympathetic consciousness, identifies with the predicament of the so-called Other, and so aligns herself or himself with the Other in challenging the status quo. Dewey showed a similar sympathy with the underclass of nineteenth-century America.

6. I have narrowed my discussion of the new cultural politics of difference to Black challenges of White hegemonic practices because, as will soon be seen, West criticizes the early Black response to such practices and I have doubts about the veracity of his criticism.

7. This endeavor may be described as the historical ancestor of the new (read contemporary) cultural politics of difference. Minus the anachronism one could even say that the early Black response constitutes at the very least the intellectual challenge that West suggests a practitioner of the new cultural politics of difference should meet.

8. It is curious, even if beside the point, that West does not identify the critics to whom he is referring. In his discussion of the art of Horace Pippin (*Keeping Faith*, ch. 4), he directs his criticism at the protagonists of the Harlem Renaissance. He denounces the Harlem Renaissance, calling it a

> self-complimentary construct concocted by rising, black, middle-class, artistic figures to gain attention for their own anxieties at the expense of their individual and social identities, and to acquire authority to impose their conceptions of legitimate forms of black cultural productions on black America. (62–63)

West accuses the protagonists of the Harlem Renaissance of the crime of denigrating the art of the ordinary self-taught Black folk (e.g., Horace Pippin, etc). And, for West, the alleged denigration consists in the characterization of the art of the ordinary folk as an expression of "primitivism" because the artists lacked formal training. In so characterizing their art, charges West, those champions of the Harlem Renaissance meant both to distance themselves from the "uncouth" Black artists and to call attention to themselves as the sophisticated "new" Negro whom the White establishment should find acceptable. It is very likely that West has the same group of cultural workers in mind in his discussion in the essay "The New Cultural Politics of Difference." In any case, it suffices for my purpose that West's criticism may apply to individuals as diverse as Alain Locke, W. E. B. Du Bois, James Weldon Johnson, George Schuyler, and Richard Wright. For an account of the politics of Black representation in the arts, see, for example, Abby Arthur Johnson and Ronald Maberry Johnson (eds.), *Propaganda and Aesthetics* (Amherst: The University of Massachusetts Press, 1979), esp. chs. 2, 3, and 5. I consider later the veracity of West's criticism.

9. By the expression "broader in extension" I mean that the number and kinds of things that are subsumable under the concept *genus* are wider than those subsumable under the concept *species*.

10. Roy D. Morrison II, "Self-Transformation in American Blacks." In *Existence in Black,* ed. Lewis R. Gordon (New York and London: Routledge, 1997), p. 38.

11. The publication of J. Herrnstein and Charles Murray (eds.), *The Bell Curve: Intelligence and Class Structure in American Life* (New York: Free Press, 1994), is proof of this claim.

12. See John Reed and Clive Wake (eds.), *Senghor: Prose and Poetry* (London: Heinemann, 1976), pp. 34–35. For a sympathetic reading of Senghor's view see Abiola Irele, *The African Experience in Literatures and Ideology* (Bloomington and Indianapolis: Indiana University Press, 1990), ch. 4, esp. pp. 76–78. John Mbiti's view is expressed in his *African Religions and Philosophy* (London, Ibadan, and Nairobi: Heinemann Educational Books, 1969). For discussions of Mbiti's view see George Carew, "A Critique of John S. Mbiti's Traditional African Ontology," *Quest: An International Journal of African Philosophy*, vol. 8 (June 1993): 170–89; and my "An Analysis of John Mbiti's Treatment of the Concept of Event in African Ontologies," *Quest: An International Journal of African Philosophy*, vol. IX, no. 25 and vol. X, no. 1 (1996): 139–157.

13. See West, *Prophetic Fragments,* p. 42 and my discussion of West's observation in the previous chapter.

14. See Cornel West, "On Christian Intellectuals" (in *Prophetic Fragments*), pp. 271–272.

15. This distinction underlies West's preference for Dewey's form of pragmatism over those of Emerson and Pierce (see *The American Evasion of Philosophy* [Madision: The University of Wisconsin Press, 1989], 5–6). For West, Dewey was an organic intellectual. West gives Martin Luther King, Jr., as another example. He says that King "linked the life of the mind to social change." See his "Martin Luther King, Jr.: Prophetic Christian as Organic Intellectual" (*Prophetic Fragments*, 3–12). In this essay, West illuminates the intellectual and existential influences on King's prophetic vision for social change.

16. In general, faculty in Black institutions are often saddled with very heavy teaching loads, they often lack the necessary research and support facilities to pursue scholarship, and their remuneration and benefits are anything but congruent with the demands on their time. It would thus be quite fair to say that they are often demoralized.

17. West gives as examples of musical legends Louis Armstrong, Sarah Vaughn, Charlie Parker, and Nat King Cole and preaching in figures such as the Rev. Manuel Scott and Gardner Taylor (*Keeping Faith*, 73).

18. I suggest that this is the reason Black institutions do not gain support from the Black community, especially the Black middle class, and not that (as West claims) the paucity of Black infrastructures for intellectual activity "results . . . from" the inability of blacks to gain respect and support from the community (*Keeping Faith*, 71). It is the other way around.

19. bell hooks and Cornel West, "Black Women and Men: Partnership in the 1990s," in *Breaking Bread: Insurgent Black Intellectual Life*, ed. bell hooks and Cornel West (Boston: South End Press, 1991), p. 15.

20. See Lewis Gordon, *Her Majesty's Other Children* (Lanham, MD: Rowman and Littlefield, 1997), p. 194; cp. 200–201.

21. Gordon mistakenly thinks the distinction in question is between public intellectuals and popular/celebrity intellectuals. His discussion rightly suggests, however, that both celebrity and noncelebrity intellectuals are *varieties* of public intellectuals. But this is not a major issue.

22. I shall ignore Gordon's mistaken ascription of a restrictivist/exclusivist conception of the intellectual to West. I have already noted West's characterization of Martin Luther King Jr. as an organic intellectual (see note 15) even as we know that King was not an academic intellectual. As if to anticipate Gordon, West describes King as "the most significant and successful organic *intellectual* in American history"(*Prophetic Fragments*, p. 3, emphasis in the original). Furthermore, we saw that West distinguishes "two organic *intellectual* traditions in African American life: the black Christian tradition of preaching and the black musical tradition of performance" (*Keeping Faith*, pp. 72–73, emphasis added). He contrasts these two forms of intellectual traditions to the academic intellectual tradition. Although all three traditions are "linked to the life of the mind," the former two, he says, "are rooted in the black life and possess precisely what the literate forms of black intellectual activity lack"—namely, a culture and mechanism to sustain it (73). The expression "rooted in black life" translates, in my view, into *being connected with praxis*.

23. Admittedly, West sometimes seems ambivalent in his critique of the Black intelligentsia. One gets the impression that he vacillates between two claims: (1) that it is the absence of the necessary infrastructure in the Black community that is responsible for the impotence of the Black intellectuals; and (2) that it is the Black academic intellectuals themselves who are detached from the community and in turn receive the contempt of the community. This ambivalence/vacillation on his

part leaves him open to a variety of interpretations, each of which has some measure of plausibility. Nevertheless, I believe that it is the first of these claims that is central to his discussion. The reason is that West generally considers the existential predicament of the individual as a function of certain forces and structures against which the individual is to struggle. The forces and structures may be political, social, economic, or, as in the case of the Black community, institutional malaise. In his view, it is these factors that need always to be reconfigured to improve the life and lot of the individual.

24. One exception is Spelman College in its African Diaspora and the World (ADW) course. Inaugurated in 1993, this course was designed with the express objective of serving as a core curriculum identity-marker that should distinguish the institution from all others of its kind. Even so, the college has not envisioned the course beyond the freshman level despite overwhelming evidence (based on positive student reactions) of the value of the course. Besides, there is an abysmal failure on the part of the college to provide the necessary resources to support the course and the incentives needed to entice faculty out of their narrow specializations to be interested in teaching the course, not to mention that the college has been extremely reluctant to commit the resources needed to recruit faculty whose formal training is in interdisciplinary studies with an emphasis on the African diaspora.

Chapter 3

1. Of course, since West believes that Black oppression in contemporary American society is inscribed within a context that includes the oppression of people of color generally, poor Whites, homosexuals, and various other groups, he would therefore insist that African American critical thought advocate also on behalf of this larger group. Such an insistence would be consistent with his humanistic motivations. Besides, there is at least one historical precedent for this motivation, namely, Martin Luther King Jr. King did not just advocate for Black workers in Alabama, Mississippi, and elsewhere, but he also challenged the American government's Vietnam war policy and challenged American capitalism at home and abroad.

2. No doubt this seems to leave out Marxism. But the reason for the omission of Marxism at this point in West's discussion is that Marxist thought is not indigenous to America; it is a European import into the American milieu. Since West's concern at this point is only to discuss the two *indigenous* American intellectual traditions that he thinks

ought to be involved in the construction and articulation of African American critical thought, it is imperative therefore that Marxist thought be excluded. I will show later, however, that West thinks Marxist intellectual tradition is indispensable to the liberating aims of African American critical thought.

3. See also Robert S. Boynton, "Princeton's Public Intellectual," (*New York Times*, October 13, 1991); and bell hooks and Cornel West (eds.), *Breaking Bread* (Boston: South End Press, 1991), p. 33.

4. Recall that it is the Emerson-Dewey versions of pragmatism that West celebrates as forms of cultural criticism; thus it is to these forms of the pragmatic tradition he is alluding in calling for African American critical thought to invoke the pragmatic intellectual tradition. See West, *The American Evastion of Philosophy* (Madison: The University of Wisconsin Press, 1989), esp. ch.1–3.

5. West distinguishes between two stripes (or streams) of the Black church. These are the prophetic (or visionary) and the priestly (or quotidian) (see *Prophecy Deliverance* [Philadelphia: The Westminster Press, 1982], p. 16). In the essay "The Black Church and Socialist Politics," he describes the former as "progressive" and the latter as "conservative" (see *Prophetic Fragments*, [Trenton, NJ: Africa World Press, 1988], pp. 67–73). Elsewhere, West notes that the former has been more visible in African American life, citing three slave insurrections in the nineteenth century led by three prophetic Christians: Gabriel Prosser (1800), Denmark Vessey (1822), and Nat Turner (1831). Says West, these slave insurrections "signify in dramatic fashion the crucial role of the black church in the Afro-American struggle for freedom" (*Prophecy Deliverance*, 102).

6. In James H. Cone and Gayraud S. Wilmore (eds.), *Black Theology: A Documentary History*, vol.1, rev. 2nd ed. (Maryknoll, NY: Orbis Books, 1993), chap. 34, p. 409. West originally published this essay in his *Prophecy Deliverance*. Unless otherwise indicated, however, my citations in the present discussion will be largely to Cone and Wilmore.

7. West lists five tasks in all, but only the task of Black liberation and social justice will concern me here. This concern itself is an amalgamation of three of the five tasks that West considers central to African American critical thought. The first and major task is to provide a historical context of the experiences of African Americans with the goal of establishing guidelines for action in addressing some of the issues

that confront contemporary African American life. The second task is
to provide a political prescription, in the form of concrete suggestions,
to facilitate the struggle for Black liberation. And the third task of
African American critical thought is to establish a dialogue between
prophetic African American Christian thought and Marxist social
analysis. The remaining two tasks are to provide a genealogy of the
cultural and linguistic roots of the idea of White supremacy and to
provide a theoretical reconstruction and evaluation of African
American responses to White supremacy (*Prophecy Deliverance*,
22–23).

8. The exception West gives is James Cone, saying that Cone's later writings reflect this critical concern (*Prophecy Deliverance*, 111).

9. For this distinction between the two strands of Marxism, see Will
Kymlicka, *Contemporary Political Philosophy* (Oxford: Clarendon
Press, 1990), ch. 5, "Marxism," pp. 160–61.

10. Kymlicka (*Contemporary Political Philosophy*) is addressing the issue
that capitalism, in the sense of private ownership of the means of production, is necessarily exploitative but that socialism is not. In light of
his example, which shows that socialism can be just as exploitative as
capitalism, Kymlicka concludes that the concern for exploitation does
not therefore justify a general preference for socializing the means of
production. Such concern should focus instead on equalizing the
means of production (182).

11. I am not even concerned here about the standard questions raised
against collectivist systems, for example, about efficiency, productivity,
innovation (or lack thereof), and the like. These questions are useful
in determining the economic merit of such systems. I shall ignore all
such issues here.

12. Bernard Boxill, *Blacks and Social Justice* (Lanham, MD: Rowman and
Littlefield, 1984), p. 54.

13. It is noteworthy that Cornel West has had similar experiences. He
records his experience of a trip to New York City. Having parked his
car in a safe parking lot he intended to continue his journey by taxi.
He soon found out, however, that no taxi would stop for him. As he
says, "After the ninth taxi refused me, my blood began to boil" (*Race
Matters*, [New York: Vintage Books, 1994], p. vx). West also shares
an experience of having been "stopped three times" in his first ten
days at Princeton University "for driving too slowly in a residential
street with a speed limit of twenty-five miles per hour" (xv).

14. See, for example, the transcript of the television program *Nightline* broadcast on Friday April 3, 1998. This routine harassment of Black motorists by White police officers is known as racial profiling.

15. It is a known fact that West always wears a three-piece suit. Indeed, the three-piece suit, together with the Afro hairstyle of the 1960s and 1970s, has come to be regarded as his characteristic professional (Du Boisean?) trademark attire. Thus, one can presume that he would have had on such a suit at the time of the New York incident, and this presumption would have very strong inductive basis.

16. West gives a litany of the intellectual blindness of Black theologians that is worth reading if only because of its humor.

17. West provides the following statistics about the distribution of wealth in America, citing an official survey conducted by the Federal Reserve Board in 1962. One half of 1 percent own 22 percent of the wealth, 1 percent own 33 percent, the lower 61 percent own 7 percent, and the bottom 45 percent own 2 percent (*Prophecy Deliverance*, 113).

18. The Reverend Jesse Jackson seems to be orienting in this direction, as evidenced in his remarks on a local television station in New York City sometime between late March and early April 1998. Mr. Jackson was commenting on an allegation that Continental Airlines had discriminated against some minority members of its staff in promotion decisions. Specifically, the charge was that the management of Continental Airlines had passed over some minority members for promotions on the grounds of their race. (Presumably, the aggrieved employees were Black.) Jackson, who had gone to New York City to meet with officials of Continental to discuss the matter, said in response to a question from a local television reporter that an effective way of avoiding such problems in the future was for minorities to buy stocks in corporations such as Continental. This would guarantee minorities some measure of control and oversight in the activities of the corporations.

19. It may be protested that whatever revisions capitalism may be undergoing are only cosmetic, not substantive; thus, one should not make too much of them. My response is that any such revisions simply prove that capitalism is not immune to revision and change, as has traditionally been maintained by proponents of Marxism. Thus, if it is possible for capitalism to undergo cosmetic revisions, it is also therefore possible for it to undergo substantive revisions.

20. It is also compatible with the views of liberal capitalists such as John Rawls, Ronald Dworkin, and Kymlicka. As Kymlicka (*Contemporary Political Philosophy*) says, "The broader theory of justice in which exploitation is [now] situated has become progressively closer to the Rawlsian theory of justice" (180). I owe the insight in this discussion to my colleague George Carew.

21. W. E. B. Du Bois, "Application for Membership in the Communist Party of the United States of America," in *W. E. B. Du Bois: A Reader,* ed. David Levering Lewis (New York: Henry Holt and Co., 1995).

22. For a discussion of Du Bois's response to the Communist Party over the Scottsboro incident see Boxill, *Blacks and Social Justice*, ch. 3, esp. pp. 52–54.

23. Du Bois noted also that the Socialist Party too fared no better. It was all too ready to sacrifice Black worker interests for White worker comforts. In "Socialism and the Negro Problem," Du Bois observes that the Socialist Party was prepared to defer the burning issues of the ten million Blacks to a later time after it would have achieved its objective of improving the conditions for the remaining ninety million White workers ("Application for Membership," p. 578).

24. It is germane to invoke Bill Lawson's observation in his essay "Social Disappointment and the Black Sense of Self" that one's reaction to any given situation is a function of the expectation one had entertained prior to and about the situation. To quote Lawson, "The greater the expectation, the greater the experience of the disappointment when the expectations are not met" (quoted in Lewis Gordon [ed.], *Existence in Black,* [New York: Routldge, 1997a], p. 151). I submit that this state of affairs was true of Du Bois.

25. Shamoon Zamir, *Dark Voices: W. E. B. Du Bois and American Thought 1888–1903* (Chicago and London: The University of Chicago Press, 1995), p. 9; cp.138.

26. Iris Marion Young identifies five ways in which groups are oppressed, of which marginalization is but one example. The others are exploitation, cultural imperialism, powerlessness and violence. See her *Justice and the Politics of Difference* (Princeton, NJ: Princeton University Press, 1990), ch. 2.

Chapter 4

1. My use of the term "ascendancy" is deliberate because of evidence that the place and negative treatment of Blacks in Western civilization goes as far back as the medieval period. See William Chester Jordan's "The Medieval Background," in *Struggles in the Promised Land: Toward a History of Black-Jewish Relations in the United States,* ed. Jack Salzman and Cornel West (New York and Oxford: Oxford University Press, 1997), ch. 2. See also Lewis Gordon, "Introduction," in *Existence in Black*, ed. L. Gordon (New York: Routledge, 1997a), p. 3. Gordon cites E. Baltazar, *The Dark Center: A Process Theology of Blackness* (New York: Paulist, 1973). Also see Chapter 6 of this volume.

2. West gives the following as examples of such principled alliances: the collaborative efforts between Du Bois's *The Crisis* and Abraham Cahan's *Jewish Daily Forward*; between Jewish leftists and A. Philip Randolph's numerous organizations; between Elliott Cohen's *Commentary* and the early career of James Baldwin; between Abraham Joshua Heschel and Martin Luther King Jr.; and between the Jewish Students for a Democratic Society (SDS) and the Student Non-Violent Coordinating Committee (SNCC).

3. Henry Louis Gates Jr., "Black Demagogues and Pseudo-Scholars," *New York Times*, July 20, 1992, Section A, Editorial Desk, cf. p .15; Cornel West, *Race Matters* (New York: Vintage, 1993), ch. 5; Adolph Reed, *Class Notes Posing as Politics and Other Thoughts on the American Scene* (New York: The New Press, 2000). See especially the following essays: "What Color Is Antisemitism?" and "The Rise of Louis Farrakhan;" *Jews and Blacks: A Dialogue on Race, Religion and Culture in America*, ed. Michael Lerner and Cornel West (New York: Plume Books, 1995); and Salzman and West (eds.), *Struggles*.

4. For a very good historical sketch of the decline in Black-Jewish relations in the cities, see Jonathan Kaufman, "Blacks and Jews: Struggles in the Cities," in Salzman and West (eds.), *Struggles,* ch. 6; and Jane Anna Gordon, *Why They Couldn't Wait: A Critique of Black-Jewish Conflict over Community Control in Ocean Hill-Brownsville (1967–1971)* (New York and London: RoutledgeFalmer, 2001). I shall draw upon these works, especially the latter, in my discussion later in this chapter.

5. The characterization of Black anti-Semitism as "top-down" is Henry Louis Gates Jr.'s (see note 3). And what I have characterized as "bot-

tom-up" anti-Semitism is only a short-hand way of referring to West's actual reference to Black "xenophobia from below" (*Race Matters*, 109). Gates uses the expression "top-down anti-Semitism" to describe what he considers anti-Semitic behavior that is espoused, sometimes openly but largely silently, by some Black intelligentsia whose goal is to project themselves as legitimate spokespersons for Black interests (15). And an effective way of achieving their goal is, he says, to attack Jews. In Gates' view, the reason for the attack is that the supposed Black intellectual leaders wish to dismantle the historical transethnic alliances that Jews and Blacks have formed as a bulwark against oppression. In so doing the attackers would then entrench themselves as the leaders of the Black community and hence present themselves as the legitimate advocates for Blacks. West uses "xenophobia from below" (what I have referred to as "bottom-up anti-Semitism") to characterize the behavior the ordinary Black person on the lower rungs of the social ladder, who believes that Jews are responsible for her or his social condition because Jews control the economy and the institutions of power in the society.

6. There is another item in the impasse between Jews and Blacks that has remained unsaid. This item, itself a subtext, is that Jews perceive Black criticism of Jews as the ultimate ingratitude, especially given the strong Jewish support for Black civil rights during the 1960s. Blacks in turn perceive (or interpret) Jewish support for (or involvement in) Black civil rights advocacy as opportunistic and self-interested. It is deemed opportunistic and self-interested because it was timely, in that its ultimate goal was to bring to focus Jewish endemic fears of White anti-Semitism. Thus, Jews appended their own sociopolitical concerns to Black demands for social justice. In any case, these oppositional viewpoints bring to focus the conflict between some Jewish leaders and some highly educated middle-class African Americans like Leonard Jeffries and others.

7. Norman Finkelstein, *The Holocaust Industry: Reflections on the Exploitation of Jewish Suffering* (London and New York: Verso Publications, 2000). For Lewis Gordon's view, see L. Gordon *Existence in Black*, ch. 5, esp. pp. 98–99. Finally, for an elaboration of the subject of Black Jews, see Howard Brotz, *The Black Jews of Harlem* (London and New York: The Free Press of Glencoe, 1964).

8. The conceptual synonymy of blackness with (being) *the* problem was first articulated by W. E. B. Du Bois, in ch. 1 of *The Souls of Black Folk* (New York: Bantam Books, 1989), the essay "Of Our Spiritual

Strivings." In the next chapter, I will draw upon this synonymy to provide a conceptual framework for appreciating the virulent opposition to affirmative action. For an existentialist analysis of the concept of blackness as the problem see L. Gordon, "Introduction," in *Existence in Black.*

9. I take up this issue of Blacks as "the problem" in and to society in my examination of West's outlook on affirmative action in the next chapter.

10. Cornel West, *The Cornel West Reader* (New York: Basic Civitas Books, 1999), ch. 43, p. 495.

11. For discussions of stereotypical views about Blacks in Western intellectual culture see Cornel West, *Prophecy Deliverance* (Philadelphia: The Westminster Press, 1982), ch. 2; Richard H. Popkin, "The Philosophical Basis of Eighteenth-Century Racism," in *Studies in Eighteenth-Century Culture,* ed. Harold E. Pagliaro (Cleveland and London: Case Western Reserve University, 1973), pp. 245–262; Emmanuel Eze, "The Color of Reason: The Idea of 'Race' in Kant's Anthropology" and Tsenay Serequeberhan, "The Critique of Eurocentricism and the Practice of African Philosophy," both in *Postcolonial African Philosophy: A Critical Reader,* ed. Emmanuel Eze (London and Cambridge, MA: Blackwell, 1997); Tsenay Serequeberhan, "Eurocentrism in Philosophy: The Case of Immanuel Kant," *The Philosophical Forum,* vol. 27 (no. 4), (1996): 333–356; and Clarence Sholé Johnson, "Teaching the Canons of Western Philosophy in Historically Black Colleges and Universities: The Spelman College Experience," *Metaphilosophy,* vol. 26 no. 4, (1995): 413–423. This list is neither representative nor exhaustive. However, in subsequent discussion I shall draw heavily upon the essays by Popkin and Eze.

12. Emmanuel Eze (ed.), *Race and the Enlightenment* (Cambridge, MA, and Oxford: Blackwell, 1997).

13. That it is not unusual for conflicts with and/or criticisms of Jews to be characterized by some in the Jewish community as anti-Semitic has been ably argued by Norman G. Finkelstein in *The Holocaust Industry.* Thus, the behavior of the UFT is in line with this practice.

14. Jurgen Habermas, *The Theory of Communicative Action,* 2 Vols., trans. Thomas McCarthy (Boston: Beacon Press, 1987); see especially Vol. 2, ch. 6. See also Iris M. Young, *Justice and the Politics of Difference* (Princeton; NJ: Princeton University Press, 1990), ch. 4.

15. Notwithstanding this observation, I show later why nonprogressive individuals, moreso than their progressive counterparts, should be included in any meeting that addresses the conflict between Blacks and Jews. West has begun to show an awareness of this point as is evident in a later work, "Tensions with Jewish Friends and Foes," in *The Cornel West Reader*, ch. 47, pp. 534–535. There, he defends against Jewish critics both his support of the Million Man March led by Louis Farrakhan of the Nation of Islam and his maintaining dialogue with xenophobic Black nationalists. For a penetrating discussion of Farrakhan's ascent to prominence and leadership both in the Nation of Islam and in the Black community, see Adolph Reed *Class Notes*, ch. 8. See also West, *Race Matters*, esp. pp. 111–115, and Lerner and West (eds.), *Jews and Blacks*, ch. 5.

16. See also Finkelstein, *The Holocaust Industry*, for a full-length devastating critique of the usurpation and appropriation of Jewish "voice" by wealthy powerful and influential Jewish organizations and individuals.

17. West gives examples of progressive Black leaders that follow upon the tradition of Martin Luther King Jr. These include Darryl Ward, president of the United Theological Seminary in Dayton, Ohio. Says West, Ward "has the largest program of training for Black preachers. Hundreds of them are part of the legacy of King. They are rarely sought out." Another such leader is Gary Simpson, "pastor of the largest Black Baptist church in America, Concord Baptist Church in Brooklyn." And West adds, "Gary Simpson's got a whole network of people who are building on the legacy of King and Fanny Lou Hamer." There is also the Reverend Mark Jacobs. Of importance, however, is West's remark, "There are many many King-like figures on the grassroots level in the Black community, but with the chasm in place we hardly ever hear about them;" see Lerner and West (eds.), *Jews and Blacks*, p. 268.

18. Lewis Gordon, "The Unacknowledged Fourth Tradition: An Essay on Nihilism, Decadence, and the Black Intellectual Tradition in the Existential Pragmatic Thought of Cornel West," in *Cornel West: A Critical Reader*, ed. George Yancy (Malden, MA: Blackwell, 2001), pp. 46–47.

19. Young brings out some limitations to Habermas's theory of communicative action in *Justice and the Politics of Difference*, pp. 117–119.

20. For a brief narrative of the Crown Heights incident, see Jonathan Kaufman, "Blacks and Jews: The Struggle in the Cities," in Salzman and West (eds.), *Struggles*, pp. 119–120.

Chapter 5

1. For some useful discussions of affirmative action, see Nicholas Capaldi and Albert Mosley (eds.) *Affirmative Action: Social Justice or Unfair Preference?* (Lanham, MD, and London: Rowman and Littlefield, 1996); Robert Fullinwider, *The Reverse Discrimination Controversy* (Totowa, NJ: Rowman and Littlefield, 1980); Bernard; Boxill, *Blacks and Social Justice* (Lanham, MD: Rowman and Littlefield, 1984), ch. 7; and Cornel West, *Race Matters* (New York: Vintage Books, 1993), ch. 5 and *The Cornel West Reader* (New York: Basic Civitas Books, 1999), ch. 43. This list is neither representative nor exhaustive.

2. Of course, the policy applied to women, and later was expanded to include other minority groups such as the disabled. However, its principal target was Blacks who, simply by virtue of race, had been (and continue to be) the victims of discrimination in the society. As Paula Giddings notes, "the Civil Rights Act [in response to racial discrimination against Blacks] . . . provided the legal foundation for women's rights—much as the Fourteenth and Fifteenth Amendments had a century earlier" (*When and Where I Enter: The Impact of Black Women on Race and Sex in America* [New York: Bantam Books, 1984], pp. 299–300). For this reason, the primary focus of my discussion will be Blacks, cognizant of the gender and other dimensions of the affirmative action issue.

3. For discussions of this issue, see for example Jerome A. Chanes, "Affirmative Action: Jewish Ideals, Jewish Interests," in *Struggles in the Promised Land*, ed. Jack Salzman and Cornel West (New York and Oxford: Oxford University Press, 1997), ch. 14; esp. pp. 295–297; Fullinwider, *Reverse Discrimination*, chs. 1 and 11; and Mosley's discussion in Capaldi and Mosley (eds.), *Affirmative Action*, pp. 23–38, and Capaldi's on pp. 65–69. Capaldi lists six issues around which revolve the problem of affirmative action.

4. As noted earlier, affirmative action was instituted initially to address Black and women's demands for social justice. However, in this study I shall limit my focus to the racial dimension particularly because the

question I wish to address is: How compatible, if at all, is West's class-based concern with Black demands for social justice?

5. West is not alone among defenders of affirmative action who are guilty of this error. The synonymy of affirmative action with preferential treatment underlies Boxill's entire discussion even as Boxill examines some objections to affirmative action. Moreover, Boxill wishes that the argument he proposes "in support of preferential treatment" be distinguished from another argument that, he says, "has a certain superficial attractiveness" (*Blacks and Social Justice*, p. 150). Albert Mosley, too, commenting on the United States Supreme Court's various adjudication of affirmative action litigation, says that, despite differences of opinion among the justices, "the Court remained consistent in allowing preferential treatment as a remedy for official findings of past discrimination" (Capaldi and Mosley [eds.], *Affirmative Action*, p. 9). Finally, Fullinwider calls attention to the following comment of Kathleen Fisher in a letter Fisher had sent to Congressman James O'Hara during the O'Hara Congressional Hearings on Affirmative Action: "The whole theory of affirmative action is to give preference to women and minorities to overcome the detrimental effects of past discrimination. That is, affirmative action is the practice of reverse discrimination" (quoted in Fullinwider, *Reverse Discrimination*, ch.11, note 2). In my judgment, all such characterizations of affirmative action as preferential treatment justifiably fall prey to the charge that affirmative action is inconsistent with the demands of social justice.

6. See Michael Lerner and Cornel West (eds.), *Jews and Blacks* (New York: Plume Books, 1995), ch. 8, especially pp. 168–176. See also note 3 in this chapter.

7. The landmark case that illustrates this opposition between merit and qualification on the one hand and racial preferencing on the other is *Bakke vs. University of California Regents* (1972). The plaintiff, Allan Bakke, a White male, had been denied admission to the Medical School of the University of California at Davis. At the same time, the school had reserved sixteen slots for minority applicants. It was alleged that the scores of some of the minority applicants were lower than Bakke's, hence the admission of these applicants constituted reverse discrimination against Bakke. Bakke thus sued the Board of Regents. The suit was decided by the United States Supreme Court, which ruled in 1978 that the school should admit Bakke. For details of the Bakke case, see, for example, Fullinwider, *Reverse*

Discrimination, pp. 2–3, and Jeffrey Chanes, "Affirmative Action: Jewish Ideals, Jewish Interests," in Salzman and West (eds.), *Struggles*, pp. 302–303.

8. There is certainly a sense in which affirmative action can quite legitimately and defensibly be characterized as preferential treatment and preferential treatment be regarded as a form of restitution. In this sense, the argument for affirmative action could be premised on the idea that the characteristic of whiteness has conferred on White males certain privileges and advantages specifically because of their race. Given that such privileges and advantages are benefits acquired as a result of race, they have therefore been obtained at the expense of other races and gender, and thus unfairly. Social justice requires therefore that, as remedy, similar and equal considerations of race and gender be accorded to all those who have been disadvantaged as a result of both whiteness *and* maleness. Affirmative action as preferential treatment for Blacks and women is just that remedy. This view is a variant of that which Boxill describes as the "backward looking" argument for affirmative action (*Blacks and Social Justice*, p. 148). Fullinwider (*Reverse Discrimination*) does not explore this line of defense of affirmative action as preferential treatment, nor does West in his characterization of affirmative action as preferential treatment; so I shall not pursue it here. I wish only to note that this line of argument can provide a legitimate moral defense of affirmative action as preferential treatment and in a positive sense.

9. There may well have been genuine instances of affirmative action as preferential hiring in the objectionable banal sense. However, I am not concerned with such cases here since, in my view, such cases could be the exception and not the rule. My present concern is the presumption of Black lack of qualification in all putative cases of affirmative action hires and the concomitant allegation of social injustice against Whites. As is clear from my discussion thus far, West left this presumption unchallenged. One can speculate in this connection that there also may be a seamy side to the banal normative sense of affirmative action. Conceivably, employers could deliberately recruit unqualified Blacks who are destined to perform poorly on the job just so as to give moral legitimacy to the position that Blacks are incapable of functioning in the requisite task(s). Such recruitment acts would be deliberately intended to cast affirmative action as *preferential nonmeritorious hiring*.

10. More recently, Lewis Gordon has aptly expressed this point in saying that in the racialized world at large, "blackness functions as an aberration that has to be explained without blaming the system in which it emerges." See Gordon, "Existential Dynamics of Theorizing Black Invisibility," in *Existence in Black*, ed. L. Gordon (New York: Routledge, 1997), p. 70.

11. Thomas Jefferson, *Notes on the State of Virginia*, ed. William Peden (Chapel Hill: The University of North Carolina Press, 1955).

12. This was a widely held view among some key eighteenth-century philosophers such as Hume, Kant, and Hegel, among others. Emmanuel Eze (ed.), *Race and the Enlightenment* (Cambridge, MA: Blackwell, 1997), is an anthology of the views of these and other philosophers and scientists of the time on the subject of raciology. James Beattie advances a very early critique of raciology in his challenge of Hume's views in the essay "Of National Characters." For Hume's views and Beattie's critique, see ch. 3 of Eze. See also my chapter 4, note 11, for some critical discussions on the issue of race in eighteenth-century thought.

13. The economic and social dominance of Whites, and hence of White superior quality of life relative to Blacks, was not limited to the market. It extended also to the sphere of education. The whole thrust of the *Brown vs. the Topeka Kansas Board of Education* decision (1954) was to overturn an entrenched, segregated, and unequal system of education between the races, wherein Whites, through the deployment of institutional mechanisms, deliberately and systemically relegated Blacks to inferior quality education. And politically, the Civil Rights protests of the 1960s were a direct assault on the institutionalized disfranchisement of Blacks (and women) in society.

14. There are constraints on my generic use of the term "women" (and cognate expressions such as "women's experiences") that I explain later. I thank George Yancy for drawing my attention to this very important issue.

15. Sandra Day O'Connor, "Women and the Law," in *Pacesetting Women of the 20th Century: National Cathedral School Centennial Birthday Festival*, October 12–15, 2000 (Mount Saint Alban, Washington, DC), pp. 31–36. Although the experiences of women that O'Connor describes are topical to the legal profession, they undoubtedly are universal in respect of the professions generally. Indeed, O'Connor says as much: "[B]ecause my own background is in the legal profession,

my remarks will describe particularly the history of women in the law. The experience of women lawyers finds its parallel in other fields as well and is illustrative of the broader experiences of women generally" (31). I will only add that if White women were excluded because of their gender, Black women would have been doubly excluded because of their race and gender.

16. See Sojourner Truth, "Ain't I A Woman?" and Anna Julian Cooper, "The Status of Women in America," both in *Feminist Theory: A Reader,* ed. Wendy Kolmar and Frances Bartkowski (Mountain View, CA: Mayfield, 2000), chs. 11 and 16, respectively. For some contemporary discussions, see: Patricia Hill Collins, *Black Feminist Thought* (New York and London: Routledge, 1991), ch. 2; bell hooks, *Feminist Theory: From Margin to Center* (Boston: Southend Press, 1984), ch. 1; and George Yancy, "Feminism and the Subtext of Whiteness: Black Women's Experiences as a Site of Identity Formation and Contestation of Whiteness," *The Western Journal of Black Studies*, vol. 24, no. 3 (2000): 156–166. This list is neither representative nor exhaustive of Black feminists who have interrogated the subject of the representation of women's experiences.

17. In Howard McGary and Bill E. Lawson (eds.), *Between Slavery and Freedom: Philosophy and American Slavery* (Bloomington and Indianapolis: Indiana University Press, 1992), ch.5.

18. I am indebted to George Yancy for formulating and motivating this objection in a conversation.

19. George Berkeley, "The Principles of Human Knowledge," sec. 20, in *Berkeley's Philosophical Works,* ed. David M. Armstrong (New York: Collier Macmillan Publishers, 1965).

20. U.S. census figures for the year 2000.

Chapter 6

1. See, for example, his *Prophecy Deliverance* (Philadelphia: The Westminster Press), chs. 1 and 2.

2. *Keeping Faith* (New York and London: Routledge, 1993), pp. 5–6; cp. 34–35.

3. In chapter 2 of *Prophecy Deliverance,* for example, West discusses what he calls the genealogy of modern racism—specifically, the inception of the idea of White supremacy in modern (read "enlightenment") discourse. He identifies two—although he claims three—stages

of this genealogy. The first is the recovery of classical (Greek) antiquity in modern intellectual discourse that found expression in the purported scientific classificatory categories of Carl von Linneaus and others. And the second stage is the rise of the study of phrenology (or the study of the skull sizes), to establish a relation between brain development and intelligence, and physiognomy (the study of facial characteristics), to establish aesthetic norms, both disciplines coated with European value-laden assumptions. These stages, says West, got "intellectual legitimacy" in the enlightenment tradition in the writings of Montesquieu, Voltaire, Hume, Jefferson and Kant, among others" (61–63). But West's treatment of the philosophers is much too cursory and therefore (I think) inadequate for a thorough appreciation of the philosophical grounding of White supremacy and anti-Black racism, and hence for the prosecution of the issue of social justice.

4. The analogy here is between the regal status as "Queen of the sciences" that metaphysics once enjoyed within the discipline of philosophy, as Kant notes, and the supremacy of philosophy in the entire humanistic studies. For Kant's view see his *Critique of Pure Reason,* ed. Norman Kemp Smith (New York: St. Martin's Press, 1965), p. 7.

5. I have already directed attention to a number of scholars who have examined the positions of key Western philosophers on the issue of race and racism (see chapter 4, note 11). I wish only to augment that list by adding the following: Harry Bracken, *Mind and Language* (Dordrecht, Holland, and Cinnaminson, NJ: Foris Publications, 1984), esp. chs. 3 and 4; and Robert Bernasconi, "Locke's Almost Random Talk of Man: The Double Use of Words in the Natural Law Justification of Slavery," *Perspektiven der Philosophie,* vol. 18 (1992): 293–318. I shall draw upon the views of these philosophers in the discussion that follows.

6. Crane Brinton, "Enlightenment," in *The Encyclopedia of Philosophy,* Vols. 1–2, ed. Paul Edwards (New York and London: Macmillan and Free Press, 1967; rpt. 1972).

7. Unless otherwise stated, all references to the views of Linneaus and the other scientists and philosophers of modernity in this chapter are from Emmanuel Eze (ed.), *Race and the Enlightenment* (Cambridge, MA: Blackwell, 1997).

8. John Locke, *An Essay Concerning Human Understanding,* ed. Alexander Campbell Fraser, 2 Vols.), Vol. 1 (New York: Dover Publications, 1894). Kant draws a similar distinction between the con-

cepts *man* and *person* with a strong moral import. See Emmanuel Eze, "The Color of Reason: The Idea of 'Race' in Kant's Anthropology," in *Post-Colonial African Philosophy*, ed. Eze (Cambridge, MA: Blackwell, 1997), pp. 105–107).

9. I will make some speculative remarks on this issue later. It is instructive, however, that Robert Bernasconi has raised the question about whether or not Locke considered Africans as persons. See Bernasconi, "Locke's Almost Random Talk of Man," p. 299.

10. For instance, Kant's epistemological concerns are a direct response to what Kant considered Hume's skepticism about our ordinary notions of causation. In particular, Hume had rejected the concept of de re necessity and instead had explained causal necessity in psychological terms. (Hume's skeptical views are formulated in Book One of his *Treatise of Human Nature,* ed. L. A. Selby-Bigge and P. H. Nidditch, 2nd ed. [Oxford: Oxford University Press, 1978] and again in his *Enquiries Concerning Human Understanding and Concerning the Principles of Morals,* ed. L. A. Selby-Bigge and P. H. Nidditch, 3rd ed. [Oxford: Oxford University Press, 1975].) Kant is reputed to have said that Hume woke him up from his dogmatic slumber over the subject of causal analysis. Thus, Kant set out in his *Critique of Pure Reason* to refute Hume.

11. The term 'morals' had a very broad extension in eighteenth-century thought. It encompassed ethics, politics, aesthetics, and logic, for all these studies concerned human beings in society, as exemplified in the subtitle of Hume's *Treatise of Human Nature,* namely, "an attempt to introduce the experimental method of reasoning into moral subjects." For a discussion of the term 'morals' in eighteenth-century thought, see John B. Stewart, *The Moral and Political Philosophy of David Hume* (New York and London: Columbia University Press, 1963), pp. 82–84.

12. See Eze, "The Color of Reason," esp. pp. 105–122. My discussion of Kant on this issue derives from Eze's penetrating insight.

13. The citation in question is as follows:

> The Negroes of Africa have by nature no feeling that rises above the trifling. Mr. Hume challenges anyone to cite a single example in which a Negro has shown talents, and asserts that among the hundreds of thousands of blacks who are transported elsewhere from their countries, although many of them have even been set free, still not a single one was ever found who presented anything great in art or science or any other praiseworthy quality, even though

among the whites some continually rise aloft from the lowest rabble, and
through superior gifts earn respect in the world. (Eze, *Race and
Enlightenment*, p. 55)

14. The capacity to reason in accordance with laws is central to Kant's
    views in epistemology, metaphysics, and ethics, as is evident from a
    reading of his *Critique of Pure Reason* and *Groundwork*.

15. Even despite his talk of "human nature" in this passage, it is question-
    able that Kant considers Africans human. I take up this matter later.

16. That Locke's concept of a state of nature is very different to Hobbe's
    does not constitute a threat to my claim. I take up this matter later.

17. John Locke, *Second Treatise of Government*, ed. Thomas Peardon
    (Indianapolis and New York: Bobbs-Merrill, 1952).

18. See Thomas Hobbes, *Leviathan* (Oxford: Oxford University Press,
    1651), chap. XIII, sect. 63, p. 98.

19. See Bernasconi, "Locke's Almost Random Talk of Man," pp.
    295–296.

20. In enlightenment discourse, notes Popkin, one of four theories pro-
    posed to explain the place of Africans in the ontological hierarchy is
    that Africans are a different species. As Popkin puts it, "A third the-
    ory was that some beings that look human are really not so, but are
    lower on the great chain of being and represent a link between man
    and apes"; Popkin, "The Philosophical Basis of Eighteenth-Century
    Racism," in *Studies in Eighteenth-Century Culture*, ed. Harold E.
    Pagliareo) Cleveland and London: Case Western Reserve University
    Press, 1973), p. 247.

21. For a discussion of this theory, see, for example, Bracken, *Mind and
    Language*, p. 42.

22. See her "Locke on Slavery and Inalienable Rights," *Canadian Journal
    of Philosophy*, vol. 25, no. 1 (1995): 75.

23. See Bracken, *Mind and Language*, pp. 42–44; cp. 56–57.

24. Elsewhere, Bernasconi speculates that possibly "it simply did not
    occur to Locke, who was above all concerned with the rights of
    Englishmen, that the chattel slavery of Africans needed justification,
    even though he was well aware of how the system operated and
    indeed profited from it through his investments." See his "Kant as an
    Unfamiliar Source of Racism," in *Philosophers on Race*, ed. Julie
    Ward and Tommy Lott (Malden, MA: Blackwell, 2002), p. 150.

25. Hume, *A Treatise of Human Nature*, Book III. ii. 2. Hume states: "This *state of nature*, therefore, is to be regarded as a mere fiction, not unlike that of the *golden age*, which poets have invented; only with this difference, that the former is describ'd as full of war, violence and injustice; whereas the latter is painted out to us, as the most charming and most peaceable condition, that can possibly be imagin'd" (p. 493, emphases in the original).

26. See Maurice Cranston, *John Locke: A Biography* (London: Longmans, 1957), ch. 12, especially pp. 153–56.

27. I have discussed Hume's theory of morality and of the relation between reason and sentiment in his moral system in my "Yet Another Look at Cognitive Reason and Moral Action in Hume's Ethical System," *Journal of Philosophical Research*, vol. XVII (1992): 225–238; and my "Annette Baier on Reason and Morals in Hume's Philosophy," *Dialogue: Canadian Philosophical Review*, vol. XXXIV (1995): 369–380.

28. See Ernest C. Mossner, *The Life of David Hume* (Clarendon: Oxford University Press, 1980), especially chs. 34 and 36.

29. Richard Popkin, "Hume's Racism," *The Philosophical Forum*, vol. IX, nos. 2–3 (winter–spring, 1977–1978): 221. For a contrary view, see Robert Palter, "Hume and Prejudice," *Hume Studies*, vol. XXI, no. 1 (April 1995): 3–23.

30. In this respect, I consider evasive Adrian Piper's inability to say whether or not Kant's categorical imperative is applicable to Blacks. See her interview with George Yancy, in Yancy, *African American Philosophers: 17 Conversations* (New York and London: Routledge, 1998), pp. 63–64.

31. See Eze, "The Color of Reason," p. 116.

32. Ella Shohat and Robert Stam, *Unthinking Eurocentrism* (London and New York: Routledge, 1994), p. 88; emphasis in the original.

Postscript

1. Julia Keller, "Poisoned Ivy," *Chicago Tribune*, January 11, 2002, Section 5, p. 1.

2. "Roiling His Faculty, New Harvard President Reroutes Tenure Track," *Wall Street Journal*, January 11, 2002, Section A1.

3. Robin Wilson and Scott Smallwood, "Battle of Wills at Harvard," *Chronicle of Higher Education*, January 18, 2002, p. A8.

4. See, for example, Shelby Steele, "White Guilt = Black Power," *Wall Street Journal*, January 8, 2002, p. A18.

5. Within the discipline of philosophy, the area of social philosophy is concerned with precisely such issues as are relevant to humans in society. Thus, we have discussions about criteria for distributing social benefits and burdens, and we examine the validity of such criteria in the context of affirmative action, merit pay in the academy, and related axiological issues. We also examine the morality of the economic behavior of corporations in creating desires in consumers.

6. Leland Ware, "Letters to the Editor," *Chronicle of Higher Education*, February 15, 2002, p. B4. Ware is a professor of law and public policy in the School of Urban Affairs and Public Policy at the University of Delaware.

7. "Letters to the Editor," in ibid., pp. B4 and B21. Detore-Nakamura is a professor of communications and literature at Brevard Community College in Melbourne, Florida.

8. There have been reports in the media that West has accepted an offer from Princeton. Ironically, it was from Princeton that Harvard recruited him in 1994.

BIBLIOGRAPHY

Abbagnano, Nicola. 1967. "Humanism." In Paul Edwards (ed.), *The Encyclopedia of Philosophy*. New York and London: Macmillan and Free Press; rpt. 1972.

Allen, Judith A. 1997. "Strengthening Women's Studies in Hard Times: Feminism and Challenges of Institutional Adaptation." *Women's Studies Quarterly* 1&2: 358–387.

Aristotle. 1941. *Nichomean Ethics*. In Richard McKeon (ed.), *The Basic Works of Aristotle*. New York: Random House.

Ault, Amber, and Eve Sandberg. 1993. "When the Oppressors Are Us." In Laurel Richardson and Verta Taylor (eds.), *Feminist Frontiers*. New York: McGraw Hill.

Ayer, A. J. 1963. *Philosophical Essays*. London: Macmillan and Co.

Barber, William J. 1967. *A History of Economic Thought*. Hammondsworth, Middlesex, England: Penguin Books.

Berkeley, George. 1965. "The Principles of Human Knowledge." In David M. Armstrong (ed.), *Berkeley's Philosophical Works*. New York: Collier Macmillan Publishers.

Bernasconi, Robert. 1992. "Locke's Almost Random Talk of Man: The Double Use of Words in the Natural Law Justification of Slavery." *Perspektiven der Philosophie* 18: 293–318.

———. 2002. "Kant as an Unfamiliar Source of Racism." In Julie K. Ward and Tommy L. Lott (eds.), *Philosophers on Race*. Malden, MA: Blackwell.

Bernstein, Richard J. 1967. "John Dewey." In Paul Edwards (ed.), *The*

Encyclopedia of Philosophy. New York and London: Macmillan and Free Press; rpt. 1972.

Boxill, Bernard. 1984. *Blacks and Social Justice*. Lanham, MD: Rowman and Littlefield.

Boynton, Robert S. 1991. "Princeton's Public Intellectual." *New York Times*, September 15, section 6.

Bracken, Harry M. 1984. *Mind and Language*. Dordrecht, Holland, and Cinnaminson, NJ: Foris Publications.

Brinton, Crane. 1967. "Enlightenment." In Paul Edwards (ed.), *The Encyclopedia of Philosophy*. New York and London: Macmillan and Free Press; rpt. 1972.

Brotz, Howard. 1964. *The Black Jews of Harlem*. London and New York: The Free Press of Glencoe.

Bruder, Kenneth, and Brooke Noel Moore (eds.) 1990. *Philosophy: The Power of Ideas*. Mountain View, CA: Mayfield Publishing Company.

Buckingham, Walter S. 1958. *Theoretical Economic Systems*. New York: The Ronald Press Company.

Calderwood, Ann, and Alice S. Rossi (eds.) 1973. *Academic Women on the Move*. New York: Russell Sage Foundation, 1973.

Capaldi, Nicholas, and Albert Mosley. 1996. *Affirmative Action: Social Justice or Unfair Preference?* Lanham, MD: Rowman and Littlefield.

Carew, George M. 1993. "A Critique of John Mbiti's Traditional African Ontology." *Quest: An International Journal of African Philosophy* 8: 170–189.

Chanes, Jeffrey. 1997. "Affirmative Action: Jewish Ideals and Jewish Interests." In Jack Salzman and Cornel West (eds.), *Struggles in the Promised Land: Toward a History of Black-Jewish Relations in the United States*. New York and Oxford: Oxford University Press.

Cohen, Carl. 1984. "Socialist Democracy." In W. Michael Hoffman and Jennifer Mills Moore (eds.), *Business Ethics: Readings and Cases in Corporate Morality*. 2nd edition. New York: McGraw-Hill Publishing Company.

Cooper, Anna Julian. 2000. "The Status of Women in America." In Wendy Kolmar and Frances Bartkowski (eds.), *Feminist Theory: A Reader*. Mountain View, CA: Mayfield.

Corrington, Robert S. 1991. "The Emancipation of American Philosophy." *APA Newsletter on the Black Experience* 90.3 (Fall): 23–26.

Cranston, Maurice. 1957. *John Locke: A Biography*. London: Longmans.

Detore-Nakamura, Joanne. 2002. "Letters to the Editor." *Chronicle of Higher Education*. February 15, pp. B4 and B21.

Douglass, Frederick. 1966. "The Nation's Problem." In Howard Brotz (ed.), *Negro Social and Political Thought 1850–1920*. New York: Basic Books.

Du Bois, W. E. B. 1989. *The Souls of Black Folk*. New York: Bantam Books.

———. 1995a. "Application for Membership in the Communist Party of the United States of America." In David Levering Lewis (ed.), *W. E. B. Du Bois: A Reader*. New York: Henry Holt and Co., 1995.

———. 1995b. "The Negro and Communism." In David Levering Lewis (ed.), *W. E. B. Du Bois: A Reader*. New York: Henry Holt and Co.

———. 1995c. "Negroes and the Crisis of Capitalism in the United States." In David Levering Lewis (ed.), *W. E. B. Du Bois: A Reader*. New York: Henry Holt and Co.

———. 1995d. "Socialism and the Negro Problem." In David Levering Lewis (ed.), *W. E. B. Du Bois: A Reader*. New York: Henry Holt and Co.

Eze, Emmanuel. 1997a. "The Color of Reason: The Idea of 'Race' in Kant's Anthropology." In Emmanuel Eze (ed.), *Post-Colonial African Philosophy: A Critical Reader*. Cambridge, MA: Blackwell.

——— (ed.). 1997b. *Race and the Enlightenment*. Cambridge, MA: Blackwell.

Feigl, Herbert. 1969. "Ethics, Religion, and Scientific Humanism." In Paul Kurtz (ed.), *Moral Problems in Contemporary Society: Essays in Humanistic Ethics*. Englewood Cliff, NJ: Prentice Hall.

Finkelstein, Norman G. 2000. *The Holocaust Industry: Reflections on the Exploitation of Jewish Suffering*. London and New York: Verso Publications.

Fullinwider, Robert K. 1980. *The Reverse Discrimination Controversy*. Totowa, NJ: Rowman and Littlefield.

Gates Jr., Henry Louis. 1992. "Black Demagogues and Pseudo-Scholars." *New York Times*, July 20, Section A, Editorial Desk, pp.15 ff.

Gates Jr., Henry Louis, and Cornel West (eds.). 1996. *The Future of the Race*. New York: Alfred A. Knopf.

Giddings, Paula. 1984. *When and Where I Enter: The Impact of Black Women on Race and Sex in America*. New York: Bantam Books.

Goldberg, David Theo (ed.). 1989. *Ethical Theory and Social Issues*. New York: Holt, Rinehart and Winston.

Golden, Daniel. 2002. "Roiling His Faculty, New Harvard President Reroutes Tenure Track." *Wall Street Journal*, January 11, p. A1.

Gooding-Williams. 1991. "Evading Narrative Myth, Evading Prophetic Pragmatism: A Review of Cornel West's *The American Evasion of Philosophy*." *APA Newsletter on the Black Experience* 90.3 (1991): 12–16.

Gordon, Jane Anna. 2001. *Why They Couldn't Wait: A Critique of Black-Jewish Conflict over Community Control in Ocean Hill-Brownsville (1967–1971)*. New York and London: RoutledgeFalmer.

Gordon, Lewis R. (ed.). 1997a. *Existence in Black: An Anthology of Black Existential Philosophy*. New York: Routledge.

———. 1997b. *Her Majesty's Other Children*. Lanham, MD: Rowman and Littlefield.

———. 2001. "The Unacknowledged Fourth Tradition: An Essay on Nihilism, Decadence, and the Black Intellectual Tradition in the Existential Pragmatic Thought of Cornel West." In George Yancy (ed.), *Cornel West: A Critical Reader*. Cambridge, MA, and Oxford, England: Blackwell.

Gould, Carol C. 1978. *Marx's Social Ontology: Individuality and Community in Marx's Theory of Social Reality*. Cambridge, MA and London: The MIT Press.

Greenberg, Cheryl. 1999. "Negotiating Coalition: Black and Jewish Civil Rights Agencies in the Twentieth Century." In Jack Salzman and Cornel West (eds.), *Struggles in the Promised Land*. New York and Oxford: Oxford University Press.

Habermas, Jurgen. 1984/1987. *The Theory of Communicative Action*, 2 Vols. Translated by Thomas McCarthy. Boston: Beacon Press.

Herrnstein, J., and Charles Murray. 1994. *The Bell Curve: Intelligence and Class Structure in American Life*. New York: Free Press.

Hill Collins, Patricia. 1991. *Black Feminist Thought*. New York and London: Routledge.

Hobbes, Thomas. 1651. *Leviathan*. Oxford: Oxford University Press.

hooks, bell. 1984. *Feminist Theory: From Margin to Center*. Boston: South End Press.

hooks, bell, and Cornel West. 1991. *Breaking Bread: Insurgent Black Intellectual Life*. Boston: South End Press, 1991.

Hume, David. 1975. *Enquiries Concerning Human Understanding and Concerning the Principles of Morals*, 3rd ed. Edited by L. A. Selby-Bigge and P. H. Nidditch. Oxford, England: Oxford University Press.

———. 1978. *A Treatise of Human Nature*, 2nd ed. Edited by L. A. Selby-Bigge and P. H. Nidditch. Oxford, England: Oxford University Press.

Irele, Abiola. 1990. *The African Experience in Literature and Ideology*. Bloomington and Indianapolis: Indiana University Press.

Jefferson, Thomas. 1955. *Notes on the State of Virginia*. Edited by William Peder. Chapel Hill: The University of North Carolina Press.

Johnson, Abby Arthur, and Ronald Maberry Johnson (eds.). 1979.

Propaganda and Aesthetics. Amherst: University of Massachusetts Press.

Johnson, Clarence Sholé. 1992. "Yet Another Look at Cognitive Reason and Moral Action in Hume's Ethical System." *Journal of Philosophical Research.* XVII: 226–238.

———. 1995. "Teaching the Canons of Western Philosophy in Historically Black Colleges and Universities: The Spelman College Experience." *Metaphilosophy* 26.4: 413–423.

———. 1996a. "An Analysis of John Mbiti's Treatment of the Concept of Event in African Ontologies." *Quest: An International Journal of African Philosophy* IX. 2–X.1: 139–57.

———. 1996b. "Annette Baier on Reason and Morals in Hume's Philosophy." *Dialogue: Canadian Philosophical Review* XXXIV: 367–380.

———. 1997. "Cornel West as Pragmatist and Existentialist." In Lewis R. Gordon (ed.), *Existence in Black: An Anthology of Black Existential Philosophy.* New York: Routledge.

———. 2001. "Reading Cornel West as a Humanistic Scholar: Rhetoric and Practice." In George Yancy (ed.), *Cornel West: A Critical Reader.* Malden, MA, and Oxford, England: Blackwell.

Jordan, William Chester. 1997. "The Medieval Background." In Jack Salzman and Cornel West (eds.), *Struggles in the Promised Land: Toward a History of Black-Jewish Relations in the United States.* New York and Oxford, England: Oxford University Press.

Jordan, Winthrop D. 1968. *White over Black: American Attitudes toward the Negro, 1550–1812.* Durham: The University of North Carolina Press.

Kant, Immanuel. 1964. *Groundwork of the Metaphysic of Morals.* Edited by H. J. Paton. New York: Harper and Row.

———. 1965. *Critique of Pure Reason.* Edited by Norman Kemp Smith. New York: St. Martin's Press.

Kaufman, Jonathan. 1997. "Blacks and Jews: The Struggles in the Cities." In Jack Salzman and Cornel West (eds.), *Struggles in the Promised Land: Toward a History of Black-Jewish Relations in the United States.* New York and Oxford, England: Oxford University Press.

Keller, Julia. 2002. "Poisoned Ivy." *Chicago Tribune,* January 11, Section 5.

Kolenda, Konstantin. 1991. "The (Cornel) West-Ward Vision for American Philosophy." *APA Newsletter on the Black Experience* 90.3 (Fall): 16–19.

Kristol, Irving. 1984. "A Capitalist Conception of Justice." In W. Michael

Hoffman and Jennifer Mills Moore (eds.), *Business Ethics: Readings and Cases in Corporate Morality*, 2nd ed. New York: McGraw Hill.

Kurtz, Paul. 1969. "What Is Humanism?" In Paul Kurtz (ed.), *Moral Problems in Contemporary Society: Essays in Humanistic Ethics*. Englewood Cliffs, NJ: Prentice Hall.

Kymlicka, Will. 1990. *Contemporary Political Philosophy: An Introduction*. Oxford, England: Clarendon Press.

Lamont, Corliss. 1990. *The Philosophy of Humanism*, 7th ed. New York: Continuum.

Lawson, Bill. 1997. "Social Disappointment and the Black Sense of Self." In Lewis R. Gordon (ed.), *Existence in Black: An Anthology of Black Existential Philosophy*. New York: Routledge.

Lawson, Bill, and Howard McGary (eds.). 1992. *Between Slavery and Freedom: Philosophy and American Slavery*. Bloomington and Indianapolis: Indiana University Press.

Lerner, Michael, and Cornel West. 1995. *Jews and Blacks: A Dialogue on Race, Religion and Culture in America*. New York: Plume Books.

Lewis, David Levering (ed.). 1995. *W. E. B. Du Bois: A Reader*. New York: Henry Holt and Co.

Locke, John. 1894. *An Essay Concerning Human Understanding*, 2 Vols. New York: Dover Publications, 1894.

———. 1952. *The Second Treatise of Government*. Edited by Thomas P. Peardon. Indianapolis and New York: Bobbs-Merrill.

Longino, Helen E. 1990. *Science as Social Knowledge*. Princeton, New Jersey: Princeton University Pres.

Lott, Eric. 1994. "Cornel West in the Hour of Chaos: Culture and Politics in *Race Matters*." *Social Text* 40 (Fall): 39–50.

Marx, Karl. 1994. *Karl Marx: Selected Writings*. Edited by Lawrence H. Simon. Indianapolis and Cambridge, England: Hackett Publishing.

Mbiti, John S. 1969. *African Religions and Philosophy*. London, Ibadan, and Nairobi: Heinemann Educational Books.

McInnes, Neil. 1967a. "Karl Marx." In Paul Edwards (ed.), *The Encyclopedia of Philosophy*. New York and London: Macmillan and Free Press; rpt. 1972.

———. 1967b. "Marxist Philosophy." In Paul Edwards (ed.), *The Encyclopedia of Philosophy*. New York and London: Macmillan and Free Press; rpt. 1972.

Moore, G. E. 1965. "Some Judgments of Perception." In Robert J. Swartz (ed.), *Perceiving, Sensing and Knowing*. Berkeley, Los Angeles, and London: University of California Press.

———. 1983. "A Defense of Common Sense" and "Proof of an External

World." In E. D. Klemke (ed.), *Contemporary Analytic and Linguistic Philosophies*. New York: Prometheus Books.

Morrison II, Roy D. 1997. "Self-Transformation in American Blacks: The Harlem Renaissance and Black Theology." In Lewis R. Gordon (ed.), *Existence in Black: An Anthology of Black Existential Philosophy*. New York: Routledge.

Mossner, Ernest C. 1980. *The Life of David Hume*. Clarendon: Oxford University Press.

O'Connor, Sandra Day. 2000. "The History of Women in the Law." In *Pacesetting Women of the 20th Century: A Symposium*. Mount Saint Alban, Washington, DC: National Cathedral School, October 12–15.

Osborne, Peter. 1996. *A Critical Sense: Interviews with Intellectuals*. New York and London: Routledge.

Palter, Robert. 1995. "Hume and Prejudice." *Hume Studies* XXI. 1. (April): 3–23.

Plato. 1992. *Republic*. Translated by G. M. A. Grube, 2nd ed. Revised by C. D. C. Reeve. Indianapolis and Cambridge, England: Hackett.

Popkin, Richard H. 1973. "The Philosophical Basis of Eighteenth-Century Racism." In Harold E. Pagliaro (ed.), *Studies in Eighteenth-Century Culture*. Cleveland and London: Case Western Reserve University Press.

———. 1978. "Hume's Racism." *Philosophical Forum* IX. 2–3 (Winter–Spring); rpt. in Richard A. Watson and James E. Force (eds.). 1980. *The High Road to Pyrrhonism*. San Diego: Austin Hill.

Rawls, John. 1971. *A Theory of Justice*. Cambridge, MA: Harvard University Press.

Reed Jr., Adolph. 2000. *Class Notes: Posing as Politics and Other Thoughts on the American Scene*. New York: The New Press.

Reed, John, and Clive Wake (eds. and trans.). 1976. *L. S. Senghor Prose and Poetry*. London: Heinemann Educational Books.

Rose, Arnold. 1944. *The Negro in America*. New York: Harper and Row.

Salzman, Jack, and Cornel West (eds.). 1997. *Struggles in the Promised Land: Toward a History of Black-Jewish Relations in the United States*. New York and Oxford, England: Oxford University Press.

Schiller, F. C. S. 1907. *Studies in Humanism*. Free Port, NY: Books for Libraries Press; rpt. 1967.

Sealey, Kelvin Shawn, and Cornel West (eds.). 1997. *Restoring Hope: Conversations on the Future of Black America*. Boston: Beacon Press.

Serequeberhan, Tsenay. 1996. "Eurocentrism in Philosophy: The Case of Immanuel Kant." *The Philosophical Forum* 27.4: 333–356.

———. 1997. "Eurocentrism and the Practice of African Philosophy." In

Emmanuel Eze (ed.), *Post-Colonial African Philosophy: A Critical Reader*. Cambridge, MA: Blackwell.

Shohat, Ella, and Robert Stam. 1994. *Unthinking Eurocentrism*. London and New York: Routledge.

Simpson, Lorenzo C. 1991. "On the Historicist Turn in American Philosophy." *APA Newsletter on the Black Experience* 90.3 (Fall): 28–31.

Spelman, Elizabeth V. 1991. "Theodicy, Tragedy and Prophecy: Comments on Cornel West's the *American Evasion of Philosophy*." *APA Newsletter on the Black Experience* 90:3 (Fall): 19–23.

Stewart, John B. 1963. *The Moral and Political Philosophy of David Hume*. New York and London: Columbia University Press.

Truth, Sojourner. 2000. "Ain't I A Woman?" In Wendy Kolmar and Frances Bartkowski (eds.), *Feminst Theory: A Reader*. Mountain View, CA: Mayfield.

Ward, Julie K., and Tommy L. Lott. (eds.). 2002. *Philosophers on Race*. Malden, MA: Blackwell.

Ware, Leland. 2002. "Letters to the Editor." *Chronicle of Higher Education*, February 15, p. B4.

Welchman, Jennifer. 1995. "Locke on Slavery and Inalienable Rights." In *Canadian Journal of Philosophy* 25.1: 67–81.

West, Cornel. 1982. *Prophecy Deliverance: An Afro-American Revolutionary Christianity*. Philadelphia: The Westminster Press.

———. 1988a. *Prophetic Fragments: Illuminations of the Crisis in American Religion and Culture*. Trenton, NJ: Africa World Press.

———. 1988b. "Prophetic Theology." In Willis H. Logan (ed.), *The Kairos Covenant*. New York: Friendship Press.

———. 1989. *The American Evasion of Philosophy: A Genealogy of Pragmatism*. Madison: The University of Wisconsin Press.

———. 1991a. *The Ethical Dimensions of Marxist Thought*. New York: Monthly Review Press.

———. 1991b. "Response (to Critics)." *APA Newsletter on the Black Experience*. 90.3 (Fall): 26–28.

———. 1992. "Philosophy and the Urban Underclass." In Bill E. Lawson (ed.), *The Underclass Question*. Philadelphia: Temple University.

———. 1993a. "Black Theology and Marxist Thought." In James H. Cone and Gayraud S. Wilmore (eds.), *Black Theology: A Documentary*. Maryknoll, New York: Orbis Books.

———. 1993b. *Keeping Faith: Philosophy and Race in America*. New York and London: Routledge.

———. 1994. *Race Matters*. New York: Vintage Books.

———. 1997a. "Walking the Tightrope: Some Personal Reflections on Blacks and Jews." In Jack Salzman and Cornel West (eds.), *Struggles in the Promised Land: Toward a History of Black-Jewish Relations in the United States*. New York and Oxford, England: Oxford University Press.

———. 1999a. "On Black-Brown Relations." In *The Cornel West Reader*. New York: Basic Civitas Books.

———. 1999b. *The Cornel West Reader*. New York: Basic Civitas Books.

———. 1999c. "The Indispensability yet Insufficiency of Marxist Thought." In *The Cornel West Reader*. New York: Basic Civitas Books.

———. 1999d. "On Affirmative Action." In *The Cornel West Reader*. New York: Basic Civitas Books.

———. 1999e. "The Political Intellectual." In *The Cornel West Reader*. New York: Basic Civitas Books.

———. 1999f. "Race and Social Theory." In *The Cornel West Reader*. New York: Basic Civitas Books.

———. 1999g. "Tensions with Jewish Friends and Foes." In *The Cornel West Reader*. New York: Basic Civitas Books.

———. 1999h. "A World of Ideas." In *The Cornel West Reader*. New York: Basic Civitas Books.

West, Cornel, and Henry Louis Gates Jr. 1996. *The Future of the Race*. New York: Alfred A. Knopf.

Wilson, Robin, and Scott Smallwood. 2002. "Battle of Wills at Harvard." *Chronicle of Higher Education*, January 18, p. A8.

Wood, Mark David. 2000. *Cornel West and the Politics of Prophetic Pragmatism*. Urbana and Chicago: University of Illinois Press.

Yancy, George. 1998. *African American Philosophers: 17 Conversations*. New York and London: Routledge.

———. 2000. "Feminism and the Subtext of Whiteness: Black Women's Experiences as a Site of Identity Formation and Contestation of Whiteness." *Western Journal of Black Studies* 24. 3: 156–166.

——— (ed.). 2001. *Cornel West: A Critical Reader*. Malden, MA, and Oxford, England: Blackwell.

Young, Iris M. 1990. *Justice and the Politics of Difference*. Princeton, NJ: Princeton University Press.

Zamir, Shamoon. 1995. *Dark Voices: W. E. B. Du Bois and American Thought* 1888–1903. Chicago and London: The University of Chicago Press.

INDEX

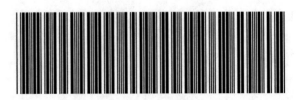